Long Way Home

The Frankie Miller Story

Davy Arthur

NEW HAVEN PUBLISHING LTD

Published 2025
First Edition
www.newhavenpublishingltd.com
newhavenpublishing@gmail.com

All Rights Reserved
The rights of Davy Arthur as the author of this work, have been asserted in accordance with the Copyrights, Designs and Patents Act 1988.
No part of this book may be re-printed or reproduced or utilized in any form or by any electronic, mechanical or other means, now unknown or hereafter invented, including photocopying, and recording, or in any information storage or retrieval system, without the written permission of the
Authors and Publisher.

Cover Design © Pete Cunliffe

Copyright © 2025 Davy Arthur
All rights reserved
ISBN: 978-1-915975-23-2

Dedicated to my mother

Agnes Milroy Darling Arthur (née Hendrie)
The coal miner's daughter who will never be forgotten

"I left my home in Bridgeton Town
With all the buildings falling down
Went to seek my fortune
Went to seek my fame
All the folks I knew so well
All the stories fit to tell
Mama said the boy child's got to roam
Lord knows when I'll way my way back home"

'Bridgeton': Words and music by Frankie Miller

Content

This Miller's Tale…	6
Introduction- A Well Respected Man	7
End of an Era	13
I Can't Change It	16
They Called It Pub Rock	25
In No Resistance	28
It's The High Life	40
Drunken Nights In The City	46
I Took a Mid-Day Plane from Glasgow to L.A.	51
Incarcerated Ecstasy	59
When I Have A couple Of Drinks On A Saturday	71
Enter Frankie Miller's Full House	79
1978 Trouble Better Get Out My Way	102
Falling In Love Darlin'	113
The 80's A Change Is Gonna Come	130
The Incredible Frankie Miller Rock Band	145
1990 The Scottish Homecoming	162
1991 I'll Call You On The Phone Some	165
Caledonia's been Everything I Ever Had	170
The Moat House Hotel Glasgow	173
In A New York Minute	176
May 2002	185
Headbangers and Heroes	194
Well, Long Way Home	197
Classic Rock Awards	207
Eagles Connection	212
Quireboys Connection	215
Frankie Miller's Double Take	219
Photographs and Handprints	231
Covers-Selected Highlights	236
A Selection of Collaborators	243
Thanks / Acknowledgments	264

This Miller's Tale Is One of Passion and Determination...

Age leaves all rock fans disillusioned. For me, one of the biggest disappointments arrived early. It was the discovery that support acts are not invariably wonderful. I had come by the delusion because the first one I ever saw, all of 53 years ago, was Frankie Miller.

The gig, at Edinburgh's Caley Cinema, was headlined by Ten Years After. All we wanted was Alvin Lee's high-octane plectrum.

But this wee guy from Bridgeton shambled on first and just blew the place away. It did no harm that he was backed by Brinsley Schwarz, Nick Lowe's proto pub rockers.

This was the era of Paul Rodgers and Ian Gillan, when all British vocalists sang like delta bluesmen. How come everyone had missed one of the very best of them?

A few hits eventually came, but nothing on the scale he deserved. Then in 1994, he was struck down by a brain haemorrhage that left him unable to speak or walk. Helped by a devoted partner and a thrawn spirit, he fought back to some sort of life, but he would never strut a stage again...

From Keith Aiken *Daily Express* 2006

Introduction

A Well Respected Man

In 1984 the phrase "Frankie Who?" "Frankie Fucking Miller, That's Who!" was coined.

It was used on T-shirts with the question appearing on the front and the answer on the back. Some years later, it was also used as the title of the Chrysalis CD box set. In the 21st century, the same question "Who?" may be directed at Frankie's influencers and contemporaries.

Who were his influencers, and in turn whom did he influence with his singing voice and songwriting talents? From his teenage years, Frankie performed with several highly talented musicians who also went on to find fame and fortune in their own right. Throughout his career, he attracted numerous quality musicians into his backing bands, top record producers, session musicians and collaborators.

Regarding his writing, his songs have also been covered by an impressive list of top stars. These were mostly self-penned but sometimes written with others.

Frankie Miller's story wouldn't be complete without looking at those who influenced him in more detail.

Most of the names will appear again throughout the book; thus this book will emphasise and justify to the reader the use of the term "Frankie Fucking Miller, That's Who!"

This book tells the story of how a talented young singer/songwriter from Scotland, who was influenced by rock 'n' roll, soul and blues music, would influence a number of his contemporaries, into the 21st century.

Having been exposed from an early age to his family's record collection, Frankie Miller became influenced especially by performers like Ray Charles, Little Richard and, later, Otis Redding. This is apparent in his singing style and the type of music performed by his bands during the mid to late 60s. The soul-band boom saw the first outlet for Frankie's talent.

In Brian Hogg's *History of Scottish Rock and Pop*, he is described as being part of a second generation of groups to perform regularly on the mid-sixties Glasgow music scene. Before them, a number had won recording contracts, moved to London and become national or international stars. These included the Poets, The Beatstalkers, Dean Ford and the Gaylords (Marmalade) and Lulu and the Luvvers who were all signed by Decca Records, a company famous at the time for having turned down The Beatles.

These acts enjoyed different levels of success and while Lulu and Marmalade became international stars, the Poets, under the management of Andrew Loog Oldham, couldn't compete with the Rolling Stones for his attention, and as with members of the Luvvers returned to their native Glasgow. Alex Harvey and Tam White are two other famous examples of "returned exiles". Fortunately these two kept going strong.

Frankie Miller's journey south would come some five years later and like those pioneers before him he would team up with various top musicians and record producers, who were attracted not only to his distinctive and powerful singing voice but also to his songwriting ability.

We should take a closer look at those who, in musical terms, influenced Frankie from a young age.

The influencers:

It is common knowledge that the music of artists like Ray Charles, Little Richard and Elvis Presley came into Scotland via imported records belonging to American servicemen based around the country. Then, thanks to a small number of specialist record shops springing up, especially at first in Glasgow, the records became part of Frankie's sisters' and parents' collections.

While Elvis Presley's first recordings in 1953 suggested a singer ready to help open the way for the emergence of rock 'n' roll, Little Richard was described as the "Architect of Rock and Roll". A young Frankie was excited not only by the charismatic showmanship and dynamic music but by the raspy, shouted vocals, for which he would also later be credited.

Little Richard was also a big influence on The Beatles and had a series of self-penned hits including 'Tutti Frutti', 'Long Tall Sally' and 'Lucille'.

Whilst the previous two had an influence in terms of rock 'n' roll on Frankie, Ray Charles was the greatest in terms of singing style. He was an American singer, songwriter and pianist who pioneered the soul music genre during the 1950s by combining blues, jazz, rhythm and blues, and gospel styles into the music he recorded for Atlantic Records. He is also credited with integrating country music, rhythm and blues, and pop music during the 1960s.

His style and success in the genres of rhythm and blues and jazz had an influence on a number of highly successful artists.

This versatility is perhaps reflected in the range of styles Frankie was to offer during his own career.

Hit singles (he released 127 of them) included 'Hallelujah I Love Her So', 'Let The Good Times Roll', 'Georgia On My Mind' and ' Hit The Road Jack'.

Music critic Henry Pleasants wrote:

"Sinatra, and Bing Crosby before him, had been masters of words. Ray Charles is a master of sounds. His records disclose an extraordinary assortment of slurs, glides, turns, shrieks, wails, breaks, shouts, screams and hollers, all wonderfully controlled, disciplined by inspired musicianship, and harnessed to ingenious subtleties of harmony, dynamics and rhythm...It is either the singing of a man whose vocabulary is inadequate to express what is in his heart and mind or of one whose feelings are too intense for satisfactory verbal or conventionally melodic articulation.

"He can't tell it to you. He can't even sing it to you. He has to cry out to you, or shout to you, in tones eloquent of despair—or exaltation. The voice alone, with little assistance from the text or the notated music, conveys the message."

Author's Note: These sentiments exactly match my feelings after the numerous Frankie Miller gigs I attended over 25 years - sometimes breathtaking but always, always filled with an emotion and intensity that came from somewhere deep in his soul... where Frankie always seemed to "cry out."

Although Frankie was to be compared to Otis Redding and others, perhaps his greatest compliment was to have one of his songs covered in 1980 by none other than Ray Charles.

So the influencer became the influenced.

Colleagues / Band Members

If the bar was set high in terms of musical influences, Frankie Miller had perhaps unwittingly also set that trend with the level of musicians he surrounded himself with from an early age.

This book will also trace the careers of his early colleagues and their fates. It will present the reader with more detailed information about where his music was recorded, by whom and with whom. These individuals ensured that the bar remained high throughout his career.

I first saw Frankie Miller perform live in June 1968 and have followed his career ever since. Our friendship later developed as a result of that.

At eighteen, he was already being described as a veteran of the Scottish music scene.

The Stoics were the name of his band and on that evening they were supported by Teargas, who a number of years later became the Sensational Alex Harvey Band.

When the Stoics signed to Chrysalis and moved south to London in 1970 (having had their name changed to Howl), it became difficult to get any news on their progress or activities. Jethro Tull, Ten Years After and Procol Harum were already some of the bigger acts signed to the label.

Not surprising then that over the next year, they would tour and share the bill with these bands, and Frankie would go on to form close personal and professional relationships with a number of their members.

He went on to release seven albums with Chrysalis and later with Capitol, Mercury and Universal.

Artists including Ray Charles, The Everly Brothers, Roy Orbison, Rod Stewart, The Eagles and many more have covered his songs.

Scottish comedian Billy Connolly is quoted in the March 2014 edition of *Mojo* magazine as saying that "The UK music press in the '70s was full of fucking idiots. They never took Frankie seriously - it was as if he was tartan first and a brilliant soul singer second."

Many examples of music journalists' work are here, either in full or paraphrased with the individual writers' kind permission.

In the book *A Hidden Landscape Once a Week*, Tony Stewart (writer and deputy editor of *NME* 1971-1985) points out "the vital role of the visual" and that the role of the photographers who worked with music journalists should never be underestimated – "If the writers signposted the way to the soundtrack of a generation, the photographers provided the showreel."

This book includes several un-published photographs which have lain in negative form for more than 45 years. They bring back to life a part of musical history that might otherwise have been forgotten about or lost. Frankie's appearances at 1970 Isle of Wight and Day for the Prisoners at San Quentin in 1975 come into that category.

This book brings together, piece by piece, an overview of his musical career based on interviews, reviews, photographs and my own memories with the sole aim of celebrating, in one publication, the true talent that is Frankie Miller.

In summary, I am sure that this book will reproduce the same maximum emotional impact for its readers that Frankie Miller has been able to achieve with his music.

Davy Arthur

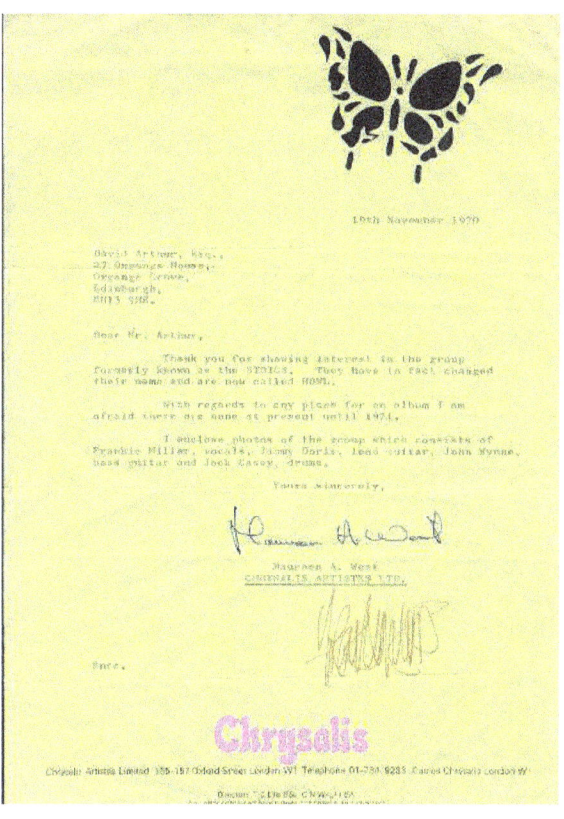

From Nobby Clark - Original singer and a founder member of The Bay City Rollers

My first encounter with Frankie Miller was at a dance club in an old cinema in Edinburgh's High Street; it was called McGoos. There were three stages in this place and I was waiting to see another Glasgow band called the Pathfinders who were set up to play on the middle stage, so my back was turned to the opposite stage when on came this guy fronting a group called the Stoics. I just heard this voice resonating round the hall and I couldn't take my eyes off him. His voice just filled the place. This was Frankie Miller. It was 1968/69. The Bay City Rollers were just taking off and spreading outwards across the country, and as our popularity grew we travelled further afield, and played on the same bill as the Stoics (if my memory serves me well) at the Flamingo Ballroom in Glasgow and the Olympia Ballroom in East Kilbride. I then made a point of going to see The Frankie Miller Band at Tiffany's dancehall in Edinburgh.

I followed Frankie's career all the years that he performed and in my humble opinion was listening to one of the greatest soul/blues singers of all time.

I salute you, Frankie Miller.

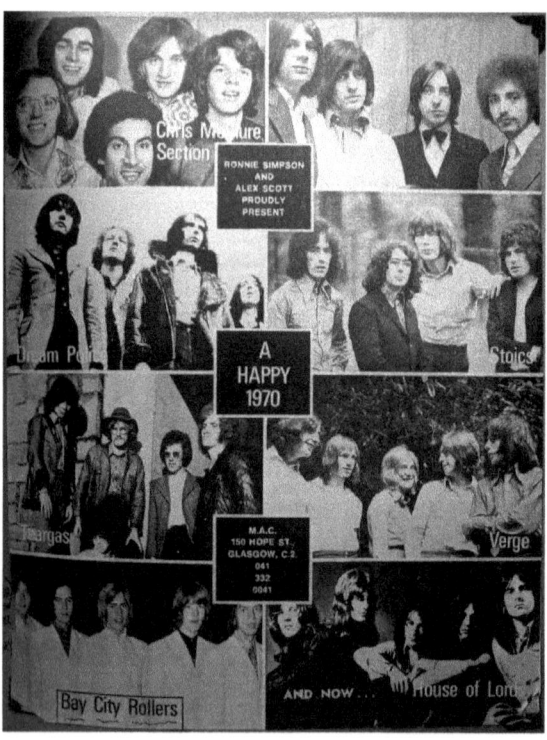

End of an Era

1980 was a watershed year in Frankie's career. Off the road since the end of the Good to See You Tour of the UK and Europe in 1979, Frankie was to return with a new album and, later in the year, a stripped-down, back-to-basics four-piece live band.

With the headline "Miller Back on the Road" *Sounds* magazine announced on 29-11-80 that:

"Frankie Miller is back on the road after a lengthy absence for a tour that continues into the New Year.

"He said this week, 'I've got some great stuff with this new band and I want people to hear it. I've got tired of people who thought "Darlin" was the only song I ever recorded.'

"Touring with him are Chrissy Stewart (bass), Ed Deane (guitar) and Malcolm Mortimore (drums)."

Chrissy Stewart
Frankie's bass player and loyal friend.

Before joining the Frankie Miller Band in 1975, Chrissy was a member of rock band Eire Apparent, who were signed by Jimi Hendrix's manager Chas Chandler. In the late 60s they toured America for four years alongside Hendrix and Pink Floyd.

Following his stint with Eire Apparent, he also played with Spooky Tooth, who featured Gary Wright of Dream Weaver fame and Mick Jones from Foreigner, Steve Miller, and Whitesnake. Apart from a short spell in 1979, Chrissy Stewart was a vital cog in Frankie Miller's various line-ups until 1994.

Ed Deane
Deane is an Irish guitarist with a career spanning six decades, from the late 1960s to the present day. He is a blues musician, playing the electric and acoustic guitar.

Ed is highly regarded as a left-handed guitarist, preferring to play right-handed guitars upside down. He replaced Gary Moore in Skid Row before joining Bees Make Honey.

He joined Frankie Miller in 1978 until 1982 and toured extensively in Europe and America.

Later, he appeared in the Mike Figgis movie *Stormy Monday* (which featured Tommy Lee Jones, Sting and Melanie Griffith). He also contributed substantially to the soundtrack and was the only featured guitarist apart from B B King. Ed also played on the soundtracks of the films *Leaving Las Vegas* and *Serendipity* (with Bap Kennedy).

Ed spent much of the 90s working with blues diva Dana Gillespie, recording several albums with her. During this period Dana was voted Best British Female Blues Singer, before being installed in the British Blues Connection Hall of Fame.

Malcolm Mortimore

Mortimore is a drummer and percussionist who has played with Arthur Brown, Ian Dury, Herbie Flowers, Gentle Giant, Spike Heatley, Tom Jones, Mick and Chris Jagger and Chris Spedding. His drumming style has been described as "free, quirky and complex" and in 2020 he replaced John Hiseman in Coliseum.

The *Sounds* article went on to say:

"Miller intends to continue playing next year and is also considering several film projects which were offered to him after his debut in BBC's 'Just A Boy's Game' on BBC's Play For Today last year. He starts work on a new album in January.

"Tour Dates open at London Dingwalls on December 3rd and include Dudley, Reading, Leeds, Sheffield, Edinburgh, Glasgow, and Ayr, finishing up again on 31st December at London Greyhound."

Carol Clark from *Sounds* openly questioned the new band's ability to take the show on to the bigger stage…

From her review:

"Frankie Miller, Dingwalls, London

"It was inevitable that when Frankie Miller achieved his biggest commercial success, his artistic acceptability plunged to an all-time low.

"It was inevitable because the song was 'Darlin', a Radio 1 'singalong' received by critics as a betrayal of everything he had done before and was capable of doing again."

The new, stripped-down four piece presented a mix of new material, old hits (no 'Darlin') and covers. The pick of these was 'Bad Case of Loving You' which was a highlight in the more aggressive moments of the performance.

The show was described as intense and intimate, and suited to the closeness of Dingwalls, although doubts were cast as to the band's ability to cope in future, in larger venues.

Author's Note : The potential problems and solutions would become clearer in the following year, as the tour progressed into Europe and America.

Frankie had released *Easy Money* in May, his eighth and final album for Chrysalis, which he recorded at Sound Stage Studios in Nashville. Perhaps aimed at the American Country Music market, with its slick production, Frankie's vocals are still full of power and emotion… and it's a shame that even with the renowned team of musicians supporting him, the album received little or no publicity or airplay in the UK.

Frankie's current situation and perceived change of style reminded me of comments written in an article by Paul Williams for *Crawdaddy!* in March 1968.

"There is confusion afoot in the rock music world, a familiar confusion that arises from lack of understanding, lack of communication, and lack of common effort in a common cause.

"It is not surprising that rock musicians, record company executives, appreciators of the music, and radio station powers-that-be should each hold separate views of what rock music should be…The performer, then, is in a difficult position. Should he (or she) try to please the public, the record company, or himself?"

I Can't Change It...

"My friends can't find some things I say
Must be the way I say those things
My friends can't find some things I do
Must be the way I do those things
I can't change it
But I'm trying to do right..."   Written by Frankie Miller

Frankie was born Francis John Miller on 2nd November 1949 in the east end of Glasgow and was influenced early on by his mother's record collection. She loved Ray Charles, while his older sisters introduced him to Little Richard and Elvis Presley. He identified instinctively with Little Richard's flamboyant aggression. "The music was alive, exciting, I loved it. I realised later that I could get my own aggression out through music. R&B and soul music, I just knew was what I really love."

Frankie started writing songs at the age of nine after being given a guitar by his parents. He composed a song called 'But I Do' which caused tears of laughter amongst his family members but Frankie was to remain undeterred.

"You know, I realised that I could sing and it would make me feel better. It was better than thumping someone on the head, which is what most people were into. I didn't realise until after I'd left Glasgow that singing was a way out. An escape from all that."

"I used to sing round the backs when I was two," recalls Miller. "I don't remember the songs but people used to throw me pennies and ha'pennies. Then I heard Little Richard and he really knocked my head off. I used to try to copy him, but at first I never knew there were any words to his songs."

His infatuation with music and his natural vocal talent took a positive form in the shape of the succession of early groups, including the Harmony Boys.

By this point Miller was barely in primary school, but by the age of nine he'd joined a local skiffle group. "They were a really good band – no name - who were into rock 'n' roll and things like Lonnie Donegan."

Frankie's tastes developed more towards soul. "I used to listen to a lot to Ray Charles, Otis Redding and Wilson Pickett," he explained through his particularly strong Glaswegian accent.

"In the early bands, we used to do a lot of Willie Dixon and R&B things. We did a lot of Ray Charles stuff." At eleven years old Frankie was a member of The Sundowners, who played at the Territorial Army Halls in the heart of Bridgeton, and two years later, he was fronting the Deljaks. "They did a lot of rhythm and blues," Frankie explains. "They used to play at a club called the Manhattan [later described by Frankie as a 'seedy blues club in Bridgeton' which he loved] and I would go and see them. They really needed a singer and my pal told me I should get up there with them. So I did." At fifteen/sixteen there was The Sabres. The Sabres gig included six months in Spain in 1966, a baptism of fire for young Miller. "That's when I started smoking and drinking. It was just far too much to handle – we were working every night and there was always chicks and booze and smoke, so I decided to come back."

Next came West Farm Cottage and a soul outfit called Sock 'Em JB which featured good friend Jimmy Dewar (Stone The Crows, Jude and Robin Trower).

Henry Wright from Sock 'Em JB wrote:
"On returning to Scotland after my last gig in Maryport with The Luvvers I met up with John McGinnis and Jimmy Dewar, starting a band which became Sock 'Em JB. The idea was to have a bigger band than usual with brass to play the soul classics of Motown, Otis Redding, Wilson Pickett and all the soul classics of the time. We asked John Waterson at the Burns Cottage if we could rehearse on a Saturday morning as there was only three men and a dog playing dominoes then. It also had a Hammond organ which was a major plus. After the first week there were few more in the place and within weeks it was packed. The icing on the cake was when John said we needed a singer and he knew a young guy called Frankie Miller.

"The impact was amazing, and from being packed it went to almost impossible to get in. We had a couple of different lineups but the most remembered would be the one with John McGinnis, Henry Wright, Jimmy Dewar, Billy Simpson, Larry Quinn and Jimmy Nairn on saxes, who went on to do very well in the clubs and cruise liners.

"We played all around Glasgow, Edinburgh and Fife. I remember an early version of Nazareth coming to see us with Dan, Pete, Daryll and Manny. This line up was going great guns when Frankie decided to leave and form his own band which meant that the band eventually just fizzled out.

"John, Jimmy and I decided to continue as a three piece along the lines of the Peddlers, and again we rehearsed at the Cottage and that was when Leslie Harvey turned up having just returned from Germany and sat in with us. He liked the rehearsals and asked if his girlfriend Maggie Bell could sit in, which was the beginning of The Power, which went on to become Stone the Crows. Unfortunately, I had been offered a job which meant I had to attend a six week course in London and I felt this would hold the band back so I offered to leave. George Grant from the Arrows took over and was eventually replaced by Colin Allen when the band turned pro."

Regards, Henry

John McGinnis and James Dewar
From Brian Hogg, writing on the Procol Harum website:
"Jimmy Dewar left Lulu and the Luvvers in 1965, returning to Glasgow to rethink his career. By 1967 he could be found in a new band, Sock 'Em JB, an exciting unit fuelled on material by Otis Redding, Sam and Dave, and Wilson Pickett.

"The vocalist was ex-Deljak Frankie Miller and the pianist John McGinnis, formerly of the Blues Council. (The latter act was one of the finest Scotland produced, revolving around one-time Alex Harvey saxophonist Bill Patrick and Harvey's younger brother, Leslie. Sadly, two members were killed when their van crashed returning home to Glasgow from Edinburgh, and the despondent survivors split up.) Sock 'Em JB were together for only a matter of months, ending when Miller formed a new group, West Farm Cottage, en-route to the Stoics. Dewar and McGinnis remained together and, by the following year, had formed a new tough-sounding band, blending blues and progressive rock.

"They were preparing to be the resident act at a new club, the Burns Howff, when Leslie Harvey and Maggie Bell walked into a rehearsal. After a jam it was suggested they join forces and Power was born. With Bell on vocals and Harvey on guitar, the unit gelled perfectly and they quickly became one of Glasgow's most popular attractions. In 1969 Peter Grant, Led Zeppelin's manager, came to Glasgow to see them and within a matter of months they had won a management and recording deal. Renamed Stone the Crows (Peter Grant is credited with christening the band after exclaiming 'Stone The Crows!' when he first saw them play) – and with the addition of ex-John Mayall drummer Colin Allen – the group recorded two excellent albums, *Stone the Crows* and *Ode to John Law*.

"Bell's passionate voice and Leslie's fluid, economical style may have defined the band's music, but Dewar's role should not be underestimated.

"His playing was always sympathetic and his earthy duets with Bell were genuinely moving. 'He's one of the finest singers I've ever heard,' she said in a later interview. However, the axis of the band had moved – the singer and guitarist were also a couple – and both Dewar and McGinnis were unhappy with the diminished role they now played in the group they had formed. Both quit in February 1971."

Eric McLean - Sabres Guitarist, now based in Nanaimo B.C.

"I was playing with The Sabres in 1964/66 and we had a residency at The Flamingo on Paisley Road West between the districts of Mosspark and Penilee.

"The Stoics were from nearby Penilee and they used to come and watch us. Really nice guys and a good band but they didn't have a front man. Jimmy Doris the guitar player would ask me how I got certain sounds and we became pally. He was a nice guy. He inherited my 1957 Les Paul Junior after I traded it back to McCormick's when I was skint. He painted it black and used it a lot. At that time The Sabres was one of the most popular bands in the Glasgow area and lots of other bands came to watch us and pick up tips because Ian Clews, our singer and frontman, was and still is local legend.

"He could pick the perfect songs of the day, great for dancing. Like The Temptations, The Four Tops, and all the great Motown artists of the day, because Clewsy saw that Motown was coming so we were always the first to pick the most popular songs thanks to Clewsy's vision. Somehow, at some point, after Frankie joined, and then left The Sabres after our fiasco in Spain, he got together with the Stoics and suddenly they had a frontman. That's another story. When Ian Clews and Ian MacMillan left The Sabres to join The Pathfinders we called Frankie in since we knew him from The Deljaks. We also brought in Ronnie Miller - no relation - to play bass.

"How and why did The Sabres go to Spain?

"Ronnie's older sister was going with Martin Frutin who owned a travel agency in Glasgow. Martin had connections in Spain because his dad had been living there for years after fleeing Glasgow, so rumour has it to escape the taxman. He used to run one of the theatres in Glasgow, maybe the Pavilion, not sure. So Martin got us this gig in the Top Ten Club in Torremolinos and off we went in around September 1966. Our van broke down in Tours in the middle of France so we had to rent a Peugeot tall van from Hertz to get us to Malaga and The Top Ten Club. Martin convinced us that we could become stars in Spain due to his 'many contacts' there. According to Martin, a nice apartment awaited us, along with TV and recording opportunities. We were playing The Top 10 Club seven days a week from 9pm to 3am, alternating hour long sets with an Irish band. Torremolinos is very close to Malaga, a major port, and we used to get lots of American servicemen coming to the club. Often we would invite some of the guys, especially the black guys, on to the stage for a few songs and that was fantastic. A bunch of young Scottish guys playing with some black guys who could really sing. We were in our element, especially Frankie, because this was the music we loved and it was great for us to play it with people who knew what it was all about.

"They loved Frankie too, because he sounded so good, just like his heroes, Solomon Burke, Marvin Gaye, and especially Otis Redding.

"At that time, Torremolinos was a hot spot for celebrities, and we had Brian Jones from the Stones drop in one time. Then another night, Frankie could hardly contain himself as he shouted to us, forgetting to back away from his mike, 'Hey guys, there's Brian Epstein!' Luckily the famous Beatles manager didn't hear this above the noise from the crowd.

"Of course, none of the promises transpired and we all started fighting. Frankie and I were the youngest at 17, far too young, and pretty soon the whole thing fell apart after a few months. The luxury apartment Martin had promised us was constantly leaking and the TV, radio, and recording opportunities never materialised. We were just a bunch of teenagers who had never been out of Scotland before and eventually we simply imploded.

"The drummer Stewart McKenzie and I had been playing together since we were 14 or 15 and Stewart and Frankie didn't get along. So when push came to shove Stewart and I left together and headed back to Glasgow while Frankie and Ronnie made their own way back later. The friendship goes back to their days in the Deljaks. The keyboard player Andy McMaster had already been fired and he was given his fare home. Andy went on to form Ducks Deluxe and then The Motors who had a couple of top ten hits including 'Airport' . We have gotten back in touch, all sins forgiven and he turned 80 this year and released another album. Amazing. You couldn't make this stuff up! I lost contact with Frankie once we were all finally back in Scotland and only saw him again close to 50 years later when we arranged to meet in London on one of my trips to the UK. I had learned of his dreadful experience with a brain aneurysm and decided that I should see him.

"It was a wonderful reunion and despite his challenges to speak, he immediately recognised me and we had a great time looking through old photos in my scrapbook. I also reconnected about ten years ago with Ronnie Miller, who I learned had been living for some time in Port Glasgow, only about 2 or 3 miles from Kilmacolm where I had grown up. Small world indeed. In the lost years in between, Frankie had joined up with the Stoics when he got back to Glasgow and then moved to England, where his career really started to take off. I always regretted that we had lost touch over the years but it was great to know that he had been successful. In the meantime, Stewart McKenzie, Ian MacMillan and I had joined The Meridians and stayed with them for a few years. The three of us had started playing together in our first band, The Boots, while in high school.

"After The Meridians, Ian went on to play with Hugh Nicholson in Blue in the 70s and now lives in Deerborne just outside Detroit. Ian Clews is alive and well, living in Topanga Valley outside LA and we keep in touch and exchange old stories."

Eric McLean

A German tour supporting Ten Years After was preceded by an appearance at The Isle of Wight Festival (as Howl). Howl performed on the main stage on the Thursday evening, August 26th. The Groundhogs, Supertramp and Terry Reid also played that day.

The highlight of the German tour was to have been the Love and Peace Open Air Festival in Fehmarn Germany. Over three days, the line up also included Taste, Procol Harum, The Faces and Jimi Hendrix. Many acts, including Ten Years After and Howl, didn't appear due a mixture of bad organisation and storms.

Howl unfortunately split before completing any recordings, when personality clashes broke up the band, and it would be the beginning of a series of frustrations for Frankie. When Frankie joined the Stoics, Jimmy Doris had been considered the main songwriter. Frankie also introduced some equally strong originals and a friction developed between them. "Jimmy and I just weren't hitting it off."

"He really wanted to do co-written songs and I felt some of them weren't good enough." Mark London, an executive from the company managing Lulu, signed Doris to a five-year publishing deal, but Frankie was a little more reserved. "I didn't like London. I thought he was a bit of a fly man and wouldn't sign with him."

Lulu would later opine of Atlantic Record honchos Jerry Wexler, Tom Dowd and Arif Mardin, the producers of her album *New Routes*: "I don't think they knew what to do with me, and the only big hit I got (off the album) was a song that I (brought in) with me" - referring to 'Oh Me Oh My…', which had been written by Jim Doris who – as Jimmy Doris – had been vocalist-guitarist for the Stoics, a band which formed in Lulu's native Glasgow in the late 1960s and whose membership had included Frankie Miller. Doris helped contribute another song to *New Routes*: 'After All (I Live My Life)' - co-written with Miller - and his composition 'Take Good Care of Yourself' was featured on the follow-up album *Melody Fair*. 'Take Good Care of Yourself' also often featured as the last song in a typical Stoics gig during the late 60s.

Reportedly, Doris subsequently went into A&R work before being sidelined by mental instability, which may have been a factor in his being killed when run over by a bus in London in the late 1980s or early 1990s.

The Stoics were a mixture of progressive rock and soul. It was simply down to two different tastes in music that drove Frankie and Jimmy Doris apart, plus the fact that both needed to be the band leader.

It is a criticism of neither of the two.

Howl 1970 Isle of Wight

By early 1971, Frankie was fronting Jude, which was formed by Clive Bunker after he left Jethro Tull, Robin Trower after he left Procol Harum and Jimmy Dewar after he quit Stone the Crows.

"I had to get Jimmy Dewar into a band," Frankie Miller told Brian Hogg in 1992. "He was doing nothing in London." The band in question was Jude. Miller had quit the Stoics, but Chrysalis, with whom he had a publishing deal, suggested he pair with guitarist Robin Trower, who had recently left Procol Harum. With Dewar on bass and Clive Bunker (ex-Jethro Tull) on drums, Jude seemed like a marriage made in heaven, but it was not to be. "I wanted to do the two-vocal thing," Miller explained, "but the vehicle wasn't right. The best thing for Jimmy to do was to sing in a power trio with Robin."

Two songs from the Jude period - written by Trower/Miller - made it on to albums. 'I Can't Wait Much Longer' featured on the Robin Trower 1973 release *Twice Removed From Yesterday*. 'This Love of Mine' featured on the 1977 *Full House* album release by Frankie Miller. "Jude got really stale," said Frankie in his still audible Glasgow drawl. "I never really felt there was never that much incentive in that band to work hard and get it on because we never seemed to be getting the right kind of reaction on gigs."

"We were together for about eight months," Frankie recalls. "We used to write songs and do them every night on the road, until we'd tire of them and throw them out. The band fell into a terrible rut and it just killed off our enthusiasm. Our manager at the time couldn't understand it - he wanted us to get about three encores on every gig, but we only used to get one if we were lucky. We really should have gone into a studio and recorded."

Unfortunately, there wasn't a lot of publicity for Jude. One or two university gigs were reviewed in the music press with very little enthusiasm.

January 1 1972 *Record Mirror*

Ten Years After announce new tour dates on the UK university circuit and will be supported by Jude in Cardiff – 19th - Brighton 25th - and Nottingham 27th January

When the members of Jude went their separate ways, most notably Jimmy Dewar and Robin Trower forming the Robin Trower Band, times were as hard then as they'd ever been for Frankie and he found himself busking to survive whilst sleeping on Jimmy Dewar's floor…"I quite enjoyed busking. Once I made £4 in four hours, but I'd always give it up as soon as I had enough money to eat. Then I'd go home and write," he recalls.

They Called It "Pub Rock"

("The name was people, especially lazy journalists, confusing style of music with type of venue" – Sean Tyla)

In a half dozen Victorian bars dotted around North London, they revived the roots of rock. While the charts were chock-full of pomp, glitter and glam, these bands took to the tiny pub stages – with the bare minimum of equipment – and stripped music back to its basics and gave it a modern makeover. Pub rock was primarily a live thing, focusing on the styles of early rock 'n' roll and R&B and you had to be there with a pint in your hand to fully appreciate the magic of it.

Frankie's rebellious attitude to the music industry and background fitted in ideally to that of the musicians around him!

He would go on to meet a few interesting musicians during this period, including Paul Carrack, Neil Hubbard and Henry McCullough… Read on and we will take you back down memory lane to the pub rock era, a movement and an environment in which, despite some people looking down their noses at it, Frankie thrived.

"Jimmy Dewar told me there was a country-rock band playing around the corner in the boozer. I just didn't believe it, 'cos I didn't know there were ANY country-rock bands in Britain at the time. We went to see them one night, and there were just four people there… sort of like, me and Jimmy and two others who weren't even listening. They (Eggs Over Easy) were just like the Band, you know, been together for years – then it started snowballing for them."

"These gigs," says Frankie, "are for the real working bands. The real musicians. You won't find any glitter bands or groupies hanging around. It's simply music and I used to get up and jam with Brinsley. I knew that musically they were very compatible to me.

"So after the Stoics broke up, and Jude and Robin broke up, we all used to go down to the Brinsleys' house – a great big place – and play around… like they had a home studio, and they said, 'Why not do an album?' So we did that first album, which was done on a really cheap budget."

Frankie's resultant friendship with the Brinsleys ended up with them recording *Once in a Blue Moon* together during '72 and touring with Ten Years After to promote the album.

1972 October dates with Brinsley Schwartz and Ten Years After

26 Hard Rock Manchester
28 Town Hall Birmingham

29 City Hall Newcastle
30 Caley Cinema Edinburgh
Nov 2 and 3 Rainbow London
4 Liverpool Stadium
6 De Montfort Hall Leicester
7 St Georges Hall Bradford
8 Victoria Hall Hanley Stoke on Trent
9 Colston Hall Bristol

Frankie got a mention by Geoff Brown at the end of his Rainbow Theatre TYA review.

"Also on the bill was Frankie Miller, who was backed by the excellent Brinsley Schwartz. Their relaxed funk complemented his style well. He can handle others' work with some style and I particularly liked the closer, Van Morrison's 'Wild Night'. With Alvin Lee on stage next, it certainly was."

Liverpool Stadium Frankie Miller Set List
I'm Ready
In No Resistance
Candlelight Sonata
You Don't Need To Laugh
Ain't Too Proud To Beg
Ann Eliza Jane
I Can't Change It
It Takes A Lot To Laugh
Wild Night
It's Over

"We had great times up there. We used to work in the evenings – seven hours at a time then sleep off our fatigue during the day."

The happiness of being left alone to make music has come across extremely well on his first album *Once in a Blue Moon*.

Commenting on it, Frankie says, "The only thing I tried to inject into this album was warmth. Brinsley are a very warm, down to earth band and I think they have helped me to do it on this album."

From Frankie Miller's first album *Once in a Blue Moon* in 1973 and throughout his recording career there has also been an impressive list of session musicians. Perhaps the lesser-known names are the real unsung heroes of rock 'n' roll. Hopefully, listeners to Frankie Miller records will listen to his recordings again with a "different ear".

Frankie's backing band on *Once in a Blue Moon* were Brinsley Schwartz.

Credits are as follows:
Frankie Miller - vocals, acoustic guitar, harmonica
Bob Andrews - grand piano, junk piano, accordion, backing vocals
Brinsley Schwarz - lead & acoustic guitars
Ian Gomm - lead & acoustic guitars
Nick Lowe - electric bass, double bass, backing vocals
Billy Rankin - drums
Bridgit, Joy and Janice - backing vocals. Collectively known as 'Bones'

Ian Gomm and Janice Carter Slater have also contributed in the following chapter…

"Without Pub Rock there would have been no punk rock in Britain. And for that alone, these bands deserve their place in Rock & Roll history."
Quote from Jake Riviera nostalgiacentral.com

1972 The Kensington, Shepherd's Bush
Brinsley Schwartz finished an incredibly tasteful rock and roll set and on stepped a short, shy Scotsman dressed in denim. "Frankie Miller turned a lot of heads that night as his ferocious voice tore into Dylan's 'It Takes a Lot to Laugh', the blues standard 'My Babe' and a truly amazing version of Van Morrison's 'Wild Night'. Miller's set also included a host of highly spirited originals, most of which can be heard on his fine debut album *Once in a Blue Moon* on Chrysalis.

"It was recorded Rockfield Studios in Wales with the Brinsleys providing a solid and flawless backing. The album's simplicity and directness gives it a rough 50s feel."

In No Resistance

Ray Telford from *Sounds* was one of the first journalists to interview Frankie after the release of *Once In a Blue Moon*.

"Right now there is one hell of a fine album on release by a tough looking young guy from Glasgow called Frankie Miller. The album… It's called *Once in a Blue Moon* gives out the first taste of the only really convincing rock and roll singer to have emerged from this country since Paul Rodgers, and the album taken as a whole is one of the strictly rocks-off collections that's been offered by any British singer so far this year."

Referring to the recent tour, Frankie said that

"The reactions we got were pretty good considering a lot of the kids who went to the concerts were there just to hear Ten Years After. Having the Brinsleys play the tour with me made it so much easier for me because they're really tight and solid and when you have that behind you feel very confident. I haven't had that feeling with many other bands."

Frankie's dream is to record in New Orleans. He is also a first-rate songwriter, as the material on his first album indicates. He calls himself a slow writer because very rarely does he complete a song in one sitting. "For me, writing a song is like having a baby in the house. I've got to nurse it along because just about all my ideas for songs come from rhythms or a certain feel and when you work like that with no real melody in your head you've got to be really careful you don't lose the feel. If I lose sight of the kind of feel I want a song to have, I can't finish it."

In 2004 Frankie's back catalogue was to be re-packaged and re-mastered by Eagle Records with bonus tracks. Ideally they would use the outtakes from *Once in a Blue Moon* sessions.

When Frankie's wife, Annette, and I got the four track tapes to Mike Howell at Eagle, they were stuck together like rolls of Sellotape and brittle, and so deemed useless.

Treasures which fans will never have the pleasure of hearing included 'Ain't too Proud to Beg' and 'I Heard it Through the Grapevine'. I was also asked to assist in building content for sleeve notes for the re-masters and worked alongside Michael Heatley to produce them.

Aside from the factual content we produced together, Michael's interviews added some interesting anecdotal stories.

Guitarist Ian Gomm recalls the era vividly. "When I think of Frankie," he says, "I have this vision of the Brinsleys doing a gig at the Hope and Anchor and, towards the end of the set, there'd be this ruction in the crowd. You'd hear this voice going 'I'm heeerrre! I'm heeerrre! Let me through!' and he'd be right at the front saying 'Let's do a numberrrr!' He'd get up with the little black hat he used to wear, get his harmonica out and insist he played. You always knew he'd find out you were playing and come along, get on stage. But he was good."

Frankie's association with the Brinsleys and delight at sitting-in led some to label him a pub-rocker, but he was at pains to point out he didn't play pub gigs in his own right. "I used to go to see bands I liked, or if I didn't know the band they might invite me up to sing, but I've never done a lot of pub work as such." His impromptu stage appearances around this period were also recalled by a fan, Billy Auld, when he visited Frankie's website. "In 1973, my brother John asked me if I wanted to go see Joe Brown and the Bruvvers playing in a pub in Hammersmith. I wasn't that keen but went anyway. When we got there I couldn't believe my eyes when I saw Frankie and (Thin Lizzy's) Phil Lynott standing at the bar!

"Halfway through the set Joe introduced Frankie and Phil and they did three or four numbers. I can't remember the songs now, but that night made a big impression on me – so much so that I put my love of live music mainly down to that gig. So, Frankie, you have my heartfelt appreciation – and even if you don't remember that occasion I always will."

When the Brinsleys and Frankie got to know each other better, they travelled down to Monmouth, south Wales, in 1972 to consign their partnership to recording tape.

"I remember Doug D'Arcy, the vice chairman of [record label] Chrysalis, coming down to Rockfield," states Ian Gomm. "It was a residential studio, so we'd been into town and got a few crates of cider and bottled Bass beer.

"Dave Robinson was producing and there were a couple of crates in the control room when we were on the second or third track. We came in to listen to what we'd just done, glugging away merrily – and Frankie, of course, was leading the debauchery!" Frankie remembered having to tape-up the mikes because they were falling to pieces and shaking the studio when he sang into them.

"It was [adopts 'sloshed' voice] 'Let's try another one then!' and straight back in the studio, but I hung back, interested to have a look at this guy in the suit. He leaned over and said to Dave Robinson, 'They're not actually going to play in that condition, are they?' He couldn't get the idea of it at all. God knows what he'd have done if we'd all been shooting up – which of course we never did!"

In fairness to band and singer, plenty of pre-production work had gone on prior to the booze-fuelled sessions. "Frankie used to come round our house and we rehearsed it all up. Our communal house was huge, the size of a school annexe.

"We had a room where we rehearsed right in the middle with mattresses all round the wall. Many's the time we'd go back and jam with the likes of Frankie, Terry Reid, those kind of people."

The vibe of songs like 'You Don't Need To Laugh (To Be Happy)' and 'I Can't Change It' were reminiscent of the Band or perhaps Van Morrison, a Miller favourite. 'Candlelight Sonata In F Major' and 'It's All Over' were nearer to the Brinsleys' own live-sounding repertoire as exemplified by the *Nervous On The Road* album which had also been cut at Rockfield that same year of 1972.

Indeed, 'I Can't Change It' was accorded what must have been for Frankie the ultimate compliment when Ray Charles covered it on his album *Brother Ray Is At It Again*. "I'm completely and absolutely jealous of the man," Procol Harum's Gary Brooker seethed good-naturedly in 2002. "I mean, he got Ray Charles to cover one of his songs! I sent the *Salty Dog* album to Ray as soon as we made it to ask if there was anything on there he could do.

"Whenever I went to a Ray Charles concert I would take along our latest record and give it to one of the girl singers or something, as close as I could get, hoping Ray might have a listen.

"Nothing ever happened, but Miller managed to get a cover!"

Aside from Frankie on vocals and guitars, the band consisted of Brinsley Schwartz (the man) and Ian Gomm, both on lead and acoustic guitars, Nick Lowe on electric and acoustic bass, Bob Andrews on keyboards and Billy Rankin on drums. Nick and Bob also supplied harmonies, while a trio of girl singers – credited as Bridget, Joy and Janice – were brought in after the album was finished. "We never met them," says Gomm. "It might have been at Olympic [studios], I don't know. They put them on afterwards, we just did the basic tracks."

Dave Robinson's production was pretty sparse and, after one more album, the Brinsleys would 'graduate' to Vic Maile of Dr Feelgood/Motörhead renown. Robinson would, however, make another mark on the rock scene by founding Stiff Records, whose house producer, one Nick Lowe, would "bash it down and tart it up" just like his mentor.

Stiff Records signed a number of artists including The Damned, Tracey Ullman, Kirsty MacColl, The Pogues, and Madness. Robinson had also managed Elvis Costello, Nick Lowe, Dave Edmunds and Ian Dury before signing them up to Stiff.

Robinson went on to manage Irish band Eire Apparent on a tour bill that included The Nice, The Move, Pink Floyd, Amen Corner and the Jimi Hendrix Experience. He went on to become a tour manager for Jimi Hendrix from his first tour of the UK until just before his death. He also managed The Animals, The Young Rascals, Vanilla Fudge, Van Morrison and Graham Parker, amongst others. Robinson also built a makeshift eight-track recording studio in the downstairs of the Hope and Anchor, Islington, and he created a network of 35 pubs in London where bands could play what they liked.

Ian Gomm and Frankie Miller's paths rarely crossed thereafter, the Scot forging onwards and upwards as Brinsley Schwartz remained around the London 'circuit'. "He took off after doing *Blue Moon*, and I can remember feeling quite flattered when, as a result, he went over to New Orleans to record with Allen Toussaint. He'd heard it, he liked it and he wanted to give Frankie his treatment. I remember thinking that was quite good, that we'd fooled him with our 'funky ethnic backing'!"

"We'd have loved to have gone ourselves," Gomm continues, "but Frankie was a solo act and Chrysalis had his publishing and recording. And he was just one guy – cheaper to send over than five. Chrysalis were quite a forward-looking company. We were with United Artists, which always seemed to be an uphill struggle."

Author's note: A number of years ago one of the backing singers from *Once in a Blue Moon* contacted me via Frankie's website. We lost touch but we recently found each other again. Janice Carter Slater from 'Bones' (or Janice Slater as she was in the time) has had a formidable career in music.

From Janice:

"By the mid '70s I'd been working as a backup singer to Cliff Richard for two years on the road with my fellow Pacific regions friends, Joy Yates (New Zealand) and Bridget Lokelani Dudoit (Hawaii). We'd formed a three girl backup group ironically named 'Bones' to keep the wolves at bay! Australian record producer David MacKay brought us together later to join Esperanto Rock Orchestra.

"By the time 'Bones' were invited to work on Frankie Miller's *Once in a Blue Moon* I was a seasoned session singer yet working with Frankie provided me with the kind of feel I'd always longed to be a part of on foreign shores. In Australia in the late 60s I'd listened to the recordings my brother Russ brought back from the USA and UK. Steve Miller Band, Buffalo Springfield, Grateful Dead, Argent, Christine Perfect/Chicken Shack were played relentlessly.

"Frankie's session brought me back to those influences and gave me the opportunity of following in the footsteps of those bands that I loved.

Frankie's heartbreaking vocals and songs were edgy, emotionally direct and a joy for us to add to. Frankie is one of the great soul singer/songwriters of all time. I feel blessed to have worked with him. I remember that the session unfolded with warmth and good humour and brief introductions to several members of the band. Years later was I to learn what formidable figures they were in the music scene. We enjoyed their ease in working with us. Now at a distance of over fifty years I can say thank you to Frankie and the great musicians on that session.

"Frankie's session unfolded in friendly introductions to a bright-eyed, long-haired lad who epitomised the grit and edge I'd yearned to be a part of when I listened to records of Joe Cocker or Leon Russell. This was a once in a lifetime gig and remains one of the most memorable. No hassles, goodwill and to die for lead vocals. We could bring our own 'Bones' vibes into the mix, those big hearted, full throttle vocals of Joy Yates and soaring soprano of Lokelani Dudoit... along with what I will call my Aussie 'twang'."

Also in Australia during the 1960s, Janice worked with Billy Preston, Bobby Day, The Easybeats, The Four Tops, George Chakiris (West Side Story), The Hollies, Johnny O'Keefe, Lesley Gore ('It's My Party'), Lou Rawls, Phil Silvers (Sergeant Bilko in *The Phil Silvers Show*), Sammy Davis, Junior, Shirley Bassey, The Three Degrees, and Trini Lopez. Janice recorded on the Phillips, Spin and Polydor labels.

In the UK she worked on numerous recordings, from Cliff Richard to Cleo Laine as well as Olivia Newton John, Cilla Black and Petula Clark. With Glenn Shorrock, she was one of the founding members of the acclaimed 12-piece progressive rock band Esperanto Rock Orchestra. That band released an album on the A&M label in 1973. (From thehistoryofaussierock.com)

"By the light of the moon, in a foggy saloon
   I was drinkin' my last piece of gold
      When a voice from behind took away my loaded mind
      And it led me to my childhood and my soul"

From 'Anne Eliza Jane' by Frankie Miller

March 17th 1973

"What Frankie needs," said a mildly drunk Deke O'Brien, guitarist and one of the three Irishmen who make up that very excellent combo Bees Make Honey, "is for him to have Steve Cropper in his back-up band, then he'd really get off. "

Deke's words were spoken in the Marquee's dusky bar only three days after the Frankie Miller/Bees Make Honey tour finally hit the road, after weeks of rumour and speculation as to whether the gig would actually be taking place in the light of business hassles involving Chrysalis, Frankie's record label, and the self-sufficient Bees.

After Frankie first saw Bees Make Honey perform at their one-time residency at the Tally Ho in Kentish Town, the impromptu jams ended up with them eventually doing a small tour together. Deke had recalled the gigs with relish.

These dates had followed Frankie's tour with Brinsley Schwartz, when they supported Ten Years After on the UK leg of their European Tour. That tour had helped boost sales of *Once In A Blue Moon* and also gave Frankie some much needed live exposure. Anyone who thought that there were no more honest-to-goodness blues singers left in the country were given a jolt.

The blues, as well as soul and R&B, have had a huge effect and influence on his life. Frankie claimed that most of his lyrics were based on personal experience, presenting honest characterisations of things like past love tussles and rough social comment. There are many examples of both in his catalogue. Frankie's delivery was also described as his most alluring quality and something which he couldn't help but project visually.

In April 1973, Frankie was booked to fly out to New Orleans to begin work on his second album, to be produced by Allen Toussaint. A studio band was organised for the sessions and some time was spent rehearsing before any recordings were made. At the time Frankie said that the two producers he always wanted to work with were Phil Spector or Allen Toussaint. He explained that tapes of the first album were sent to Marshall Seahorn, Toussaint's manager, and the response was that they would be happy to produce the next album. Frankie had songs already written for the album (or he had figured out in his head what he wanted) after hearing that the Meters, who had recently worked with Dr. John, could be involved in the backup work. Frankie also described how bands like the Meters had lots of space in their music, and that was what he had liked about working with Bees Make Honey. The plan was for Allen Toussaint to be doing the horn arrangements and, in Frankie's words at the time, "They're gonna have to be pretty well spaced out because I need that kind of room."

Before setting off for the States, Frankie further reflected on his tour with Ten Years After and their knockout appearance in Edinburgh. He was disappointed that they hadn't played in his hometown of Glasgow because of the energy there generated by rock 'n' roll audiences.

Frankie reflected that enthusiasm and strength of soul in his singing and had come to the conclusion that it was the direct result of his past experiences, both musical and otherwise, in Glasgow.

"The vibe in Glasgow right now," said Frankie, glum faced and deadly serious, "is that the people want to get the government, line them up against the wall, and shoot the lot of them. That sort of attitude breeds a very special kind of energy which is reflected in the kind of music they dig."

So with *High Life* recorded but as yet unreleased, Frankie hit the road again.

In spring 1973 Brinsley Schwartz/Frankie Miller were the support band on the Wings tour. Paul and Linda asked them to be on the tour after seeing them perform at London's Hard Rock Café's opening night a few weeks previously.

Leicester Odeon
The Odeon bar was once described as a kind of sanctuary for rock bands and the Brinsleys had taken advantage of that and partied hard for at least an hour before they were due on stage. Frankie joined them for a couple of songs, including 'Ain't Too Proud To Beg'.

The atmosphere created in the bar had carried along with them into the show.

Afterwards Frankie commented that Wings were getting better and better all the time and that he loved the way Paul McCartney played bass, describing him as "a mover".

There were already rumours that Henry McCullough might be splitting from the band, maybe because of his highly individual approach (which would be in conflict with the rest of the band) or perhaps because he was unhappy about the long period of inactivity before the tour.

Author's note: Some years later I actually asked Henry, in a quiet moment, why he had left Wings and he answered – tongue in cheek in his lovely soft accent – "too much fuckin' oohin' and aahin'."

That answer could only come from an Irishman!

Some interesting stories from these few days with Wings come from Dave Robinson in *Be Stiff: The Stiff Records Story*. On this support tour, there was an obvious publicity opportunity for Brinsley Schwartz (and Frankie) but Wings manager Vince Romeo wanted them to pay for the privilege and perform for no fee.

Henry McCullough (previously managed by Dave Robinson in Eire Apparent days) was able to step in and persuade Mr Romeo to give the Brinsleys £125 a night plus travel in McCartney's tour bus. The tour schedule also suited because they could play their support slot and still make it to some of their pre-arranged headline shows.

There was an obvious gulf, though, between Dave Robinson's and his band's ambitions. He felt perhaps that they were not putting as much effort into it as he was and it came to a head one night when Nick Lowe went out for a drink and appeared on stage halfway through the show at the Liverpool Empire.

Dave Robinson went on to say that he was frustrated, not at the lack of success but at the lack of effort. He had observed how hard Paul McCartney was working (when he didn't have to) and was trying to polish up and improve his music while his lot were in the pub…

Later in the year Frankie again made an appearance at Dingwalls with Bees Make Honey.

Three pub rock gigs from August were covered by *Sounds* on 1/9/1973 in which Frankie featured.

"Bees Make Honey continued their Tuesday night visits to Dingwalls last week and turned in yet another fine performance."

Despite being without their pianist, guitarist and sax player Ruan O'Lochlainn, it was reported that they had put on a decent show. The highlight of the evening for everyone was an appearance by Frankie Miller. He reportedly "stormed through four or five songs—the most memorable of which was 'Walking the Dog'—and the crowd loved it". The band obviously did too.

Ducks Deluxe were also reviewed:

"Ducks down the Lord Nelson - the thought of that is enough to set the pulses of the *Sounds* office workers racing, and their feet dancing down the road to the local."

It was reported that the venue was packed out and the band had whipped up a great atmosphere during their first set.

Frankie Miller was spotted during the break, after having been asked to get up and sing, having a discussion with Martin Belmont in which he was trying to persuade the band to do Allen Toussaint's 'On Your Way Down'.

Frankie got up and after a hurried conference with the band, launched into 'Walking The Dog'. It sparked the Ducks into life again, and then came 'On Your Way Down' "which was really beautiful with Frankie singing his heart out and the band playing sparse lines but really funky - they sounded like Free at their height." Glenroy from Greyhound then joined them for the Rolling Stones' 'It's All Over Now', alternating verses with Frankie as well as the two singing in harmony while spurring each other on to greater heights.

And Brinsley Schwartz:

"Thursday night at Dingwalls Dance Hall saw Brinsley Schwartz in fine fettle."

With Brinsley himself sometimes on saxophone, it was reported that the "bounce-off between him and guitarist Ian Gomm was excellent" as was the keyboard playing of Bob Andrews. The fluent rhythm section of Nick Lowe and Billy Rankin was also appreciated by the reporter.

Frankie Miller got up to sing a couple of numbers, which was a high a point as usual.

Author's Note: Frankie always seemed to stand out when he appeared as a guest with these bands, which is a far cry from the claim made later that he was "A joke in the London bars before *Full House*." Who could have made such a claim, I wonder?

October 1973

By now Frankie and Henry McCullough were starting to put something together and with some other ex-Grease Band members, and others, played a warm-up gig at the Finsbury Hall in London.

It had been arranged to give Frankie the opportunity to play a none-too-frequent full show and with an admission charge of 40p it seemed like a great deal!

The band was made up of Henry McCullough and Neil Hubbard on guitars, Alan Spenner on bass, Ruan McLochlain on sax, Mick Weaver on piano, and Average White Band drummer, Robbie McIntosh.

The venue's acoustics were questioned as it was reported that Mick Weaver could only be heard on the slower, moody songs and Henry's guitar licks couldn't be heard on the fast, rockier songs.

As well as songs from *Once In A Blue Moon*, Stevie Wonder's 'Superstition' was a highlight of the show.

There was some mis-timing and lost cues during the show but as Frankie explained afterwards, they had only rehearsed once and he wasn't sure who would actually be turning up to play. He was also the first to admit that after the high praise given to his first album, it hadn't done him too much good not being on the road with his own band.

According to reports, Chrysalis were currently sitting on a second Frankie Miller album, which was recorded the previous spring in New Orleans and Atlanta with Allen Toussaint arranging and producing. The association with Toussaint, Frankie said, "ran very smooth and promised that the new, as yet untitled album would turn a few ears."

But it was noted that "to get the full extent of Miller's talents you have to see him live, and for this reason, the sooner he gets a band around him the better."

Ace (fronted by Paul Carrack) Roundhouse

This was billed as a "jolly yuletide jam" by a multitude of Real Musicians as Dave Robinson once dubbed them.

The band consisted of (sax section) Paul Bailey (Chilli Willi), Barry Richardson (Bees Make Honey) and Brinsley "Bert" Schwarz, operating as the "Electricians".

On drums were Pete Thomas (Willis), Billy Rankin (Electricians), and Fran Byrne (Ace). Tex Comer (Ace) played bass and Alan King (Ace), Martin Stone (Willis), Jimmy McCulloch (Wings) and Ian Gomm (Electricians) strummed guitars.

Bob Andrews (Electricians) played organ and Phil Lithman (Willis) started on piano moving later to violin, and if you've ever heard a fiddle swinging through 'Walking The Dog' you'll get some idea of the quality of the latter part of the icing on this Chalk Farm Christmas cake.

Lastly the vocalists. There were a lot, but to pick out the "stars" Frankie Miller, of himself, sang best lead vocals while Phil Harris and Paul Carrack of Ace, plus Various Others, wrestled for mike space.

Neil Hubbard

First met Frankie Miller in the mid 70s and featured in various line-ups with Frankie between 1977 and 1994. Neil is a British guitarist who has performed with Juicy Lucy, The Grease Band, Bluesology, Joe Cocker, Roxy Music, Kokomo, Alvin Lee, B.B. King, Kevin Rowland and Tony O'Malley, and played on the original 1970 concept album *Jesus Christ Superstar*. He can be heard on Roxy Music's *Flesh and Blood* and *Avalon* albums and a notable guitar solo by him features on the hit single 'Slave To Love'.

Henry McCullough

Northern Irish guitar player Henry McCullough joined the Frankie Miller Band in 1975 along with bassist Chrissy Stewart, keyboard player Mick Weaver and drummer Stu Perry. Having appeared at Woodstock as part of the Grease Band with Joe Cocker, Henry was asked by Paul McCartney to join Wings and features on classic songs like 'Hi Hi Hi', 'Live and Let Die' and 'My Love'. He walked out of the *Band on the Run* sessions and teamed up with Frankie Miller to record *The Rock* album in San Francisco.

Mick Weaver

is an English session musician, best known for his playing of the Hammond B3 organ. In the late 60s his band performed as Wynder K. Frog. He joined Traffic when Steve Winwood left to join Blind Faith. He also recorded with solo artists such as Buddy Guy, Dave Gilmour, Joe Cocker, Eric Burdon, Roger Chapman, Steve Marriott, Gary Moore and Taj Mahal.

Mick Weaver at San Quentin

"It's The Highlife"
Lookin up…Lookin up…"

From 'High Life' by Frankie Miller

It's into 1974 though before Frankie starts to get a bit more publicity in the music press and his relationship with Allen Toussaint takes him to another level.

"New Orleans? Ever since I can remember, you know how you get these songs on your mind. I've had it on my mind since probably before I can remember.

"It's just incredible, you know. Especially in the French Quarter where I was. Everything's happenin'."

An early Chrysalis press release launched *High Life* as follows:

Frankie Miller's High Life
Take one Scottish-born singer, mix well with the king of New Orleans, black music, simmer gently with a remix in Detroit and you've got a new recipe for Miller's *High Life*.

The Ingredients
Miller is a 23-year-old, Glasgow born Scot who has been influenced by classic Black vocalists such as Ray Charles, Otis Redding and Sam Cooke, along with the pioneering work of Allen Toussaint. Thus, when he recorded his first album (*Once In a Blue Moon*, with Brinsley Schwartz, originally only released in the UK, Miller sent a copy to the Black songwriter/producer in New Orleans) Toussaint's reaction was immediate: he wanted to see Miller, pronto.

"Miller just does not sing; he wraps himself mercilessly around a song and tackles it with the intensity of early Joe Cocker"—*The Guardian*

Things began to happen. Miller flew to New Orleans: the rapport was instant. He rehearsed and wrote side by side with the legendary Toussaint.

It was a somewhat strange collaboration—a young Scot sweltering in the heat and humidity of the South, blending the tough romanticism in his voice around the tunes of a master pianist, writer, arranger and producer. It worked.

"Frankie Miller is very real; he doesn't have a pre-fab voice. It's just the real nitty gritty. Not only his voice but his feeling. He feels these songs"—Don Davis

Next, Miller went to Atlanta for a rendezvous with musicians handpicked by Toussaint, and here, his and Toussaint's songs were laid down by the young Scot.

The tapes were taken to Detroit for a re-mix by Don Davis, who like Toussaint, has long associations with many prominent Black recording artists.

"Likely to be one of the toughest, most soul-searching singers you've heard in a long time."—*New Musical Express*

The outcome of this long but productive journey is Frankie Miller's *High Life*—a convincing display of rock 'n' roll by a young singer, with a little help from his friends. "I'm very happy about the Frankie Miller session," says Allen Toussaint. "I think that's one of the best projects we have. Frankie is a good singer and he writes some great songs."

(Interestingly though, some time later it became apparent during interviews that Frankie wasn't totally happy with the Don Davis mixes.)

It was to be summer 1974 before the music press reviews and interviews were published.

In *Sounds* magazine, Edward Pouncey (a.k.a. Savage Pencil) wrote that "Frankie had already proven himself to be a remarkable songwriter with a strong, gritty voice and a unique style of phrasing - a kind that sounds effortless and natural but takes extraordinary twists and turns."

He also reflected on Frankie's numerous guest appearances with Brinsley Schwartz and Bees Make Honey, pointing out that the singer had proven himself equally effective when handling other people's songs - Rufus Thomas's 'Walking the Dog' and Allen Toussaint's 'On Your Way Down' being two of his party pieces.

It was noted again that because Frankie hadn't a regular band to work with over the last couple of years, he wasn't able to get his teeth into the type of songs that he liked to perform live.

With *High Life* he had "emerged not only as a songwriter with a good voice but as a commanding singer who can work different styles into an album that remains identifiable as Frankie Miller."

Edward Pouncey also noted that to an extent, Allen Toussaint had put Frankie "through the hoops" several times on the album, with "challenges of style and pace that bring out an astonishing versatility which proves him to be an assured, commanding and inspired singer. There are few enough of those around."

Reflecting on his time in New Orleans, Frankie looked back fondly on the experience of working with Allen Toussaint. "He made me realise that I should be laid back some of the time. At the start maybe I used to scream a bit instead of singing. I don't think that happened on *High Life,* which is the way it should be."

James Johnson described Frankie in July '74 *NME* as "a tough Glaswegian who's always been dedicated to the roughest most raunchy black music. Also maintaining a dour, almost surly persona and a fairly basic attitude towards his role as an artist."

Frankie explained that he felt in the UK the music industry was more interested in glitter and sensationalism. He had gone to a Lou Reed gig "because Ducks Deluxe were on" and "couldn't believe how bad it was, both musically and stagewise, but a lot of people go to see that kind of thing."

Part of Frankie's time in New Orleans was spent living in Bourbon Street, where he had the opportunity to check out places where his heroes like Dr. John and Lee Dorsey had learned their trade.

He recalled actually meeting Lee Dorsey and was "knocked out" to meet him. As for his time with Allen Toussaint, Frankie said that he had been great guy to work with and didn't write anything down. It was all carried in his head the whole time.

While 'Brickyard Blues' has been selected by many as one of Frankie's finest performances and featured in his live shows for some years afterwards, he had some reservations about the album.

When Frankie was asked what sort of sound he wanted for *High Life*, he told Toussaint "Rough as we can get."

The result was a "really punchy" album until it was sent to United Sound Studios in Detroit, where it was re-mixed, because the "Philly" sound was in.

It left Frankie sad and disappointed, because he "hated that stuff". He didn't want anything to do with the album and he was again without a band or a hit record, despite 'Shoorah Shoorah' getting a few covers.

At the time, Thin Lizzy were working on their *Night Life* album and Frankie lent drinking buddy Phil Lynott a hand in writing and performing on a track. So the classic 'Still In Love With You' was born and Frankie still jokes to this day that Phil owed him a fortune after leaving him off the writing credits!

Whilst in search of new musicians to work with at this time, Frankie and Andy Fraser got together to try and form a new band. After leaving Free, Andy had started a band called Sharks with guitarist Chris Spedding and after that folded he was left looking for a new front man. Frankie fitted the bill as his soulful vocal style had often been compared to Paul Rodgers.

They then spent over a week auditioning musicians at the Hope and Anchor in Islington.

"We got on well together as far as jamming and even writing went, but as a band it never clicked."

The band was unofficially named the Rumbledown Band and joining Andy and Frankie were Mike Kellie on drums (ex Grease Band/Spooky Tooth) and Nick Judd on piano (ex Juicy Lucy/Audience), with Frankie handling guitar duties. Recording sessions had taken place with Andy and Frankie playing all the instruments themselves.

Because Frankie wasn't really a lead guitarist, Robin Trower and Paul Kossoff did some sessions with Jimmy Dewar doing backing vocals.

In Frankie's words, "There was a lot of energy but we were just wasting time."

Their search for a permanent lead guitarist had led them to ex-Grease Band and Wings member Henry McCullough, but Andy didn't get on with him.

Andy moved on, taking Nick Judd with him, leaving Frankie and Henry to make their own plans.

During an interview with Rob Mackie from *Sounds* on 6th July the conversation somehow meandered away from the Miller/Fraser project as Frankie reminisced about bigotry in New Orleans and his home town in Scotland.

Frankie managed to turn a very serious subject into something quite hilarious...

He explained that in New Orleans "the blacks and white live in separate areas because they both want to, but when they socialise on evenings and weekends, they mix well." He referred to Jerry Lee Lewis recording a Little Richard or Chuck Berry song but refusing to share a dressing room with them. He said that he was very surprised by that and that it was just ignorance. "Like the Scots hating the English," he said. "Most of them don't know any!"

Frankie went on to relate a story about having a grandfather who played for both Rangers and Celtic, as well as Scotland. (Rangers discovered he was a Catholic, which was against their signing principles.) He was called Archibald Kyle, but they called him 'Punch'. "Because he played like Jim Holton?" "No, because he drank a lot."

Frankie had the traditional love-hate relationship with his hometown, Glasgow, a place where he was thankful for his upbringing and loved going back to, but always realised he had to get away from.

He reflected on how hard his parents had worked, with not a lot to show for it. He described their home as a slum – just a room and a kitchen with no toilet.

He criticised the planners by saying that when they pull down the slums, they just build skyscrapers, "and those are fuckin' slums too. Aye, they never really re-built Glasgow, they were too busy re-buildin' Edinburgh for the tourists."

High Life Postscript

Allen Toussaint organised the musicians for this album, and provided Frankie with some of New Orleans' top session players.

Allen Toussaint - piano, organ, conga

American musician, songwriter, arranger, and record producer. He was an influential figure in New Orleans rhythm and blues from the 1950s onwards. Passed away in 2015.

Joe Wilson - guitar, slide guitar

Joe Wilson was born on 5 May 1943 and was gigging around the New Orleans clubs from the beginning of the 60s. He was also a soul singer and was once described as follows: " 'When A Man Cries' is an exquisite deep soul ballad, brim full of emotional power from Joe's light high baritone and featuring one of Wardell Quezergue's most heartfelt string arrangements – superb guitar fills as well."

Tom Robb - bass, conga

American session bassist who is best known for his work with acts like Dionne Warwick, Little Richard, Dolly Parton, The Marshall Tucker Band, and many others.

Mike Huey - drums

American drummer and producer, earning 18 gold/platinum top ten awards. He has played with a diverse group of artists in genres including rock, pop, country and R&B such as Glenn Frey, Joe Walsh, Juice Newton, Etta James, and Lindsey Buckingham.

G. C. Coleman – drums

During his career he drummed for Otis Redding and Curtis Mayfield.

Auburn Burrell - dobra guitar

Also did session guitar work for Joe South and Leo Sayer.

Barry Bailey – guitar
Once played in the backing band for Roy Orbison then became part of the Atlanta Rhythm Section, who supported the Who and the Rolling Stones on their USA tours in the mid 70s.

Horns:
Lester Caliste – trombone
American trombonist, born in New Orleans, Louisiana. Played with the world famous Preservation Hall Jazz Band and recorded on Allen Toussaint and Patty Labelle recordings.

Clyde Kerr Jr – trumpet
His early career included work as a studio musician for national acts such as The Jackson Five, The O'Jays, Aretha Franklin, Tony Bennett, Allen Toussaint, Dr. John and the Neville Brothers.

Gary Brown - tenor saxophone
His repertoire includes a long list of collaborations with some the world's biggest musicians. He recorded and toured with Otis Redding, Marvin Gaye, Joe Cocker, the Bee Gees, Dr. John, Irma Thomas, Wilson Pickett, and many more. In addition, he recorded the instrumental soundtrack 'Alone At The Drive In Movie' for the motion picture *Grease*, starring John Travolta.

John Longo – trumpet
Played in the Duke Ellington Band and featured as part of the backing band in *Diana Ross Live! The Lady Sings... Jazz & Blues: Stolen Moments*.

Alvin Thomas - baritone saxophone
When Paul McCartney and Wings came to New Orleans during the *Venus and Mars* sessions, Alvin Thomas added saxophone to the mix at Sea-Saint Studios, which was a music recording facility co-owned by musician, producer, and arranger, Allen Toussaint.

In December it was announced that Henry McCullough, formerly of the Grease Band and Wings, was in the studio working on his first solo album, which would involve people with whom he had been working, including Tim Hinkley, Neil Hubbard and Frankie Miller, who would play some guitar and backing vocals. The plan was to play some live dates in the near future with a mid-January date being set for the Hope and Anchor. Other band members were to include John Halsey (ex-Patto) on drums and Jimmy Leverton (ex-Fat Mattress) on bass.

Drunken Nights in the City

Barbara Charone remains one of the most respected women in the music business and is joint director in one of the world's top music PR firms, MBC. Clients include Madonna, Rod Stewart and Keith Richards. She also worked as a music journalist in the 70s for *Rolling Stone*, *NME* and *Sounds*, before writing Keith Richards' authorised biography. Barbara kindly approved use of the following:

In December '74 she reviewed a gig which took place at the Greyhound, Fulham, during that month. The line-up was Dave Thompson on piano, Jimmy Leverton on bass, John Halsey on drums, Neil Hubbard on rhythm guitar, Henry McCullough on lead guitar and Frankie Miller's vocals.

Barbara commented on the current climate in rock 'n' roll with "overpriced concert tickets and over-the-hill rock and rollers and the fact that there were no limousines waiting out front. Yet the music played on the small stage far surpassed most of the rubbish heard at the Empire Pool."

She went on to describe 'Band on the Run' playing over the club PA as Henry casually sauntered in whistling to the tune. Meanwhile Frankie was spotted in the bar before the show, "Grinning cherubic smiles and looking healthy."

It was Frankie's first live date since the previous October, when both men had stubbornly fought for centre stage, in what Barbara Charone described as an "ego infected performance". But this time everything worked out smoothly, despite it being a one-off gig. Frankie's vocals were described as "Just as potent as those of a certain R. Stewart."

"The band kicked off in a style reminiscent of Wilson Pickett or Booker T. with clean guitar leads surrounding very black vocals."

Barbara decided that the evening belonged exclusively to McCullough and Miller, "where the band performed the classic '634-5789', which was followed by standout numbers 'Ann Eliza Jane', 'Trouble' and the divine 'Brickyard Blues', giving off large chunks of rock and roll magic and R&B funk that instantly reminded the listener of days spent listening to the original Jeff Beck Group or Joe Cocker and the Grease Band.

"Remnants of Henry's stint with Wings were provided by his pop star sequinned jacket, but the notes coming out of his guitar were far from phoney. It was the real thing.

"Wings wasn't the right vehicle for Henry but with this band his solos were right there, in every number, proving that he is one of the top guitarists playing today. Anyone who has heard his 'My Love' solo already knew that.

"What the gig easily proved is that Frankie Miller is superb. More bands like this one and rock and roll might survive.

" 'Frankie is the dirtiest singer I've ever heard,' one girl ecstatically mumbled when it was over. She just might be right."

In a *Sounds* interview by Barbara Charone in January 1975, the headline joked

"We've had Sonny and Cher and Simon and Garfunkel but we've never had anything like Frankie and Henry."

"In a good humoured exchange, conducted in their favourite watering hole in London's West End, the pair outlined their intentions in no mean fashion.

" 'There's no band that's doing it except for us,' the courageous Scot boasts. 'I've looked around, seen everybody. If Otis (Redding) were alive today he'd be the one; he'd be doing it, singing the truth, the real nitty gritty. Otis was so fucking truthful,' Miller says of his idol.

" 'Naw,' Henry disagrees. 'Otis might have ended up in Vegas, just like Elvis.'

" 'Otis was too real for that,' Frankie insists, playing the straight man...

" 'What was good about these records was the rawness. Cause ya know I don't think it's down to having a great band, an amazing P.A. system. It's down to where your roots are. You can forget the rest of it,' Henry announces. 'People talk about taste but it's the most artistic people that lose out.'

" 'I'm in the business for the preservation of music," McCullough continues, slowly adding momentum to his words. 'It's fine and good playing to 20,000 people but it won't be any fucking different than playing in the Hope and Anchor.

" 'I'm in it for the love of the music more than anything else. We'll never become stars and be all different. You've got to have your ego trip and a sense of reality as well.' Typical of these two characters, the band presently exists in a permanent state of loose chaos. Like Henry says, they 'don't have the money or whatever' to elevate them to the big time. What they need is an industrious, honest manager, if indeed such a thing exists, to shake them out of their pub circuit slumber and into the Rainbow. They are that good.

" 'All we need is a manager that's behind us 100%. We know the band is good. WE know the band is good. WE know the basic structure is gonna be baad. I'm dying to go to America and just rip it apart. I can feel it.'

"Frankie stops short, caught up in the euphoria. 'There's no way we'll be sitting about in May saying let's do Dingwalls, let's do the Hope and Anchor.'

" 'Yeah,' Henry continues. 'There's a reason for doing these gigs and they'll never be repeated. Once around and that's it - if we can't make an impression we'll go elsewhere. I hope by the time we run out of pubs someone will see us. It's just a case of rehearsing the band in front of an audience instead of spending four weeks in rehearsal.'

" 'And there's no better place to rehearse than the pubs. But ya know what good are the pubs? Frankie shouldn't spend his life singing in pubs. This really is the best band I've worked with and we really haven't had a chance yet. See, there was no one prepared to put the money in except Nigel Thomas (Management representation for Kiki Dee, Joe Cocker, The Kinks).' At which point Frankie winced and reached for a brandy.

" 'We will do an album once someone gets us out of this stagnation. The only people that are doing something for us are ourselves. We have to be heard. It's time everyone knew how good Frankie Miller is. What we need is a good manager. We need someone to read your article and say,' Henry's normally lethargic speaking voice is animated, with American slang, 'Hey man we know what you cats are about, let's give you a 100 million dollars. Someone's got to give us the money so we can keep the right musicians in the right place. Right now we're just stumbling about in the dark.'

"The latest plans are for Henry to finish off his solo album before the notorious duo unite in the studio.

" 'Henry's got a load of great songs and this is the first chance he's had to sing and play them. There's one song on his album – "Irish Country Rose" - that's a dead ringer for my voice, but Henry does it brilliantly,' Frankie enthuses.

"Both Miller and McCullough have spent a lot of time reaching their common ground. If the potential isn't exposed to the general public it will be tragic."

Barbara Charone finished her piece by stating that "The time is right now. Frankie Miller, he's the one with the amazing vocal chords, and Henry McCullough, he's the one with the hot licks, are an unbeatable combination."

(Reproduced with kind permission)

In the same month (March), Frankie appeared with Procol Harum at the Over the Rainbow concert at the Rainbow Theatre. It was the last concert before the venue shut for several months for refurbishment. They did seven numbers together: 'The Devil Gun', 'Brickyard Blues', 'If You Need Me', 'It Takes a Lot To Laugh', 'He'll Have To Go', 'Shoorah Shoorah' and 'It's All Over'.

OOR magazine came over from the continent to interview Frankie after previously choosing *High Life* as their album of the year.
Frankie is ready.

Their opening statement was as follows….

" 'Ladies and Gentlemen, Scotland's number one poet, Frankie Miller!' With these words Procol Harum's Gary Brooker introduced the white soul singer Frankie Miller to the fans at the Rainbow. After listening to complex music for hours, the audience could finally stand up and get active. The very direct, aggressive and catchy sound of the Scot made people get up and move. What a victory for Rock and Roll."

Frankie was already popular in Holland thanks to some appearances at Boddy's Inn in Amsterdam in 1972 with Brinsley Schwartz and Ducks Deluxe.

I had the original interview translated from Dutch into English and I have to say that journalist Constant Meijers did a brilliant job with a series of well researched, sensitive and incisive questions, to which Frankie responded in a way that belies his evasive reputation.

Here are some examples, with Meijers touching on Frankie's views of life in the Scottish music scene at the time, a reflection on *High Life*, and his (eye-opening) thoughts on future band members for him and Henry McCullough. (Reproduced with Kind permission: Constant Meijers.)

"Frankie, time and time again we're seeing very good soul bands show up from Scotland. Do you have an explanation for that?"

"It could be that it's rather dismal and sad over there. Especially in Glasgow and Dundee. Those are really messed up cities, that you could compare to American ghettos. The place where a lot of the black ghetto music comes from. Bands from Edinburgh differ quite a lot from Glasgow and Dundee bands. Glasgow and Dundee are like a different world. Edinburgh is a tourist city and it's very clean. That might play a role in influencing our music."

"Which artists would you say were your biggest influences?"

"Otis Redding, Ray Charles, Solomon Burke, Bobby Bland and Little Richard."

"When searching for new band members with Andy Fraser, were the people not good enough or did you set the bar too high?"

"The last one. Look, I had already seen a lot and now I just wanted the band around me to be THE band. While reaching for that I've been without one for two years. To find the one I want I'll go to America soon."

"Why America? Aren't English musicians capable enough?"

"Oh sure, there are many excellent people here. But those are stuck in bands. Take B.J. Wilson, the drummer of Procol. He is the best drummer here, astonishingly good. But he is committed to his band. To find similar people these days, you have to go to America. Mick Weaver, who just left Joe Cocker, will join my band on keyboards. He is fantastic and lives in America now. The same goes for Henry McCullough, who will probably come to play the guitar.

"He was already up for it in the past, but due to all kinds of business difficulties he had to do something else for a couple of weeks. After that, I hope he will join us again."

"Does that mean you want to settle in America?"

"Yes, I feel more for America than England. *High Life* was played quite a lot in America. I know it has been played a lot on the radio, so now I plan to do a promotional tour of 3-6 months."

"Starting from that basic group, the rhythm section becomes particularly important. It seems difficult, at least to me, to find the right people for that. "

"I have my eyes on a drummer who played for Ike and Tina Turner, Stu Perry. The guy is incredibly good and lives in LA. Someone like Al Jackson is the type of drummer that I like most. Do you know Al Jackson? He played on all Otis Redding records. Or Bernard Purdie, and, not to forget, Zig (or Zagabo) from The Meters. If you could find someone who'd combine the talents of the three of those, you'd have found the best - within the limits of what's possible. The new band is going to be one of the best bands in the world, man. A lot of people are waiting for it and I'm ready."

"I Took a Mid-Day Plane from Glasgow to LA….
where the bad ol' stewardess frowned in shades of grey"
From 'Free and Safe (On the Road)' by Frankie Miller

June '75

Andy McConnell from *Sounds* was another of the 70s music journalists who "got" Frankie and accompanied him to the States, where he witnessed the activities first hand.

I succeeded in making contact with him in 2020 and got an amazing and enthusiastic response. His subtle wit, enthusiasm and intelligence shone though in his writing.

He interviewed Frankie after Mr. Miller had jumped on stage un-invited to join a band, as witnessed by the "Fourth Cream Member", Felix Pappalardi, and his wife, as follows:

"Gail Pappalardi asks curiously, 'Do you know anything about Frankie Miller? We saw him the other night.' 'Yeah, we were watching the Section at this club in North Hollywood, when this little guy gets up on stage, absolutely out of his mind, and starts singing. The band looked completely amazed then finally threw him off,' continues her husband Felix, bassist and vocalist in Mountain and the former Cream producer. 'I said to Gail, we've got to find out who he is because he has one of the strongest voices I've ever heard. He's got balls too. I want to work with him.'"

He'd been planning an outfit with Henry McCullough in England, but that fell through after a row, then almost inevitably, they came back together again for this American jaunt.

"I originally met Henry through the Brinsleys actually," recalls Frankie, the afternoon after his evening with the Section. "I was up singin' with them an' he came up an' said 'Get yourself a good Celtic band together,' an' I said 'Nice one' because I've always dug his playin'. He's exactly what I want, a really raw player."

Henry had been forming a band with Mick Weaver in San Francisco last year when he called Joe Cocker and discovered he was needed to help form a new band for his old pal, bringing Mick along for the gig. They went up to a ranch in Santa Barbara and rehearsed one song in six months, 'With a Little Help From My Friends'.

In a quote from *Irish Folk and Trad Blues*, Henry says, "The bass player was into smack, the drummer Jimmy Karstein was into guns and I was drinking tequila for breakfast with a teaspoon of mescaline.

"A few psychedelic freaks, a smackhead and the drummer into guns: it makes a fucking great combination! And Joe was trying to keep his belly in by lying on a bottle of Courvoisier. Everybody was just too out of it."

In later years, a biography of Joe Cocker, *With a Little Help from my Friends* by J.P. Bean, alleges that Henry pulled a gun on Cocker at one point!

Yet when it comes to drinking, Frankie is no Mormon abstainer himself. Writing in *Let it Rock*, Myles Palmer said, "It's no secret that he's fond of a little light refreshment. Who isn't? But if I hear one more story about him being carried out of the Marquee or Hope and Anchor, I'll personally go round to his flat and hold him out of the window by his ankles."

Indeed, many suggest that but for his drinking habits, Frankie would be the latest in a long line of world-acclaimed British R&B vocalists. As it stands Frankie remains virtually unheard.

Remarkably and thankfully, it appears that Frankie has toned his drinking down. Frankie explains, "We played two nights at the Hope & Anchor and the first night I didn't have much to drink. Then we went partying until nine o'clock the next morning and I was so ill I couldn't look at another drink. When I got up on stage that night I knew where things lay."

"I did some dates with Procol Harum and never touched a drop... ok, maybe one or two... but no getting' out of it, that's not where its at... "

When Frankie officially appointed his new manager, Joe McCourtney went searching out new deals for Frankie and Henry in LA, and he found companies didn't want to know about the combination. Reputations travel across oceans.

"Well I don't care two fuckin shits about any record company. We're both in this band and if they don't like it they can fuckin lump it," Frankie insists furiously.

But they're now in San Francisco searching out their elusive bass player and drummer, and considering recording with Neil Young's producer, Elliot Mazer.

Elliot Mazer

Frankie recorded *The Rock* at His Masters Wheels studios in San Francisco with audio engineer and record producer Elliot Mazer. He was best known for his work with Linda Ronstadt, Neil Young, Bob Dylan, The Band, and Janis Joplin.

He worked on *The Last Waltz* (by The Band), which turned out to be their farewell performance. That album went along with the documentary film of the same name by Martin Scorsese, on which Mazer worked as audio engineer.

Neil Young called him "a master in the studio." He added that his work on *Harvest*, "is one of my most recognised recordings and it all happened because of Elliot Mazer."

Frankie's excitement prompted him to burst into his famous Glaswegian accent with a couple of bold statements:

"When I finally get this band on the road, it's gonna be fuckin'…watch out America," he exclaims, almost shouting, confidence exuding from every joint. "I mean it, man. Watch out. This is the place to do it, even though they canny understand what I'm talking about. We're gonna go out there and kill 'em."

If Frankie Miller can get it all together, give him half a chance and he'll be layin' waste to America!

With the nucleus of the band established and the opportunity of being produced by Elliot Mazer of Neil Young and Janis Joplin fame, it became easier to recruit a top notch rhythm section with ex Ike and Tina Turner drummer Stu Perry accepting the offer to join, along with Chrissy Stewart on bass. Chrissy was a colleague of Henry's from Eire Apparent.

Chrissy flew in with his entourage, which included his wife Sheila, brother Dennis and a young neighbour by the name of Davy Shannon. Now resident in Toronto, here are some of his recollections, which came to the author by email.

Hi Davy

I found a small collection of photos from San Francisco in July/August 1975. I say small because although they have been kept in a cabinet all these years and in total darkness, the prints have turned either orange or faded out. I have prints from the sixties that are totally fine. Maybe it was the fact that the SF ones were originally printed in SF and were not good. I never had the negatives. That would have been great but not to be.

In fact there was a second roll of film taken that I didn't get copies from because the negatives could not be found by Denis. The other thing I see from the scan are dots (like pixels). Looking at the prints up close, they were done on matt paper, hence the bumpy texture coming through. The studio ones were taken without flash as not to distract the guys. All of them were taken by me with Denis's 35mm camera and the two smaller ones on a Kodak Instamatic. Seems so dated now. I did the best to restore the colour. You can maybe Photoshop them to improve the images.

The background...

When we arrived, Chris (as we knew him growing up) was sporting a plaster cast on his right arm. He never told us what happened and so we didn't think we'd ask! He had it removed about a week later, hence no cast in some of the studio shots.

Henry, Chrissy and their wives were staying in a house that looked like a castle, complete with a turret, on Vallejo Street. Denis and I slept in the turret! I believe it must have belonged to Elliot Mazer as music mags and mail had his name on it at that address (I still have a magazine from there with his name and address on it). There was a courtyard and that is where some photos were taken.

From what I remember being told was that a long time ago there were three brothers that built a house each behind a wall with the resulting treed courtyard in the middle. Frankie was staying in an apartment closer to downtown.

Henry had the master tape of his solo album with him and was playing it on a reel to reel at the house/castle. I asked what the title was going to be and he said, "Mind your own business." I think he enjoyed telling people that as it embarrassed them for asking. Then he said, "No, really, that's what it's called."

One day a guy from Dark Horse Records came over and the two of them went for a meeting. His album was signed to them that day. They had various other musicians that would drop by when they were there, including Van Morrison.

The photos of the guys at the Oakland Coliseum were taken on August 3rd 1975 at a Day on the Green concert staged by Bill Graham, who died in a helicopter crash in 1991. You probably know that. The concert was also known as "The British are coming" and featured Fleetwood Mac, Gary Wright, Peter Frampton and Robin Trower.

We were invited as guests by James (Jimmy) Dewar who was with Robin Trower at the time and a good friend of Frankie. Jimmy also did backing vocals on *The Rock* album. The connections all go back to Jude. I only learned recently that he too had passed back in 2002.

I know you're already aware of all this but it was just to justify why we were all at the Coliseum that day. I didn't know at the time whether the girl with Mick Weaver was temporary or permanent at the time so maybe that part of the photo may be irrelevant. Stu Perry was also a great guy. You can tell from the photos that they were all a happy bunch (most of the time). Frankie always had his professional musician look, no matter who was taking the pictures.

Stu Perry   Bill Rose   Frankie Miller

Chrissy Stewart did actually play a gig with his arm in plaster and it took place. It was at the Keystone in Berkley which, along with other Bay Area nightclubs, became a haven for music lovers who felt detached from the music in large stadium settings.

Elliot Mazer was okay in those days. He seemed laid back and friendly but also serious about what needed to be done. He kept Jeremy Zatkin, the other engineer, on his toes. His T-shirt says, "All Quads Children" in reference to some of the audio pioneering he did. He was famous for his live recordings and you can see that there was minimal sound barriers or booths for the musicians. Some plexiglass around the drum kit but pretty much that was it.

Henry McCullough Stu Perry Chrissy Stewart

Next door was Alembic/Stars Guitars. Alembic originally owned the studio and sold it to Elliot Mazer in 1974. I remember us standing in there one day and Chrissy saying "Do you know that guy standing next to you?" I didn't recognise him but it was Carlos Santana checking out a guitar.

Recording The Rock at His Master's Wheels

And for Davy Shannon's sake he was actually in Winterland with Frankie on 4th August.

Frankie Miller / Slade / Ten Years After
San Francisco Monday 4th August 1975

San Francisco's Winterland is the only one of the town's old rock venues not to have moved or closed down, and there Bill Graham continued to put on shows for the audiences of the Bay Area.

The Winterland gig came just two days after the completion of *The Rock* and the recording and rehearsing had really damaged Frankie's vocal chords.

If he was in agony at the gig, it didn't show as the band drove him into 'Brickyard Blues'.

From the *NME*

"To sing as Frankie does, and get away with it, a performer has to be both original and convincing. You must be able to identify him completely with the spirit of his songs so that you really believe his longing for something I can understand, otherwise he'd just sound like an imitation of someone older, sadder, and probably blacker.

"Professional in an abrupt way ('Thankin' you - and now I'd like to do a John Lennon number – Jealous Guy - if somebody'll give me a plaictrum -') and never polished, never bland. But for me, when Frankie sings 'Jealous Guy', I forget big John ever sang it; and the man I'm listening to now has wiped everyone I've ever heard in San Francisco right off the stage.

Some weeks later, after the release of *The Rock*, The Frankie Miller Band hit the headlines with news of a very special up and coming concert.

Miller for San Quentin
by Todd Tolces in San Francisco (*Melody Maker* Bureau Chief SF)
The Frankie Miller Band, after making their first American showing at Winterland a few weeks ago, will undertake another show this week, but not for the public. Miller and his band will play the most notorious and most dangerous prison in the United States: San Quentin.

They will be backed by local honkers Lettuce Prey and the show is being produced by "John" of the Hell's Angels. Sounds like fun? You bet!!!
Todd Tolces
Frankie Miller Band San Quentin

Incarcerated Ecstasy

San Quentin, California: There it sits, right at the foot of Marin County, at the beginning of the Richmond Bridge, in its own little world. It can be seen from almost anywhere in the Bay Area and everybody knows what it is and what it stands for. San Quentin Correctional Facility (as the State prefers to call it) is the most feared and most dangerous of all California prisons.

The inmates here, numbering up to 2,300, are almost all second-time offenders and almost all for violent crimes. A better audience for a rock and roll show could not have been found anywhere.

This show has been put together entirely by the Hell's Angels, not only for the multitude of Angels held within the prison walls, but for everyone else who cared to come out to the baseball field for an afternoon of music.

About 500 prisoners opted for the show, which included the Firedomes, Lettuce Prey, and the Frankie Miller Band. 500 more were locked up and unable to attend. The rest just didn't particularly care.

Just after ten in the morning, the bands were admitted through the three checks and then filed out towards the laundry, which borders the ballfield.

Surrounding the entire yard, a 20ft high walkway hosted a score of unsmiling, gun toting guards; their eyes riveted on the doings below.

Many of the guards on the "rail" are there because they've shot and killed prisoners in the past. They are removed from the ground security because they run a higher risk of getting their throats slit than all the other guards.

Frankie Miller grins when informed of this oddity. "I've played all the prisons," he professes solemnly. "They're all the same."

And, by a strange gust of co-incidence, Frankie's new album is called *The Rock* as a reminder to bloody Alcatraz. Frankie is dedicated to the cause of prison reform and if his music can help ease the pain of incarceration even slightly, he's personally satisfied and outwardly ecstatic.

Walking into the large yard, a resounding cheer goes up from the audience as the band comes into sight. Accompanying the band are a half dozen go-go girls in skirts and dungaree cut-offs that could have been mistaken for belts. They were invited by the Angels to add a little spice to the show.

The first notes to crackle over the P.A. that day were from a loosely conglomerated band of inmates. Two guitars, bass, a few horns and an especially tasty drummer known only as Dan comprised the make-up of this Latin-funk orientated group.

After two numbers they left the stage to no applause to make way for Firedomes. The inmates were keeping their energy in reserve for the outside visitors. But at least they played original material, which is more than you could say for Firedomes, an Angels band who stuck mainly to progressive standards like ELO's 'Showdown' and the banal 'C.C. Rider'.

However, with the implementation of "outside music", the girls were brought onstage to dance and tore the place up in seconds flat. Ugly incidents have been know to arise in the past with situations like these, but the girls were able to let it hang out (literally) and keep the boys under control at the same time.

Lettuce Prey wasn't all that musically inspiring either, from a critic's point of view, but when you haven't heard live music in literally ages, you really aren't in such a great position to complain. So, Lettuce Prey trudged along for about 45 minutes and then took a break to set the stage for Frankie Miller.

Not unexpectedly, the band's overall performance was far superior to their Winterland show a few weeks back. The overall execution of the tunes was much tighter and the sound, even for an outdoor gig, was far and away better than the previous outing at Bill Graham's ex-ice rink.

Miller's vocals are a unique blend of raw rocking strength with a Scottish flair and precision uniquely his own. His tunes are earnest and sometimes brilliant combinations of a multitude of popular styles. For instance, his version of John Lennon's 'Jealous Guy', which still stands out as the highlight of the programme, is executed in a slower, more devastating field than the original. McCullough's guitar work knifes through the arrangement like a hot cleaver through soft cheese. Mick Weaver accompanies beautifully on organ as well. But it is Frankie's vocals that continually stand out as the superstar of his show.

He's not into a big trip. He's got a great band, winning tunes, and most of all he can sing. Sing with the best of them. Other arrangements like 'Brickyard Blues' and the title cut to the new album 'The Rock' were performed with finesse and set the inmates off into incarcerated ecstasy.

(Reproduced with kind permission)

Since meeting Henry McCullough (and, via Frankie's website, Davy Shannon) the author decided to contact Todd Tolces in the hope of receiving more detailed information on the day at San Quentin. The reply was astonishing.

Hi Davy!
Yes, I'm the guy. I remember it sort of O.K. Frankie wore a black bowler hat I think. The inmates were nuts about the girls onstage... and we may have some pictures of the event. If you like I can reach out to my photographer and see if he has some prints or jpgs to send you. Good to hear from you! Let me know if I can help you further.
Cheers
Todd Tolces

Then, a few days later...

Dear Davy,
Todd Tolces forwarded your Frankie Miller Gig email to me, and I thought I'd give you a response. I was Todd's photographer for that 1975 San Quentin gig, and I believe some of my pictures were used in the gig review appearing in *Melody Maker*. It was a very memorable occasion, since it was the first and only time I've ever been inside the notorious "Q"! As I recall, I was the only member of Frankie's entourage that mingled with the inmates gathered in the South Yard.

The inmates were selected to attend this prison entertainment based on good behaviour, but I recall them as appearing impressively hard and tough. This audience was strictly segregated into three groupings: the Aryan Brotherhood, the Mexican Mafia, and the Black Guerrilla Family.

This white guy photographer mingled in all three! My association with Todd Tolces as his photographer dates from about 1972-1976. I was a Computer Science undergrad at UC Berkeley, and an amateur photographer using my dorm room as a darkroom. When I met Todd, he was hustling his writing about the SF Bay Area music scene, to *Melody Maker* and other publications.

He got press passes to rock concerts, and offered to take me along if I would take pictures and print them up for his articles. There wasn't much pay involved, and the expenses easily exceeded that, but to get access to these Rock 'n Roll Gods - that was golden.

I ended up becoming a software engineer, writing video games for Atari (I did "Millipede" for the Atari 2600). But I kept all the negatives from that era, stuffed in a drawer, disorganised and poorly catalogued. It wasn't until recently I decided to scan and catalogue some of these. I've spent many hours digitising and researching, and still I'm less than half done. I've taken a break from the project for about six months now.

Things keep coming up, like wildfires in Northern California, and a world-wide pandemic. Very distracting! The San Quentin negatives are still unscanned, but if you're really interested in those photos, I could resume my grand project.

As you indicated, you have a clip of the San Quentin Frankie Miller article. Do you have the exact date that occurred? Any chance I could get a scan of this clip? I am willing to provide you with hi-res scans of photographs for your book, if I'm given picture credit.

Best wishes,
Dave Staugas

And next, the same day (24th) and only a few hours later…

Hi Davy,
I just ran across more images of the Frankie Miller Band you might be interested in. I can reliably date these 36 images to 4-Aug-'75, when the band performed at Winterland. The San Quentin gig must have been around the same time. Ten Years After was the headliner and I got nice shots of them as well.

The amazing Dave Staugas also sent me this story - an insight into the workings of the business…

Here's something I've been thinking about while working on these: In the pictures, there are many identifiable inmates. I recall something about not taking pictures of the inmates, by order of the San Quentin authorities. They said that any inmate appearing in my pictures would require a release form to be signed by the inmate and an authorised correctional officer.

Here we are, 45 years later, and it would be almost impossible to get a release from the identifiables! So it's not going to be a problem getting a release.

I now recall a big reason why I never made any effort to examine or reprint these negatives again in the intervening 45 years.

I had some bad blood in the aftermath after the gig, and it had nothing to do with Frankie or the great San Quentin adventure itself. It involved the promo man from Chrysalis Records (I can't remember his name) who was in Frankie's entourage when we entered the prison. After the show, he approached me and asked if he could get prints of my pictures (I was the only photographer present).

He said he would pay me $75 if I would select six or so of my best images (my pick) and mail them to his Chrysalis office in L.A.

I promptly developed and printed six 8x10 glossies of my favs, and mailed them to the address provided by the promo man, with a bill for $75.

After a long interval of time, I heard no response from Mr. Promo-man. So I called and asked him about it. He said he received the prints, but he couldn't use them so he wouldn't pay. I told him that we had an oral contract and I fulfilled my part of the deal. He just said "tough luck."

So I filed suit in small claims court in Marin County (where the oral contract was made), and had my L.A. friend serve the dude with the summons. He would have to come to Marin County (the scene of the crime) to attend a hearing or forfeit and pay a judgement. After the papers were served, I got an angry phone call from this jackass telling me that my photos sucked, he didn't have to pay, and that "You'll never work in this town again."

He acted like L.A. was the town in question, but I reminded him that San Quentin prison was the site wherein the contract was engaged. Finally, he relented and said he'd "pass the hat" at the office and get me $50. I did get a check for $50, but not before being humiliated and insulted by this asshole.

I've heard from many sources that the music business is really rough and that conmen and hustlers abound.

You hear so often about the artists getting ripped off by unscrupulous businessmen. This taught me a big lesson about trying to make money with photography. For me, I only do it now for the love of photography; money is to be made by other means.

Dave Staugas
Photographer

I also thought it would be interesting to look more closely at some of the venues Frankie had played in out there and I was shocked and amazed at what I found.

The history of the Showcase Theatre (previously the Eastown) is an interesting if shocking one when you compare the scale of what went on to, say, any average UK town and its music venues. After reading a piece on Frankie from Detroit based journalist Susan Whitall, it inspired me to look a little closer at its background. Maybe San Quentin was a picnic compared to Detroit...

"Patrons of the Eastown Theatre went from downing popcorn to downing tabs of LSD. The theater is the last survivor of Detroit's four major neighborhood movie palaces, but its legacy was made as one of the city's most notorious drug-infused rock venues."

After closing as a cinema in 1967, the Eastown re-opened in May 1969 and became one of the foremost places to see rock 'n' roll in town -- and one of its most notorious concert halls. Major artists who appeared included The Who, Yes, Fleetwood Mac, the Faces, Cream, Captain Beefheart, Steppenwolf, King Crimson, and Joe Walsh.

Among the locals, the MC5, the Stooges, Mitch Ryder and the Detroit Wheels and Bob Seger all took its stage. Ted Nugent and The Amboy Dukes recorded their live album *Survival of the Fittest* at the Eastown, and Joe Cocker began his "Mad Dogs and Englishmen" tour there.

The *Detroit Free Press* quoted rocker Alice Cooper in August 1997 as saying that the Eastown was "the best audience in the world. And I'm not saying that just because you're writing it down. Any other city, people went home from work to put on their Levis and black leather jackets for a concert. In Detroit they came from work like that. The Eastown -- those were pure rock 'n' roll times."

While the Grande had a hippie vibe, the Eastown was all blue-collar - and it was rough. "I remember stepping over a body that had overdosed in front of the backstage door on my way in to talk to Alice (Cooper)," Bill Gray recalled in the *Free Press* in 1976.

The venue was described as "a veritable drug supermarket" and major nuisance for the local authorities.

It was also described as a "musical dope den" and was associated with two deaths in four months. Despite that, and several drug arrests, Fire Dept violations and operating without a business licence for a year, the Eastown kept putting on rock shows.

Its capacity was legally 1,727, but some nights it drew crowds of 3,000. It was reported that between September 19, 1969, and December 17, 1971, the theatre received six violations for overcrowding. It also was no secret that the Eastown was a haven for drug taking.

Detroit police and city officials knew about it, "but fear that any move to stop the drug traffic will provoke a riot" allowed the thriving, unchecked drug dealing to continue, the *Free Press* wrote in December 1971. The final straw came after the *Free Press* launched a month-long investigation in November 1971 into the Eastown. "More than a dozen dope dealers" operated every weekend "with almost no fear of the management, the theater's security force or the Detroit police," the paper wrote that December. (Reproduced with kind permission Dan Austin.)

The Rock CD Sleeve Notes By Michael Heatley and Davy Arthur

Released in September 1975, *The Rock* marked the debut of the Frankie Miller Band – the singer's first ever solid backing unit. His 1973 debut album *Once In A Blue Moon* had found him fronting pub-rock favourites Brinsley Schwarz, while follow-up release *High Life* had been a strictly studio affair combining his Celtic vocal talents with the cream of the New Orleans music fraternity. With no band to call his own, the talented Scot had been obliged to co-opt Procol Harum, then at a relatively low commercial ebb, as an occasional instrumental unit. Sadly, little recorded evidence of that collaboration has surfaced, though tapes of a set from the Rainbow Theatre in March 1975 are gathering dust on the shelf.

The Frankie Miller Band included two ex-members of Eire Apparent in Henry McCullough and Chrissy Stewart. The Irish progressive outfit had enjoyed (if that's the word) a whirlwind experience of fame thanks to the patronage of one James Marshall Hendrix. Changing their name at his manager's suggestion, they'd supported Hendrix on a Stateside tour as well as selling a number of copies of 1969's long-playing *Sunrise* on the strength of his name as its producer. Sadly, this gilt by association didn't last and, disillusioned, Eire Apparent quickly disbanded.

Since then, McCulloch had passed through the Grease Band and enjoyed a worldwide profile as a member of Paul McCartney's post-Beatles Wings project, but again gave superstardom the sidestep by quitting on the eve of sessions for *Band On The Run*. Stewart, meanwhile, had replaced the Humble Pie-bound Greg Ridley as bassist for highly regarded progressive rockers Spooky Tooth before relocating to the States to play with Joe Cocker's touring band and record with the future Grateful Dead pairing of Keith and Donna Godchaux.

The other members of Frankie's band were Mick Weaver on keyboards and Stu Perry, an American, contributing drums and percussion. Weaver's history alone could fill a book, never mind a sleeve note: his best-known pre-Frankie gigs were as temporary replacement for Steve Winwood in Traffic (who then played as Wooden Frog), Keef Hartley, the Grease Band and his own outfit, Wynder K Frog.

Perry, meanwhile, had been part of the Delaney and Bonnie family tree as well as playing with unknown US bands like Blue Rose, Jellyroll and Uncle Jim's Music. He was recommended by Robin Trower, who had recently been auditioning drummers for his eponymous power trio. Jimmy Dewar, Trower's long-time bass player and vocalist, had been a long-time pal of Frankie's and would contribute backing vocals here.

The Rock was recorded in San Francisco, in sight of the famous Alcatraz prison, appropriately situated on a rock in the Bay. Frankie commented that it was only music that had saved him from that kind of fate and dedicated the album to Jimmy Boyle. Boyle, a feared Glasgow gangster, spent years in solitary confinement and was considered totally beyond redemption. Once released from prison, he became an acclaimed sculptor and author who married the psychiatrist employed to assess him and lectured in prisons and schools to try to prevent others from following the path he once took.

The recording location for *The Rock* was His Master's Wheels and the producer Elliot Mazer, whose greatest claim to fame was having supervised the recording of Neil Young's 1972 best-seller *Harvest*. He'd also be called upon by symphonic rockers Barclay James Harvest to produce their *Time Honoured Ghosts* album, released in the same year as *The Rock*, but appears to have been very much the choice of the record company.

Nevertheless, Mazer's connections led to two prestigious musical teams making an appearance on the record. The Memphis Horns were recruited to add brass (they'd do likewise on Frankie's 1977 effort, *Full House*), while the Edwin Hawkins Singers of 'Oh Happy Day' fame were more than happy to supply vocal backing.

The album was judged a great success at the time ("a tight band and great little songs – definitely Frankie's best yet" read a typical review) and remains so, but as with *High Life*, his collaboration with Allen Toussaint, Frankie confessed himself disappointed with the technical (production and engineering) side of things. "Nothing personal against Elliot, he was a great help, but...when we talked about how we wanted the album, I said, basically live, no overdubs."

Frankie's love of American music was undoubted – "Apart from the bagpipes it's the only thing that's ever said anything to me," he once boasted – so it's no surprise he found his spell in the States conducive to creativity. "I wrote a lot of songs in California, especially in Sausalito," he told *Hot Wacks* magazine editor Bert Muirhead. "*The Rock* was about Alcatraz. I've always been into prisons and prisoners, 'cos I know a lot of people from a certain place where I come from in Glasgow – a lot of them are still in prison and I don't think it was anything to do with them, I think it was due to their surroundings. And there's hundreds of millions of towns with people not aware of things like that. Maybe if I can say something through *The Rock* and make people aware, that's good."

Frankie and band suited actions to words when they followed in Johnny Cash's footsteps and played inside San Quentin's notorious walls. "It was unbelievable," Frankie recalled. "There's been so many stabbings inside the prison that there hadn't been any concerts there for two years."

The album kicked off confidently with 'A Fool In Love', co-written by Frankie and former Free bass player Andy Fraser. The pair had attempted to put a band together two years previously but gave up after ten months of writing, rehearsing and recording. "They were great times in the studio," Miller said, "there was a lot of energy there but, at the end, we were just wasting time..."

'A Fool In Love' was something good to have emerged from their collaboration; indeed, it's said both raced to get their own version out first! Frankie's winning interpretation enjoyed a lot of radio airplay on both sides of the Atlantic when simultaneously released as the album's first single backed with 'I Know Why The Sun Don't Shine'. It was also a sizeable US hit, helping put Frankie Miller's name under the noses of the Stateside public. A vocal resemblance to Otis Redding certainly didn't harm its prospects, while Texan Delbert McClinton was impressed enough to cover it.

After 'The Heartbreak' comes title track 'The Rock', which received a sleeve dedication from Frankie "to Jimmy Boyle and the plight of prisoners." It would also become the album's second single, though curiously almost a year afterwards in July 1976.

'I Know Why The Sun Don't Shine' was another holdover from the Miller/Fraser Band, having originally been cut in March 1974 by Miller (piano, guitar, vocals) and Fraser (organ, drums, bass) along with a guest appearance from ex-Free guitarist Paul Kossoff. The original has only briefly appeared on a Kossoff compilation, *Blue Soul*, credited to the Rumbledown Band, and makes a fascinating contrast with the longer, slower version here.

'Hard On The Levee' is a great example of Frankie using American terminology - as with Led Zeppelin's 'When The Levee Breaks'. He admitted, though, that only now he'd come to the States did he understand some of the things his musical heroes had sung about. "Things like going down to the union hall... I never knew what one was until I came (to America) and asked somebody, but I'd been singing it all my life! When you come here you can finally associate the real thing with the words that people use." (A levee, for the record, is an earth or sand embankment, often naturally created, that holds back water.)

Hot Wacks's Muirhead likened 'Hard On The Levee' to Bob Dylan's 'Highway 61', also detecting a Dylanish 'Ballad Of A Thin Man' feel to 'I Know Why The Sun Don't Shine'. It was an easy comparison since Frankie had covered 'Just Like Tom Thumb's Blues' on his first album, 1973's *Once In A Blue Moon*, but it took a brave man to suggest any similarity to his face.

"Dylan, d'ye say?" he responded craggily. "Actually I see more Hank Williams in 'Levee'. It was written in New Orleans. 'I Know Why The Sun Don't Shine' – I mean the riff is a standard, like Ray Charles' 'I Believe To My Soul'. My notes, were never ever done... you can check it – Thin Man' or 'Believe To My Soul' never was it. I read a review that mentioned 'Thin Man', I was trying to figure out for ages where it came from."

If Frankie's songwriting was his own, then track six, the self-penned 'Ain't Got No Money', was to become by some way this album's most covered song. Cher, Chris Farlowe, Jo Jo Zep and Bob Seger – the Detroit rocker Frankie was so often compared with Stateside – are all known to have cut versions. Little surprise, then, that it received belated single release, if only in 1979 as the flip of 'When I'm Away With You' (the latter a new track from the *Falling In Love/A Perfect Fit* album).

'All My Love To You' was another Otis Redding homage, while the romping 'I'm Old Enough' was covered by Johnny Halliday, the 'French Elvis', and the Ramblers while Texan blues singer Lou Ann Barton liked it so much she titled an album after it.

Track nine, 'Bridgeton', was named after the tough suburb of Glasgow in which Frankie, born in 1949, had grown up with his two sisters, Ann and Leticia. He had been raised a supporter of Glasgow Celtic football team, often wearing their striped football shirt on stage, and final track 'Drunken Nights In The City' is said to have been written for his late-night drinking buddy, Celtic and Scotland winger Jimmy Johnstone, although it could also relate to nights on the town with Henry McCullough!

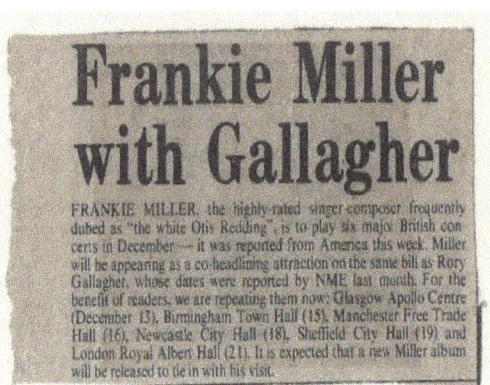

The Frankie Miller Band's American tour of late 1975 was an unqualified success. Despite never rising higher than second on the bill, they blew the likes of Quicksilver Messenger Service off stage. (The group had re-formed without mercurial guitarist John Cipollina to push a reunion album, *Solid Silver*, and by all accounts were feeling his loss.) But back in Britain, a December UK tour as special guests of Rory Gallagher fell apart. Henry McCullough had also dropped out to record a solo album, *Mind Your Own Business*, for George Harrison's Dark Horse label, leaving Frankie (who inevitably guested on that album) to lick his wounds and travel to Holland to sing with Procol Harum.

When I Have A Couple of Drinks On A Saturday...
Los Angeles be-e-elongs to me...

With *The Rock* album on release Steve Clarke joined the story, with his humorous "I Belong to Glasgow" headline...

At the Showcase gig in Detroit, Frankie did manage to pull some reaction out of the crowd and although the reformed Quicksilver Messenger Service were headlining Miller says it was he and his band who came out top dogs.

"We tore the house apart," he boasts. Then, in cooler vein: "Well, that's not for me to say. It's just that we got more reaction than the two bands we were on with."

In the interview Frankie was able to recount some of his experiences of San Quentin. He explained that prison concerts are organised by the local Hell's Angels. The convicts were allowed three concerts a year, one country, one folk and one rock. For some reason there hadn't been a rock gig for two years, then the Angels heard about Frankie's new album which had been dedicated to "the plight of prisoners".

Frankie accepted the gig despite the rigorous security and being told that the band couldn't wear blue denims on stage because it would clash with the convicts' uniforms. While joking that they hardly had anything else but denims, they were advised that they would be surrounded by machine-gun carrying guards.

He spoke about *The Rock* album and Elliot Mazer.

Frankie knew the name but admitted that he hadn't paid much attention so when they met up Mazer was asked if he could "cut a live band live." He said "Sure."

"There's talk that on *The Rock* I'm like Otis, and I can see what people mean – especially on 'All My Love To You'. When I was writing that I definitely had Otis in mind, as a feeling."

Frankie explained that 16 tracks had been recorded with the minimum of overdubs and to date the album was the first album to capture his true personality.

One track he didn't want on the album was 'Drunken Nights In The City'. He was drunk when he recorded it and didn't think it was going on but Elliot Mazer thought the fans would like it so it went on.

Frankie recalled that the last verse was written around the time he stopped heavy drinking, explaining that it was one of the few songs on the album that he had written in London.

"Everybody goes through it, you wake up in the morning and you think you're going to die. You say to God, 'I'll never drink again.' "

The inspiration for the title song 'The Rock' came from Frankie's time living in Sausalito (on the other side of the San Francisco Bay) when he regularly sailed past Alcatraz on the way to San Francisco.

He knew about the reputation of one of the world's toughest prisons and thought of people he knew back in Glasgow who were in prison.

Frankie was adamant that it was not their fault but society's. He also maintained that he could have been there if it had not been for the musical path that he had chosen.

Andy McConnell accompanied Frankie and his entourage on the Chrysalis promotional evenings that took in Atlanta, Los Angeles and San Francisco with the headline "Above Average White Band".

The evenings would prove crucial to getting *The Rock* across to all the local radio stations.

On the previous evening at the Rainbow Bar and Grill somebody joked that they had never seen Frankie smile so much and be so nice to so many people at once!

Next day, on the flight from L.A. up to San Francisco, Frankie also spent the time chatting up Kathy Nelson, the promotions lady who was organising the evening's event.

The party was held at Columbia Studios on Fulsom Street. It was regarded as the most important of the three because it was where the album was recorded and where the band had been living, but also, as Chrysalis pointed out, it was the city that "broke" Robin Trower.

If Frankie could win over a couple of key radio stations, notably KSAN, the word could spread out of the city like wildfire. The programme was the same as in L.A. and Atlanta: play an album or two until most of the guests arrive; then show a five minute film made for *Top Of The Pops* featuring Frankie and the band playing the single, 'A Fool In Love'; play the album through until people begin to leave, then repeat the film. During the entire evening Frankie, Jeremy Salmon (Frankie's manager), band members Henry McCullough, Mick Weaver and Chrissy Stewart and the Chrysalis reps wandered around chatting up the guests.

It was tiring work, but after the booze, food and visitors were gone the consensus was that it was the most successful of the three, having got across to a large number of radio and press personnel. Then it was time to put the feet up for a while and unwind.

Frankie and Jeremy Salmon headed for 'The Castle' where bassist Chrissy Stewart and Henry and Sheila McCullough lived. It was an incredible house; built in the thirties, by the look of it, and a replica of a

Scottish castle. The only remaining question was: is the world ready for the Frankie Miller Band?

The night after the party, KSAN radio DJ Richard Gossip announced over the air: "Here's somebody who's impressing me very much at the moment." Then he proceeded to play 'Ain't Got No Money' and 'All My Love To You' with Otis Redding's 'Down In The Valley' sandwiched between them.

"That's Frankie Miller," Gossip proclaimed at the end. "And he's incredible."

Frankie Miller Band   San Francisco 1975

Meanwhile, 'A Fool in Love' had been released as a single back in the UK.

Frankie Miller "Eight plays a week"
A Fool in Love/I Know Why the Sun Don't Shine
Week One
Chrysalis plugger Geoff Goy considered that Frankie Miller's 'A Fool in Love' stood a 50-50 chance of getting on the BBC Radio One playlist, the key factor in whether or not a single becomes a hit record. It was released on September 18th, and overall radio response during the first week was good, with no negative reaction at all.

At this point promotion chief Chris Stone hoped that the record would in fact be playlisted on the BBC the following Tuesday - the day when the BBC playlist meeting is held, under the chairmanship of Doreen Davies.

In fact 'Fool in Love' wasn't playlisted on Radio One for this week—really it would have been unusual if it was, seeing how Miller was an unestablished artist—but it was played as a "New Spin" on the Noel Edmunds and Johnnie Walker shows.

It had an airing on Radio One's two review programmes, Rosko's Roundtable and Ann Nightingale's show, and in each case received a very good review.

Rosko's producer, Dave Price, was particularly impressed and played the record on Rosko's Saturday morning show. John Peel played it on one of his early evening shows. London's Capitol Radio listed it on their "Extras", meaning that although it was neither in their charts or in their "Climbers", it was still on the playlist and received some seven or eight plays a week.

Sounds – Pete Wingfield September 20th
Frankie Miller - A Fool in Love
Chrysalis
"Now here's a surprise. Not the old Ike and Tina Turner classic, this self-written opus by long underrated Scots soulster Frankie Miller sounds vaguely familiar... was it recorded previously? Elliot Mazer produced, getting a particularly horns and tom-tom sound. I suspect it's a track from an as yet unissued made in the U.S. album. The feel's nearer to Otis Redding or Sam and Dave than today's sophistifunk heroes: rough, rough and a solid delight. Marathon, bluesy flip. The riff reminds me of Ray Charles 'Believe to my Soul'. I just can't get this record off the turntable. Great... Great... Great."

The big break begins here... excerpts from a review by Steve Clark
"Paul Rodgers once said that his main musical ambition was to turn on people like Otis Redding had turned him on.

"It wouldn't surprise me if Frankie Miller has the same thought, because the two of them, like several other British singers, have gained the vast majority of their inspiration from Otis."

The consensus was that Frankie sounded more like Otis than Rodgers had done with his rougher and dirtier voice.

It was also noted that the band played with so much aggression that they were bound to be lethal live.

One of the tracks in particular - 'All My Love To You' - was compared in style to that of Otis Redding, with Henry McCullough's playing style compared to Steve Cropper on 'I've Been Loving You Too Long'. The tone of the horns and Frankie's vocals on that number were highlighted.

This album was further proof that white men can sing and play the blues, especially if you're Scottish!

From Bud Scoppa, *Phonograph Record*, 1975

"Vocally, Miller's gruff but flexible voice and aggressive attack place him in the Otis Redding school - a fact Elliot Mazer underscores through his use of the Memphis Horns in their classic ensemble style. His 'All My Love to You' is a startlingly precise replication of the Redding mode, and it's obvious that Frankie is getting a thrill from finding himself at the mike in the middle of an Otis arrangement.

"Miller's got better equipment and better moves than any rock vocalist to emerge in the last year - all this forceful, intelligent young writer/singer lacks is an audience. The rock is bound to take care of that.

"Without doubt, Miller's Killer Album."

The Memphis Horns - horn section

The Memphis Horns were an American horn section, made famous by their many appearances on Stax Records. The duo consisted of Wayne Jackson on trumpet and Andrew Love on tenor saxophone. They lent their sound to 83 gold and platinum awards and over one hundred high charting records, including Otis Redding's 'Sitting On The Dock of the Bay', Al Green's 'Let's Stay Together', and Elvis Presley's 'Suspicious Minds'.

The Edwin Hawkins Singers - backing vocals

Edwin Hawkins (as leader of the Edwin Hawkins Singers) was probably best known for his arrangement of 'Oh Happy Day', which was included on the Songs of the Century list. The record sold more than 7 million copies worldwide, for which Hawkins won a Grammy award. The Edwin Hawkins Singers made a second foray into the charts exactly one year later, backing folk singer Melanie on 'Lay Down (Candles in the Rain)'.

In the UK, *New Musical Express* published the Rory Gallagher/Frankie Miller tour dates for December, to include the Glasgow Apollo and the London Royal Albert Hall.

Then came the shock news on Friday 5th December via the Scottish *Daily Record* that the Frankie Miller Band had broken up and Frankie had returned to Glasgow.

"Everyone was having a swell time and as usual, Keith Richards was feeling no pain. A small unshaven, scruffy lad was brought into the company by Rod Stewart and the notable Rolling Stone said, 'Who's he?'

Whereupon Mr Stewart turned sharply and said, 'You, Keith, have the pleasure of addressing Frankie Miller, who only happens to be the greatest rock singer in the world.'

"In the past few weeks he and the band have toured the States in a series of live performances. Two of these were with Rory Gallagher's band – with whom he is billed to be supporting later this month in a British tour. But the Frankie Miller Band will not be on that tour. 'When we played with Rory Gallagher in America, the audiences gave us a bigger reception than them. We blew Gallagher off the stage man !' "

Henry McCullough

I first met Henry in year 2000 while helping out with Jings Promotions, a company who booked gigs around the Fife area in Scotland.

The Sunday gig was an afternoon session at The Yard in Rosyth and was great - a mixture of country/blues and rock including a range of Henry's self-penned songs and some interesting covers.

As the band made their way through to the bar to watch the World Cup Final, I introduced myself to Henry and as I shook his hand I informed him that I was a close friend of Frankie Miller. Well, his face turned white with shock and he immediately turned to his partner Josie and said, "Give this man me address and number, he's coming to Ireland!" I was amazed and immediately proud that Henry had reacted in this way and it was the start of another series of adventures and friendships in both Ireland and Scotland over the following years.

The Irish trips included a couple of visits to the Derry Jazz Festival and one year at a lovely venue called Sandino's. The show was recorded by a local radio station and Henry did a few interviews for them. It wasn't long after the release of his *Unfinished Business* album, which was partly a reflection of his past career, featuring songs by Ronnie Lane, Paul McCartney and Frankie Miller. When the interviewer got round to asking Henry what was the most enjoyable time in his distinguished career, he replied, "Frankie Miller."

He said that while Joe Cocker was "soulful", Frankie Miller's "root was really deep."

First trip to Ireland 2002

My own favourite story about their time together in Sausalito was a wild night out for Frankie and Henry which resulted in a few nights in jail for Henry for a driving offence!

I had read the story on some sleeve notes years before but was keen to hear it from the horse's mouth and one day I got the chance to ask him. "I was driving and Frankie was in the passenger's seat, both of us totally out of it," says Henry.

"I drove up the ramps on to the Freeway and after a while realised that we were heading into oncoming traffic. In other words we were on the wrong side of the road!" I will never forget how Henry calmly described the next part of the story...

"The first people who came to help were the police!!"

He also told *Hot Press*: "They took us out and put us up against the wall, the real American trip and the fact that I was the driver and slightly under the influence meant they just told Frankie, 'right, fuck off,' so Frankie staggered off into the night.

"They handcuffed me and put me into the back of the car. I had an oul' purple geansai on me with a chunk of black dope in the folds. I thought I'm in trouble now but I somehow managed to manoeuvre the piece on to the back seat and ate it, and it was fairly decent 'chunk'."

Henry described his cell as "a cage within a cage", complete with a sloping floor and central drain for urinating in.

Being dressed in his rock 'n' roll gear - "green velvet jacket and leopard skin shoes" as he described them - he was the centre of attraction amongst the other prisoners caged in beside him! "Mexicans, Puerto Ricans and a couple of black pimp-types."

Meanwhile, back at the ranch, Frankie had been so pissed that he'd gone home and forgotten all about it, and over the next couple of days, Henry was becoming conspicuous by his absence. When the other band members began asking as to his whereabouts, "our Frankie" couldn't remember. It was only after a couple of days that Frankie realised: "Henry's in jail!"

Henry finished up the story by saying that Frankie never ever apologised, instead calling him a "Wee Scottish Gurrier!"

The Collins English Dictionary definition of "Gurrier" is "Dublin dialect" for a low-class, tough, ill-mannered person…

Enter Frankie Miller's Full House

The early to mid 70s was to prove a real stop-start ride for Frankie, but on returning to the UK at the end of 1975 he went back to the drawing board to emerge with a completely new outfit comprising Ray Minhinnett (guitar), Charlie Harrison (bass), Jim Hall (keyboards) and Graham Deakin (drums).They were christened Frankie Miller's Full House and during their relatively short time together would cut an album of the same name and tour extensively.

Equally important was the appointment of Procol Harum's lyricist Keith Reid as Frankie's manager.

In a *New Musical Express* interview of the time, Frankie credited Reid with putting his career back on track. "I've always liked Procol. I used to be in a band in Scotland called the Stoics, and we used to play *A Salty Dog*, the album, all the time. I've always liked Keith's words. When I came back from America at the end of '75, I was looking for a manager, so when Keith came along that was great – because he's an honest person." For Reid, the first step had been "to get a band together for Frankie and get him out on the road. The guy had never performed – he'd just made records sporadically, done a couple of dates and that was it. He was such a great performer, people had to see him." The results would be a year of hard graft for Miller, the first concentrated roadwork he'd experienced for some time.

"Keith's a bit of a slave-driver, but I'm not complainin'; its been great." Minhinnett and Hall had both been in a north-eastern band called Highway, which had recorded albums for EMI and Elton John's Rocket label. Ray was also friends with Mick Grabham, who became Procol Harum's guitarist, and was in his company the very first time he met Frankie Miller. "I was at the Royal Festival Hall one night to see Procol and was sitting with (drummer) BJ Wilson and Mick in the dressing room when the door opened and Frankie fell in!" Fortunately he'd seen the singer in more favourable circumstances supporting Ten Years After at the Rainbow and had loved his voice. So when Keith Reid came down to Dingwalls in Camden to ask Highway if they'd like to be Frankie's new backing band, the answer, from Ray at least, was very much in the affirmative. "The bass player didn't want to do it, so I pulled in a mate, Charlie Harrison, who'd been with Judas Jump. We auditioned drummers and Pete Van Hooke got the gig, but these were early days and the wages weren't great so he decided to stay with Van Morrison. We carried on auditioning and found Graham

Deakin, who had just left John Entwistle's Ox; that was how the band came about."

Six weeks of rehearsing by day at the famed Hope and Anchor pub-rock venue in Islington preceded 18 months of solid gigging, beginning with a 50-date UK tour that kicked off in May 1976, and would finish with a triumphant show at London's Victoria Palace Theatre on 27 June.

My first Full House gig (the fifth show on the tour), was at Tiffany's on 21st March in Edinburgh, and after watching support band, Meal Ticket, we headed for the toilets before Frankie was due on stage.

We went out into the long corridor and who is walking towards us and taking up the whole width of the corridor but the five guys in Frankie Miller's Full House, with Frankie in the middle... It was enough to stop us in our tracks, as first to speak was Frankie Miller, who grinned in our direction: "How's it goin', wee man?"

It was hilarious, not only because he was in full swagger mode but also because he was wearing the famous hat that looked to be almost level with the top of my head!! He knew my mate Tiny who had been a roadie back in the days at The Cavendish so it was exciting to meet everyone and get autographs into the bargain...

Not long after, Frankie appeared on stage alone, armed with a 12-string acoustic, and announced: "I've got a drink and you huvnae!!" (no late bars for us in those days) followed by a 'thump-thump' coming through the P.A. It was Frankie kicking the metal base of the mike stand to the beat of 'Drunken Nights in The City'.

The most exciting aspect of it was the fact that here was our very own Scottish rock star, back from the USA, with three albums under his belt, up close and only a few metres away, on the famous Tiffany's sunken stage!

'The Devil Gun' followed as Frankie was joined by his new Full House band. Tight, aggressive and a perfect platform for Frankie's voice. Other highlights for me were 'Brickyard Blues', 'A Fool In Love', 'It Takes a Lot to Laugh', 'The Rock', 'Ain't Got No Money' and 'Sail Away'.

As the tour progressed that summer, there were BBC Radio broadcasts including an In Concert' in June plus John Peel sessions. In Europe, there were Dutch radio broadcasts and in Germany, via WDR, a Rockpalast live in concert from Cologne... and an appearance at the Montreux Jazz Festival.

Later on came appearances on *Top of the Pops* and *The Old Grey Whistle Test*.

Also as a result of this activity, there was more publicity for Frankie Miller in the music press.

There were also many references to the off-stage activities in America from the previous year, but more importantly some rave reviews for Frankie's new Full House band's performances.

One of the more enthusiastic writers was Angie Errigo, with her headline:
"Still Sensational Still Underrated"
Weybridge College
Frankie Miller is a great example of a galling phenomenon in a business that quite regularly rewards boring artists with riches and fame - the outrageously talented performer who is bafflingly obscure and neglected.

When Frankie rolled on in his beat-up, medicine man's hat and moaned his way aggressively through the gritty 'Drunken Nights in the City', the audience virtually ignored him and carried on drinking their beer.

Their transformation during the hour-long set from uninterested spectators to stamping, cheering participants was one of the most exciting and pleasing mood shifts one ever hopes to see in a rock performance.

From the appearance of the band, Miller was on his feet and fighting with confident power. He has the nerve and the mastery to attack great numbers like Dylan's 'It Takes a Lot to Laugh, It Takes a Train to Cry', Wilson Pickett's 'If You Need Me', and Randy Newman's 'Sail Away', fighting with the song, screaming and grappling with the lyric, making it his own.

His own compositions are compulsively raunchy - straightforward, black-hearted rock and roll - delivered with the graceful but wrenching force only Paul Rodgers and a few others can put out. 'Ain't Got No Money' 'I'm Old Enough', 'The Rock' and 'A Fool in Love', as examples, are irresistible stomps to the core, real electric-tingles-up-the-ass-to-the-spine-through-the-floorboards stuff rendered marvellous by Frankie sweetly coiling around the words with his rasping vibrato. Having completely won the crowd over, Frankie and his band were shouted back twice for honest to God encores, and when the journalists dragged down for the occasion are among those banging on the floor hollering you KNOW it was sensational. Three days later I'm still buzzing from the dynamite barrel through Buddy Holly's "Rave On"- as good as rock and roll can ever be.

Bloody fantastic.

Full House interrupted their tour to fly over to Cologne on June 3rd and recorded a TV show for WDR Rockpalast. Some years later it was released on CD, vinyl and DVD.

Pro. Manfred Becker kindly sent a number of previously unpublished photos, including soundchecks and the actual performance.

Drunken Nights in the City Sways Critic
Frankie Miller Victoria Palace

Steve Clarke from *Sounds* described Frankie in his "Drunken Nights Sways Critic" piece as arguably rock's "most recalcitrant performer/non-performer, who had come up with some above-average albums". He also pointed out that "apart from a half-hearted attempt at touring the States," his appearances had been restricted to "impromptu gigs around the London pub/club circuit."

The Full House tour finished up at the Victoria Palace in London, where a sceptical London journalist ended the night being positive and excited by Frankie's performance.

Frankie's singing was described as having a "beautiful roughness," while he sang "his own urban blues with maximum conviction in a voice which is as good as any British rhythm and blues singer you care to name, be it Rod Stewart, Paul Rodgers or Joe Cocker." He also established "a rare rapport with the audience" while he opened the show acoustically on 12-string guitar with 'Drunken Nights In The City'.

When joined with his band, Full House were described as a "swaggering blues-rock outfit who are in total sympathy with what Frankie does" even though three quarters of them were "unknown." They were compared to early Free and "often crude but never inept."

As the show progressed Frankie's voice was described as being charged with a "rare emotional intensity" as he "wowed the audience with numbers from his excellent *High Life* album including 'Brickyard Blues', 'Shoo Rah Shoo Rah' and the very dramatic 'Devil Gun' which played with nagging intensity."

Steve Clarke finished his piece by declaring that it was "a treat seeing excellent R&B performed in an intimate setting" and that Frankie Miller's "Time had come—Hallelujah!"

From Allan Jones
"Miller's talents as a writer (often overlooked) are evident from his compositions featured on *The Rock* – what a great song that is – but he is also an interpretive singer of brilliance. His arrangement of Randy Newman's 'Sail Away' is a minor masterpiece of rock drama, which builds through Minhinnet's fiercely splendid chord thrashing to a climax of overwhelming tragedy.

"The deserved applause and demands for another number were still echoing around the theatre when the safety curtain was lowered."

From Barbara Charone: "Full House Wins: Hands Down"
"The evening began with Frankie accompanying himself on acoustic guitar. 'It's supposed to be out of tune,' he announced. Full House joined for a rousing 'Devil Gun' where Miller proved what an impeccable singer he really is, excelling at each verse with immaculate phrasing.

"Drummer Graham Deakin is the pivot around which Full House revolved. Deakin supplies supple, hollow rhythms that perfectly complement Miller's aggressive vocals. The rest of the band include bassist Chrissy Stewart, guitarist Ray Minhinnet and keyboard player James Hall. The guitar and piano solos were pleasantly adequate but the rhythm section was superb.

"The band kept a relatively low profile, leaving Frankie full rein at the throttle. He has become an even better singer, flaunting a full scale attack on 'Brickyard Blues', 'It Takes A Lot To Laugh',' Sail Away' and ' Shoorah Shoorah', consistently bettering the originals. That's a true vocalist."

Looking back on how Frankie was portrayed by the London based music press regarding his partying and Glasgow tough-guy background, it's interesting to read Angie Errigo's take on the subject. Her headline was "Tough Nut Reveals Soft Centre" as she interviewed him after the Victoria Palace soundcheck. She was one of the journalists who actually admitted being a little intimidated by the thought of meeting Frankie.

"Frankie Miller's a nice fella, a bit of a teddy bear really. Like he tries to stick to the story that he got his beat-up hat off a dead man in Chicago, and that the hole in it is a bullet hole. He had previously told a reporter in

Sounds, Giovanni Dodomo, 'that there was a guy lying shot dead through the head. And everybody took no notice of him. And I see the hat lying there so I just took it.' [Pure Glasgow humour if you ask me!]

"I thought he was supposed to be some kind of heavy, hard drinking wild man, and I tend to find Glaswegians intimidating anyway, probably because I can't understand half of what they say - and that makes me edgy."

In his set, he does numbers by Dylan and Randy Newman.

What other writers' material does he see himself covering?

"There's a lot of Stax stuff which I could do, but you canna really add much to Stax. I would never sing an Otis Redding song, nor a Wilson Pickett. Well I have done, sung a few Wilson Picketts, but there's certain singers I would just never even... like Ray Charles. I'd never do a number by him because he's done it, and if he's done it it's gotta be the best singing that's ever been. I've never heard anybody better a Ray Charles thing, Never.

"There's a lot of people who say – specially in America – that I'm very much like Bobby Bland. Singing's a spiritual thing, even in the studio. It's to reach a spiritual level which gets higher all the time, always has gotten higher with me.

"There's some things that you do and like you nearly pass out, you know? And that's good. That's why I love singing.

"Once or twice in America, Winterland especially, I nearly passed out with the reaction. It was a bit frightening. I had to come down a wee bit, tell a few jokes."

"You project this image of being a Glaswegian toughie along with the hard drinking bit." I accused.

"I don't! Other people do." Well, there's certainly aggression in the way he comes across on stage.

"Ah well, maybe so. But I'm far from being a Glasgow toughie. Maybe it's because the place that I come from in Glasgow is a rough place. I was never aware of it till I came out of it. I go back because I love it... I love the people there. It's very rough, but it's great. And maybe aggression for me is the idea that, instead of hitting somebody, you sing it and get it out.. To me that's something that you've got to get out of yourself. I get it out singing. Sometimes..."

Meanwhile, the comparisons with other vocalists and superlatives for the Full House performances were flowing like confetti.

Allan Jones again from *Melody Maker* on 25th September with the headline: "No More Mister Bad Guy"

Allan Jones was once described (from the stage) by Roger Waters as a "stupid shit" after giving "The Wall" live show a scathing review. Jones went on to launch the *Uncut* magazine after becoming disenchanted with *Melody Maker*.

In an interview entitled 'If You Ask Me', Allan Jones was interviewed by *Press Gazette* in July 2007 . It contained these two paragraphs:

"In 1974 *Melody Maker* advertised in *Time Out* for 'highly opinionated' writers under 21 with a good knowledge of music. A 22-year-old Welshman called Allan Jones replied with a scathing letter about the magazine's coverage, signing off with: '*Melody Maker* needs a bullet up its arse. I'm the gun – pull the trigger.'

"Despite, or perhaps because of, his criticism, Jones was taken on as a reporter. It was the first step on a 30-year journey in music journalism that has taken him around the world interviewing some of the world's best – and worst – bands."

He says: "The idea for *Uncut* came from my own disenchantment about what I was doing with *Melody Maker*. There was a publishing initiative to make the audience younger; I was getting older and they wanted to take the readers further away from me. It seemed like an impassable bridge."

He also had run ins with people like Van Morrison and Lou Reed but thankfully had kind words to say about Frankie… which resulted in a great interview with a talkative Mr Miller!

Excerpt from the interview, which focused on the previous year's activities…

Frankie Miller stared hard across the table. "Yeah," he said. "I am an aggressive little cunt; you just have to be in this business, if you want to succeed. And I'm determined to succeed. And I won't allow this business to fuck me up.

"Too many people have been screwed up. I'm prepared to take my time and when my time comes, I'll be prepared. I'll be a success, and it'll be on my own fuckin' terms. I'm not bitter that it's taken so long. I have a name. A reputation. The people who have heard me appreciate me. If I haven't made it then it's my own fault. But I will make it nae problem."

Roy Harper once said that he was not so much underrated as an artist, merely unheard. Much the same could be said of Frankie Miller… His reputation as being one of the greatest white rock singers is based on three albums: *Once in a Blue Moon* (1972), *High Life* (1974) and *The Rock* (1975). Prolific he isn't but these records possess quality in abundance.

Frankie always enjoyed reminiscing about Glasgow and Scotland and about the clubs there that he frequented as a teenager. He was 14 when he went to the Scene Club to hear bands like the Blues Council who he described as being "A F****n amazin' wee band" and being enthralled by the music and the people.

Again touching on *The Rock* he gave an insight into how the song 'Bridgeton' came about. It evokes memories of where Frankie grew up in Glasgow and had been written in New Orleans at five in the morning. Frankie had been out and about in all the bars and clubs and wrote the song when he got back to where he was staying. He had been thinking about Glasgow and the song came to him very easily.

He also spoke about Los Angeles, where he had stayed for about nine or ten months the previous year and was becoming homesick. He loved the city but was aware of getting "sucked into all the weirdness." He was missing family and friends and wondered if he was ever going to make it home. But thankfully he made it.

Leith Theatre Edinburgh
Frankie's second trip to Scotland in October '76 and I bought every ticket for the front row.

This was not long after his appearance on Supersonic and led to one or two attempted heckles from a loudmouth who asked where Frankie's "Supersonic suit" was, to which Frankie responded: "Gie' him a bottle of whisky and shut him up!"

Embarrassing for me because the guy in question was a flat mate of mine at the time…

Towards the end of the year, Full House were ready to record, and in Ray Minhinnett's words:

"Keith put us in the studio after promising Chris Wright at Chrysalis a hit record within the first two years. "

This album combined Miller originals with choice cover versions. Andy Fraser's 'Be Good To Yourself' kicked off proceedings, just as the Miller/Fraser composition 'A Fool In Love' had its predecessor, and would eventually give Frankie his first ever UK chart single when it reached number 27.

More superlative comments were to come Frankie's way in the first batch of press releases for the new album.

From a Steve Clark review:
"Frankie Miller sings with more commitment than ever on *Full House*. Just listen to him on Lennon's masterpiece 'Jealous Guy', which Miller and his band have turned inside out. In their hands it becomes a tortured piece of

R&B in contrast to the reflective tranquillity of the original. Miller wails with anguish, a victim of the green-eyed monster, splitting his vowels the way Otis used to.

"Two thirds through the band change direction, throwing the song's original structure to the wind, coming on with all the swagger of classic Free. A minor masterpiece. 'I always thought he (John Lennon) could have been angrier,' commented Frankie of the original."

The song had been featured in Frankie's live shows in 1975 and could have appeared on *The Rock* but didn't.

Two other songs were resurrected from Frankie's recent past. Chris Thomas had always liked 'Take Good Care Of Yourself', written by Jimmy Doris in the Stoics days, but 'This Love Of Mine' took Frankie to another level. Compared to Otis Redding's peerless 'I've Got Dreams To Remember', it was co-written with Robin Trower in the early 70s.

Frankie admitted that he had Otis in mind when he was writing the song, dedicating it to him internally, but he never said much about it.

For this album, the additional musicians to Frankie's band are listed as Guests as follows:

Chris Spedding – guitar is an English musician, singer, guitarist, songwriter, multi-instrumentalist, composer, and record producer. In a career spanning more than fifty years, Spedding is best known for his studio session work.

Notable examples of his guitar solos on Frankie Miller albums include 'Let the Candlelight Shine', 'Jealousy' and 'Gladly Go Blind'. He has also recorded with Jack Bruce, Roxy Music, Joan Armatrading, Harry Nilsson and many others.

Rabbit – keyboards
John Douglas "Rabbit" Bundrick (born November 21, 1948 in Houston, Texas) is an American–English rock keyboardist. He is best known for his work with The Who and associations with others including Eric Burdon, Bob Marley and the Wailers, Roger Waters, Free and Crawler. Bundrick is noted as the principal musician for the cult film *The Rocky Horror Picture Show*.

Gary Brooker – keyboards was an English singer and pianist, and the founder and lead singer of the rock band Procol Harum.

The Frankie Miller connection goes all the way back to the 1960s and lasted all the way through Frankie's career, and therefore Gary Brooker features throughout this book. 'A Whiter Shade of Pale' is the worldwide hit for which Procol Harum is best known, but on *Full House* Brooker was responsible for the arrangement on 'Love Letters' on top of his keyboard contribution.

The Memphis Horns are also featured on the *Full House* album.

Chris Thomas

As well as producing *Full House* for Frankie in 1977, Chris Thomas worked extensively with the Beatles, Pink Floyd, Procol Harum, Roxy Music, Badfinger, Elton John, Paul McCartney, Pete Townshend, Pulp and the Pretenders. He has also produced breakthrough albums for the Sex Pistols, the Climax Blues Band and INXS.

Notable singles produced by him include 'Love Is the Drug' by Roxy Music; 'Let's Stick Together' by Bryan Ferry; 'Anarchy in the U.K.', 'God Save the Queen', 'Pretty Vacant' and 'Holidays in the Sun' by The Sex Pistols; 'Brass in Pocket', 'Talk of the Town', 'I Go to Sleep' and 'Back on the Chain Gang' by The Pretenders; and 'Blue Eyes', 'I'm Still Standing', 'I Guess That's Why They Call It the Blues', 'Sacrifice', 'Can You Feel the Love Tonight' and 'Circle of Life' by Elton John.

Because of illness on Frankie's part towards the end of the year, the rest of the tour came to an abrupt end with a number of cancellations.

A period in hospital suffering from laryngitis followed. After lying low for a few months, during which time the new album was recorded, Full House were back on the road in March/April for a UK tour of over 20 shows booked.

There were relatively few headlines during the first month but an interesting review was published, covering the first night at Oxford Polytechnic.

In it the journalist highlighted the up-and-coming threat of new-wave and punk and its influence on young music fans of the day. He - Pete Silverton - also focused on Frankie's rapport with the audience.

Oxford, March 2nd 1977

Frankie Miller's concert on a sweltering night last summer at London's Victoria Palace was exceptional, the singer establishing a rapport with his audience and singing his soul out – as ever.

The Oxford Poly gig was the first gig proper and there was a strong undercurrent of animosity between performer and certain segments of the crowd throughout the set.

There were a couple of seconds during his intro rap to what turned out to be a magnificently tortured version of J. Lennon's 'Jealous Guy', the band playing with all the venom of Free on an angry night as the song strayed away from its originator's scheme, where Miller gave the audience the kind of looks that kill.

That aside, after a potent start with his own almost classic song, 'A Fool In Love' – a number that could have been plucked straight from *Otis Blue* – and 'Brickyard Blues', and a predictably moving version of his soul ballad 'With You In Mind', things began to slide nigh on irrevocably downhill.

Miller has a particularly strong repertoire, which is boosted by his excellent choice of other people's material he's yet to record.

Full House are good solid players – especially drummer Graham Deacon, who came on both visually and musically like Simon Kirke. They did show their mettle on the final two numbers, at last performing with a sense of taut urgency, Miller singing as well as any other British R&B singer.

The hour is frighteningly late, especially in the wake of the new-wave, for Miller to achieve the commercial success his talent deserves, and he and Full House must tighten up and broaden the scope of their material. All the necessary talent is there: it's more a question of attitude.

Pete Silverton (reproduced with the kind permission of Pete Silverton)

Author's note: Regarding The Stare: I have been on the wrong end of it many a time but I came to realise that sometimes Frankie would use it on me from the stage as a form of "Hello I know you're here." And I burned with pride.

Also, having heard a number of recordings of Full House shows in England, audience members stagefront can be overheard mimicking Frankie's Glaswegian accent. Not a very clever thing to do in his earshot...

Frankie was criticised for his performance at the New Victoria Theatre, where the focus was on his comments about one Maggie Thatcher. He called her a Nazi.

When asked later if he really believed that, he replied "Yes," but later stated in an interview that it was wrong to use the stage as a platform for these comments. Not to be totally put off, Frankie would regularly dedicate 'Ain't Got No Money' to Mrs Thatcher.

Three New Victoria reviews may give a balanced perspective. One from London, one from Scotland and an eyeopener from a Detroit based lady (you've got to love her... tough, admiring and extremely humorous).

From Allan Jones:

"A little over a year ago Frankie Miller's Full House played a concert at London's Victoria Theatre whose exuberance was created by the band's commitment to unpretentious rock and roll and full-bloodied R&B. The panache of Full House, charged by the muscular guitar of Ray Minhinnet, provoked Miller to an extraordinary performance.

"Last Saturday the band returned to Victoria, but across the road this time to the more prestigious New Victoria theatre, and the story was different. Fire and verve were virtually entirely absent. Miller looked curiously distracted, with Minhinnett frequently lost beneath the rhythm section and pianist Jim Hall was frequently inaudible. With a voice as potentially large as his, such an abuse of natural talent is as unforgivable as it is depressing."

Charles Catchpole in his piece for the *Daily Express* described the show as "Miller Magic" and seemed impressed that "Half of Glasgow" had turned up for the gig!

"Glasgow must have been very quiet on Saturday night. Half its population seemed to be in the New Victoria Theatre to see Scotland's latest cult hero Frankie Miller. It was an amazing reception for an artist who is not widely known, and I am still at a loss to explain the Miller phenomenon. His voice has enormous raw power, his songs are gutsy, his band, Full House, are tight and mean. Yet his stage presence is, to put it mildly, low-key. He just stands there, legs splayed, one knee bent, like a latter day Gene Vincent, and rips through one raunchy rocker after another."

Frankie Miller: High Life and Times
Susan Whitall, *Creem* magazine

THE LAST time I was in London Cass Elliott deep-sixed on a ham sandwich in a Mayfair hotel. Spring 1977, and Sylvia of the Three Degrees took one handful of downers too many and was rushed to the hospital from a hotel just down the road...where I was staying while doing a story on Frankie Miller.

Superstitious? Nah. I was too busy trying to regain use of my typing fingers after discovering the liquor supply that came with my hotel room. This is what I found after I threw my tape recorder onto my bed: 2 small bottles of cognac, 5 bottles of scotch, 4 bottles of vermouth, 5 bottles of vodka, 2 bottles of Evian water, 2 bottles of Lowenbrau, 2 cans Watney ale, 2 bottles Moet et Chandon champagne, 3 splits Moet et Chandon, ginger ale, orange juice, Pepsi, quinine water, bitter lemon and Laughing Cow cheese cubes.

The cheese cubes were a nice touch. Not only was this hotel ready for a journalist, they were ready for... a Frankie Miller interview. But first I made my way to the New Victoria Theatre.

There I witnessed a singular cultural phenomenon; I thought I was back in Cobo Hall in Detroit, and to prove it – there was Esther walking by, and Air-Wreck and Milos and Carol. Then people started yelling at the stage, and blew it. I couldn't make out most of the heckles unless they were song titles ('Sailin' Awoi', for instance).

Even so, unless there's someone flying transatlantic once a week just to make sure the kids at the New Victoria match the kids at the Garden, I don't understand it. Large unkempt youths roamed the aisles, there was the obligatory pool of vomit in the Ladies', the lad next to me had biologically active hair, and scattered music fans would flop onto the floor every once in a while, like chemically soaked flounder.

I felt right at home. My blood sugar was right up to American concert standards, too, and you'll pardon me for saying that it was an aesthetically correct way to experience Frankie Miller onstage.

Frankie had obviously dipped into the sauce before the show; of course, I didn't think he was acting the drunk particularly (reading the music papers the next week told me that) – I thought that was the way he always acted, and I liked it. But then, I'd had enough vodka earlier to keep up with my English hosts, which is ten times too much for any American.

If Frankie wanted to be drunk, I was very receptive. The audience was of the same mind (chemically and philosophically); they greeted their favourite songs – which included everything – with screams, yowls, and singing of their own. Song requests, encouragement, and just "Frankie" when they couldn't think of anything else.

"Love letters" Frankie called them later. Between songs he hooted back at them good-naturedly: "Shaddup! Give us peace! The man at the door let in all my friends, I can see. And he better let them OUT before some damage is done to the seats!" (More screams, more "Shaddup!")

There was thankfully a minimum of stage theatrics, just the songs – including 'The Rock', Randy Newman's 'Sail Away', 'Ain't Got No Money' – all delivered in Frankie's impassioned howl... and the ad libs.

Before 'Jealous Guy' he called out for everybody in the audience who was jealous to yell. A few girls shrilled. Frankie yelled "Doesn't anybody out there get jealous? I said, doesn't ANYBODY OUT THERE GET JEALOUS ONCE IN A WHILE? I do!!"

"And I'm jealous RIGHT NOW!!" Screams. "How many of you will admit you're JEALOUS?" A great howl rose from the crowd. "I AM! I'm so jealous right now I could get a gun! You'd best believe I wouldn't SING it if I didn't feel jealous RIGHT NOW!" I was jumping on my seat then, cheering for the gun.

Then he segued into the song, and beat the crowd into even more of a froth. By this time he'd abandoned the bowler hat he'd come out with, and his jacket came off to reveal white shirt and vest, his trademark onstage and off. The band was hot and steamed through each number with an exquisitely controlled chaos I thought I'd seen the last of when I saw the Faces' show.

If that sounds like the kiss of death, understand that before I was a paid rock critic that was the kind of good time I used to shell out my wine money for. Raw but tight. I am also one of the few people I know who listens to Faces albums all the way through (except Lester). And I thought they were great when they were drunk; self-mocking, idiotic, full-throated and out of their minds with juice.

Just like tonight; Frankie's guitarist and bassist grind out the beat with the joy and sweat of newlyweds; Frankie winds up 'Jealous Guy' with savage moans of "I'm gonna SHOOT somebody" like a he-animal with his heart being ripped out. Dirty filthy pumping rock 'n' roll – the kind of stuff our mothers tried to keep us away from. The dedication of 'Let's Spend The Night Together' to Keith Richard was the capper.

I was mildly amused to read the *Sounds* review the next week, which talked about Frankie's unprofessional drunk and disorderly stage act. So promising, and he had to get self-indulgent and ruin everything... the old Soul Singer Burn-out. Ha ha ha. When Frankie made his way up to my room to chat I was ready.

Any dent I had made in my liquid refreshments had been cunningly replaced by the maids with the fresh sheets and soap. Indeed, when I threw open the supply of goods I thought I caught a glint in Frankie's eye... but just as quickly he suppressed it and explained that he was confining himself to white wine... just what I didn't have.

We compromised with beer and settled down to talk while his manager sipped Scotch and soda. (Heartless.) I'd heard rumors Stateside that Frankie couldn't cut a long tour because he always got too deeply into the bottle. And he was involved in the rout at the Speakeasy Club in London in early spring '77 which put guitarist (and fellow Scot) Brian Robertson out of commission for Thin Lizzy's American tour.

What happened was quite simple: Brian had gotten between Frankie and a broken glass a chap was about to meld with Frankie's face. Frankie in fact was all ready to call in reinforcements down from Scotland, but he realized that "it would have turned into a full-scale war."

As he told Tony Parsons of the *NME*: "I've got a bad reputation but I don't play it up. It would be bullshit if I did. It's just that the hard stuff makes me crazy."

"Ahhh, bullshit," Frankie dismissed it later. "I'm not interested in politics. I'm only interested in American politics." In fact, anything American. He reminisced cheerfully about Detroit for my benefit: "The drugs, man!"

"These chicks gave us some synthetic heroin! We said hey, let's stick around here for a while. One time somebody knocked on my hotel door, I crawled over to open it...and they crawled into the room. That's Detroit!" He also spoke warmly of buying drinks in the middle of the night, the different music scenes in every city, etc. Especially New York.

"But Frankie," I offered. "Have you ever seen *Taxi Driver*? THAT'S NEW YORK!"

"Yeah," he said, grinning. "I love it!" What he's not so fond of: Bruce Springsteen ("I couldn't understand the words and I didn't like his singin'. I guess I should have listened to his words more."), London at the moment, punk bands ("I like their energy, but they can't play! They put down the Stones and yet try to play 'Satisfaction' – they can't even play it!").

Gabba Gabba hey. At this point Frankie grabbed a copy of *CREEM*, professed not to know the magazine the other writer was from (he almost got the cover for that), and left me with these thoughts:

Black soul music these days is more often chunka chunka disco sludge than not. As for the white soul boys, Joe Cocker's producing more vomit than anything. Rod's voice sounds as smooth, lush and passionless as a L.A. nymphet. Who else is there? Paul Rodgers, Robert Palmer (too pretty, eh?)... Otis Redding's widow wept when she heard Frankie Miller for the first time. And the Scottish bastard took my last copy of *CREEM*.

© Susan Whitall, 1977 Reproduced with kind permission of the author.

June 19, 1977 Bottom Line New York
The Original Booker T and the M.G.'s
Featuring: Steve Cropper, Booker T Jones, Donald 'Duck' Dunn, Willie Hall
Also appearing: Frankie Miller Band

Frankie and his band appeared at The Bottom Line supporting Booker T and the M.G.'s, probably the most prestigious club venue in New York.

During the evening Steve Cropper asked Frankie if he would like to come and jam with the band (they had never been able to replace Otis Redding) and maybe even do some material together.

Interestingly, they were able to discuss the Stax tours of the mid 60s in which Booker T and the M.G.'s featured. Frankie explained that the style of his set had been "consciously based" on these tours and the fact that all the songs were taken faster than they were on record.

"Didya ever listen to people like Wilson Pickett and Otis live? 'Cos they just go dah-dah-dah-day." (Frankie taps out a fast beat.) "Now if people know the number you're doing, they get a buzz; but if they hear it done like..." (He taps it out again.) "That's an extra buzz. And I picked that up from listening to those records."

The band then played two nights at the Bijou Club in Philadelphia. Chrysalis had arranged a press party for after the second night and one prominent guest was *Star Wars* leading lady Carrie Fisher. In later interviews it was reported that Otis Redding's widow had come backstage in Los Angeles after she broke down and cried after hearing Frankie sing.

When Frankie was asked what music he was listening to these days he could only talk about the Eagles' *Hotel California*.

"When I was in California in 1975 we were staying at the Riot House [rock'n'roll slang for the main rock hotel, the Continental Hyatt House] and I couldn't take it so I moved downtown to where the people are.

"I saw Bobby Blue Bland for the first time down there - he's one of my heroes. I learned a lot from him, especially style and approach. There was a single out from his *Dreamer* album then called 'I Wouldn't Treat A Dog The Way You Treated Me' and the first time I heard it, it was on a jukebox in a bar and me and Henry [McCullough] just kept on playing it until I were driving people out of the place."

Full House finally disbanded after the very long, west coast leg of the American tour, but the stars had come out for the Frankie, Bob Seger and Rod Stewart among their number.

"Rod came down for two nights down at the Roxy in Hollywood," recalled Ray Minhinnet, "and there was a big party at his house, all sorts of good things happening. But I think it went to our heads a bit. We were all drinking a lot, doing things we shouldn't've... Frankie had this name of being that way anyway but I've never heard him sing out of tune, not once.

Full House MK2 a Winning Hand?

One headline from *NME* entitled "Miller Throws In A Winning Hand" claimed that Frankie had fired his Full House men, but an unrepentant Frankie told them: " I think there was need for a change. It's now gotta get better."

Reports elsewhere implied that the Scottish singer had "callously dismissed guitarist Ray Minhinnet and drummer Graham Deakin." But Miller claimed this accusation was "harsh".

Frankie also explained that his decision was not as sudden as it first appeared. He said he had gradually been disillusioned by the group's performance during the US dates, and believed that all members were aware changes would have to be made on their return to Britain.

As far as he was concerned the band was not working as it should. When they recorded their last album it was necessary to bring in session players, including Chris Spedding and Procol Harum's Gary Brooker, and Miller would prefer to front an outfit which could record without this embellishment.

Discontented, Jim Hall had quit the group just before their American dates. Minhinnet and Deakin were forced to leave for similar reasons. Recording with additional help "caused a bit of resentment" added Frankie. "They didn't feel too good about it, which is understandable. I don't want that to happen again."

Ray Minnhinet commented: "I just had a call from him saying it was all over. Just a few words, that's all. Full House took him away from being a joke in every bar in London and worked for a year to get him some respect. Suddenly bang it was all over."

Full House MK2 at the Reading Festival
The 17th national jazz, blues and rock festival
1977 August 26/27/28th
Headliners: Golden Earring, Thin Lizzy, Alex Harvey
Weekend tickets: £7.95

The night before the festival sees thunderstorms. Mud covers the entire site and the crowds are forced to witness performances knee deep in mud, but respite comes via Aerosmith, Thin Lizzy and The Alex Harvey Band. The *NME* says of the festival "It's cold and it's wet and it's bloody miserable."

Frankie had returned from the USA, and refreshed his Full House line-up by replacing Ray Minnhinet with Neil Hubbard and bringing in BJ Wilson on drums. Paul Carrack came in on keyboards plus a horn section of Chris Mercer, saxophone, and Martin Drover, trombone.

BJ Wilson

Barrie James Wilson was an English rock drummer. He was best known as a member of Procol Harum for the majority of their original career from 1967 to 1977. He had a powerful, distinctive style – he sat very low behind his kit (often side-on at the side of the stage) and was once referred to as being like an "octopus in a bathtub." He declined an offer by Jimmy Page and Robert Plant to be the original drummer for Led Zeppelin and later became a member of Joe Cocker's touring band.

The recording I have of this show brings us a glimpse of Frankie in an upbeat mood and he seems impressed that the fans have lit fires to keep warm. Showtime was scheduled for 8.40pm, after The Doobie Brothers, with Alex Harvey headlining at 9.45.

The set list is 30 minutes on the recording. Neil Hubbard takes over lead guitar duties for the evening.

'Devil Gun'

Neil Hubbard's chunky riffs dominate the sound on here, backed up by Barrie Wilson's technically brilliant drumming and nicely arranged horns in the background but Frankie is on form, no doubt about that. Paul Carrack is soloing away like mad in the background too.

'Brickyard Blues'

Paul Carrack comes to the fore with a nice intro and piano solo, which is taken at a perfect pace with nice slide playing from Neil Hubbard.

'Hard on the Levee'

Taken at a fast pace, there are some great bass lines in here from Chrissy Stewart. Another great version of this song... not often included unfortunately. There is a vibrancy and freshness about this line-up for sure. If this doesn't warm up the wet and freezing crowd I don't know what will. They are loving it anyhow, going by their enthusiastic responses!

'This Love of Mine'

Led by the horn section, Frankie does his best Otis and that's something to treasure. It sounds like Frankie is loving the backing from this band and a sax solo thrown in too... Feel it getting stronger...goes on forever! Powerful stuff indeed.

'Shoorah Shoorah'

Neil Hubbard, the horns and Frankie's rhythm section have this nailed perfectly too, making it easy for him to deliver the song confidently over an expert backing... and another sax solo for good measure! Frankie is really up for this.

'Double Heart Trouble'

Introduced as a possible new single and a heavy Neil Hubbard guitar riff opens the number - and as Free-like as Frankie ever sounded but with the addition of a great horn backing which really dominates as the song progresses. Another number appreciated by the partying crowd.

'Down the Honky Tonk'

Frankie introduces this as a "Glasgow song" (in tribute to his old local The Treble Two). Another fast paced rocker from the *Full House* album with Neil Hubbard and horn section in perfect harmony once more, with guitar and piano solos bringing the set to a dramatic end. A great show which underlines just how Frankie could rise to the occasion when part of such a star-studded bill.

After the Reading Festival, with Mickey Moody replacing Neil Hubbard on guitar, it's difficult to find very much about the second USA tour, but one gig in Detroit was supported by Crawler in the beautiful old Royal Oak Music Theatre, sadly demolished now.

Micky Moody
is an English guitarist, and a former member of the rock bands Juicy Lucy and Whitesnake.
A quote from mickymoody.com:
"I played in Frankie Miller's band at various times in the 70s and 80s. He will always be considered one of the greatest."

Rolling Stone did a piece but it was not very well researched, with Mikal Gilmore going over old ground (drinking, and comparing Frankie to other singers) rather than actually reporting on the show. Gilmore interviewed Frankie in the bar at his Sunset Strip Hotel (the famed "Riot House").
"I think where I'm coming from," says Miller, pouring his last glass of wine, "is like a fusion of everybody, including Solomon Burke and Randy Newman and Bob Dylan. They're all great singers. But I've not actually imitated anybody consciously. Well maybe once or twice - I can't tell a lie…If it happens to come out like Otis Redding, that's good enough."
I wonder if Frankie realised he had been interviewed by the brother of Gary Gilmore…

Back in England the music press were out in full force again.

Lanchester Poly, Coventry
"The unpredictable Scotsman is back on the road again and both he and his new Full House line-up are really blowing. Rarely will you see a band hit such a peak and such togetherness on the opening night of a tour. The craggy voice is as powerful as ever. The hat and waistcoat are still there. Each and everyone adding something to the overall sound of the band.
"Carrack seems so much more adaptable than even the talented Jim Hall ever was. But the most notable and influential newcomer must be the horn section. They make the House Full.
"Catch Full House if you can… they're on fire."
Jim Evans

And so back to London and the Rainbow Theatre, where the journalists lie in wait with sharpened pencils (or is it knives in the back?). Rosalind Russell, a fan, described the packed, enthusiastic crowd as being full of "drunken sons of Caledonia…"

While another went on about "the muddy and haphazard P.A. sound. "

But back to Rosalind Russell.

"I truly believe that Frankie Miller is a musical genius, but in only giving parts of it to his audience, he's relying on their consideration and on the fact that they will make allowances for him. He began well, building his set, knitting it together with his excellent six piece band. The brass was brought right to the fore right from the start, but it's always been the piano breaks that I've liked best about Frankie's music - apart from his voice of course.

"His voice just tears me up on the sad songs. Piano was played by ex-Ace member Paul Carrack. 'Jealous Guy' was just a cracker, unbelievable. Frankie at his most emotional. It's performances like that, that convince me he is a genius. He maintained the energy more or less until the end of the set, with an excellent ending. When it comes down to it, he has the same effect on me as everyone else - it's worth it to be present at the strokes of brilliance.

1978 "Trouble better get out my way"

Miller in "Trouble"

Frankie Miller releases a new album on April 1 and becomes the first British act to have an album produced by top US producer Jack Douglas of Aerosmith, Patty Smith etc. fame. Recorded at Air Studios and Record Plant in New York, the album features B.J.Wilson, Chrissy Stewart, Paul Carrack, Chris Mercer, Martin Drover, Ray Russell and Aerosmith's Stephen Tyler on harp and backing vocals.

The material will be premiered on BBC's *Sight and Sound* programme at 6.30pm on April 1st.

Jack Douglas

Double Trouble was recorded at the Record Plant in New York and produced by Jack Douglas. During his career, he worked with John Lennon and Yoko Ono, Patti Smith, Cheap Trick, and the New York Dolls, among other rock artists in the 1970s and 1980s. He also produced three successful albums for Aerosmith. He engineered John Lennon's *Imagine* album in 1971 and worked closely with him from then on.

Ray Russell

Guitarist-composer Ray Russell has enjoyed two distinct careers: one as an esteemed session player and award-winning film and television composer, another as an ingenious guitar experimentalist and free-thinking collaborator. Russell made his professional debut as Vic Flick's replacement in the John Barry Seven, with whom he twanged the famous James Bond theme in several Barry-scored films, beginning with 1962's *Dr. No*. He went on to play a stew of jazz, R&B, and other styles with Georgie Fame and the Blue Flames, the Graham Bond Organisation, and the Mike Gibbs Band, where he worked alongside Chris Spedding and Jack Bruce.

As an indefatigable session musician, he has recorded and/or toured with Alex Harvey Soul Band, Lulu, Paul McCartney, Cat Stevens, Van Morrison, Bryan Ferry, David Bowie, Phil Collins, Scott Walker, Art Garfunkel, Marvin Gaye, Heaven 17, and Tina Turner (check out 'Let's Stay Together' on *Private Dancer*).

The news that Frankie had gone back to the USA to record his next album didn't reach us in Scotland until the end of March when it was announced that the Frankie Miller Band would appear on BBC's *Sight and Sound* on

April 1st. *Sight and Sound* was a new concept where the show was transmitted simultaneously on BBC Radio and TV so, much to my parents' horror, I had a hi-fi system rigged up and huge pair of Rigonda speakers which stood either side of the TV that evening!

It meant that I had a great stereo cassette recording of the TV show as a souvenir!

"Saturday night and I'm drinking and thinking of you"... Wow!! With Paul Carrack co-writing a number of the songs, I loved this particular period in Frankie's career, although he told me years later that he couldn't afford to keep them together on the road for long and consequently never made it up to Scotland.

Double Trouble took shape at the Record Plant in New York with the emphasis this time on a harder rock approach, which was reflected in the choice of Aerosmith man Jack Douglas producing. Frankie took his own band to the studios, including Paul Carrack, who co-wrote five of the ten songs.

L to R Chris Mercer BJ Wilson Frankie Miller Front Jack Douglas and Assistant

Photographer Carlo Chinca, who had also covered the Rainbow gig in December, took these shots in the Record Plant...

Over to you Carlo:
Frankie Miller - Air Studios

"Working as a freelance with Chrysalis Records PR department one of my many live coverage photo shoots with some of their bands was with Frankie Miller's Full House at the Rainbow Theatre in Finsbury Park, London. This was December 1977 and due to the success of my pictures from that concert Chrysalis asked me to cover the mixing at Air Studios of Frankie's new album *Double Trouble* a month later.

"I spent a couple of hours there with Joe, the Chrysalis PR man, making pictures of Frankie and the band hanging out around the mixer desks and shot just one roll of film. I found Frankie very cool and approachable and on my way out he was stretched out on the reception sofa with a bottle of Blue Nun wine in his hand. 'Hey Carlo,' he said as I was about to exit, 'thanks for photographing this and have yourself a glass of wine!'

"I left with the intro to 'Have You Seen Me Lately Joan' pleasantly circling around my head.

"What a great song and impressive album! Never forgotten. "
Carlo Chinca

Double Trouble Sleeve Notes By Michael Heatley and Davy Arthur

Long before Stevie Ray Vaughan adopted the name for his world-beating blues band, Frankie Miller was getting himself into *Double Trouble*. It would take a heart of flint not to be amused by the dramatic cover photos, which give a clue as to the man's extrovert character, but within the sleeve resided an equally powerful collection of songs. The emphasis this time was on a hard-rocking approach. And that was reflected in the choice of producer, Aerosmith man Jack Douglas.

The Record Plant in New York was where *Double Trouble* took shape. And while he'd used session musicians on his first Stateside sojourn, as with *The Rock* Frankie brought his own band with him. And it was an impressive one indeed.

Ray Russell on electric guitar was a highly-rated session player, while Irish bassist Chrissy Stewart had appeared on both of the previous two albums.

Drummer Barrie 'BJ' Wilson had been left high and dry with the dissolution of Procol Harum, a band Frankie had often played live with in the past. A hard-working two-man horn section of Chris Mercer and Martin Drover added no fewer than four instruments between them – tenor and baritone saxes, trumpet and flugelhorn.

But perhaps the most impressive recruit of all was Sheffield-born keyboardist and vocalist Paul Carrack. He'd mined his own soulful groove with Ace and, as well as adding his vocal and instrumental skills to the mix, would have a hand in writing five of the album's ten songs. Its release in April 1978 would put Carrack back on the map after his Ace success; he was lead singer on their 1974 hit 'How Long', and would also contribute to Miller's 1979 release *Falling in Love* before throwing in his lot with Squeeze.

Carrack had played with Frankie at the Reading Festival in August 1977, just two months after the appearance of the *Full House* album. This was a major surprise, since the backing band of the same name had appeared to be a solid working unit. But press reports suggested the singer had been unhappy the likes of Chris Spedding and Procol Harum's Gary Brooker had been called in by producer Chris Thomas to guest: according to *New Musical Express*, "Miller would prefer to front an outfit which could record without this embellishment." Accordingly, Reading had seen him backed by a temporary line-up of Neil Hubbard (guitar), BJ Wilson and Chrissy Stewart, plus horn-players Mercer and Drover. Carrack supplanted Procol Harum's Chris Copping, himself a temporary replacement for the departed Jim Hall. By the time Miller set out on a major four-week tour in November, Neil Hubbard had given way to Micky Moody, but with Micky bound for heavy-metal heaven with David Coverdale's Whitesnake it was Ray Russell who'd make the Stateside trip to cut *Double Trouble*.

A choir of backing vocalists recruited from New York's finest included Karen Lawrence, Lonnie Groves, Eric Troyer, Richie Supa and Stephen Tyler. The latter was, of course, no session man but the lead singer of Aerosmith, which has made *Double Trouble* a must-buy for their fans. It's not possible to be definitive as to which tracks Tyler is on, but it's likely his background vocals appear on 'You'll Be In My Mind', 'Love Is All Around' and 'Goodnight Sweetheart', while 'Love Waves' may well showcase his harmonica skills.

But it was, of course, Frankie Miller who was squarely centre stage in what was clearly intended by record company Chrysalis as the album to launch him in the States. Joe Cocker, a similar kind of blues-influenced singer, had done well early in the decade, but on the back of extensive touring – and Frankie realised he, too, would have to become familiar with the turnpikes and freeways of the land of the free.

"The thing about this place," he told *Creem* magazine's Toby Goldstein, "is if you want to crack it right you have to work on the road – and, if you're any good at all, people will pick up on it. It's a lot of hard work in this country, but that's why I like it."

"I've always been influenced by American music," continued Frankie. Yet he admitted that only now did he understand some of the things his heroes had sung about. "Things like going down to the union hall... I never knew what one was until I came (to America) and asked somebody, but I'd been singing it all my life! When you come here you can finally associate the real thing with the words people use."

It was in some senses a Coals to Newcastle exercise, but Frankie felt he could make it on the back of *Double Trouble*. He was certainly impressed with Jack Douglas, calling him "the most positive producer I've ever met." The harder edge of the music must, he felt, be matched by a more forceful delivery from himself. "And if Jack can pull more aggression than I can and get it out of me I'll be a happy man."

Promoting *Double Trouble*'s predecessor, *Full House*, in the States had seen him supporting country-rockers the Outlaws, a match that was hardly made in heaven. He preferred to headline smaller venues, clubs like the Roxy and the Bottom Line, where there was more audience contact and he could be certain they had come to appreciate his unique brand of blues-rock music.

The album kicked off with 'Have You Seen Me Lately Joan', the only solo Miller song on the track list and a real statement of intent with squealing guitar from Ray Russell and a driving rhythm from Stewart and Wilson. The album took its title from 'Double Heart Trouble', one of two tracks here written by former Free bassist Andy Fraser.

Miller and Fraser had briefly been bandmates in a project that had preceded 1975's 'The Rock', and though nothing came of it they clearly remained friends.

That the result was very reminiscent of Free (or their spinoff band, Bad Company) should have come as no surprise; indeed, the verse chords are all but identical to Free's 'The Stealer'. It's worth checking out the 'original' version of this song which appears on the first Andy Fraser Band Album, released in 1975.

Track three, 'The Train', was the first of the five Miller/Carrack co-writes, while 'You'll Be In My Mind' saw guitarist Russell and producer Douglas join in the songwriting.

Both have an AOR (adult oriented rock) feel to them that suggest they were aimed towards the American airwaves. There seemed more chance of a fair hearing than in punk-obsessed Britain, so bending Frankie's music and voice to fit a format was a calculated risk.

"The record company had a great talent in their hands they weren't quite sure what to do with," Paul Carrack reflected in 2003, "so they tried to force him into a pigeonhole." Now a star in his own right, Carrack believes Frankie "was and is one of our best soul shouters."

'Good Time Love' was simpler, a piano ballad with Paul Carrack's talents to the fore, and perhaps more in keeping with what fans of *The Rock* or *Full House* might have expected.

A fine track to end the vinyl side one, which could only have been improved by more prominent horns. Flipping the disc revealed 'Love Waves', a slighter song perhaps that may well, as previously hinted, include Steve Tyler's harmonica talents. 'Breakaway (I Can't)' is notable for more horns and a fabulous Ray Russell guitar solo.

The choice of single from the album almost inevitably fell on track eight, Marvin Gaye's 'Stubborn Kind Of Fellow'. The up-tempo rock version of the Motown classic held few surprises, but Creem magazine acclaimed it as "forcing Miller to sing with the fury that burns inside him." And few would argue with that!

Andy Fraser's second songwriting contribution to the album, 'Love Is All Around', was given an arrangement based around BJ Wilson's drum patterns and heavy wah-wah guitar from Ray Russell. At just a touch below five minutes, it was the album's second longest track and featured backing vocals from Steve Tyler. This was a track that dated back to the days in 1973-74 when Miller and Fraser had attempted to form a band together but abandoned the concept, leaving a treasure trove of songs to plunder separately. Indeed, Fraser had included his version on his own first solo album and it makes an interesting comparison.

'Goodnight Sweetheart' certainly won the prize for the oldest song on the album. It was performed in 1954 by the Spaniels, a black doowop group from Gary, Indiana (coincidentally the home town of the Jackson Five) and became a massive R&B hit. Frankie's version has more in common with the original than the McGuire Sisters cover for the 'white' pop market. The comments of Chris Mercer, who played tenor and baritone sax on this album, offer an insight into the recording industry in the 1970s.

"This band had some heavyweight players, Chrissy, Ray Russell the noted 'studio gun', Paul Carrack, the late, great BJ Wilson, Martin Drover and myself on horns. The album was produced by Jack Douglas from New York, which was typical of the era when record companies hired 'hot' producers, regardless of their feel for the music being created. A tragic exception of course was the wonderful album Frankie made with Allen Toussaint, which never got the recognition but was the right thing to have done.

"On *Double Trouble*," Mercer continued, "the horns were pitifully under balanced in the mix and Douglas didn't even use the dynamite section parts we recorded on 'Goodnight Sweetheart'. The album has some very powerful playing and singing but is very rockish, whereas Frankie's gift was R&B." Long time Miller fans would probably agree with that assessment.

Certainly both band and songs were even better live, as Steve Simpson of sometime opening act Meal Ticket confirmed. He was so knocked out with what he heard and saw he resolved to work with Frankie at the earliest opportunity – and would get his wish within a few months.

"One of the great perks of Meal Ticket was that we did some great supports: we did the Atlanta Rhythm Section, Bob Seger and the Silver Bullet Band, Ry Cooder and Frankie Miller. An earlier version of the band had featured Henry McCullough, who was an absolute hero of mine and became a dear friend. So I always wanted to follow my friend. During the course of us touring together I told Frankie 'One of these days I'm gonna work with you' and he said 'I hope you're serious.' So when Meal Ticket came to an end and Full House had had its moment, I got the call to go and work with the boy."

It was a regret of Simpson's at the time that a live album never transpired. "On stage he was frighteningly good and he was good with an audience. He could entertain them and he had that old classic Scottish way of dealing with hecklers. He always had the power…but he created that. If any musician was acting up he'd say 'Hey listen—all eyes on my shoulders!'" But if he gave you space to loon about, that was a different thing. Occasionally I'd play fiddle on stuff and he really liked me to get into it. He was always very generous in that respect as long as you remembered he was the boss!"

There were a couple of eye-catching headlines for a show at The Paradiso in Amsterdam - "Double Dutch Trouble" and "Going Dutch With Frankie" - and during the interviews, Frankie's dry Glaswegian humour shone through alongside his often frank and honest views on the music side of things.

During the *Double Trouble* tour Frankie was able to reflect on the break-up of Full House, with the music press wondering if one day, Frankie Miller was going to "make it". It was pointed out that perhaps he had attracted more support from rock writers than anyone else, and had stretched journalistic tolerance to the absolute limit!

Double Trouble would either, in their opinion, make him or finally kill him off. Of course, Frankie was indignant that he should be given this ultimatum to 'break through' and pointed out that after the release of *Once In A Blue Moon*, a friend in Glasgow had suggested that if he didn't make it with that album then "That's it." Frankie said that that was the most ridiculous thing he had ever heard, and that he would do anything to be successful except sell his soul.

Looking back over the previous two years, when Procol Harum's lyricist Keith Reid first took over his business affairs, and Frankie formed Full House, it was felt that that was when he finally looked ready to achieve recognition. The group established a reputation that complemented the critical respect for Miller as one of Britain's greatest R&B singers.

It appeared to everyone that the breakup of Full House came as a surprise but as Frankie explained, even he had misgivings about killing off an obviously effective formula. "At one time I was real happy," he explains, "and there was a real good band atmosphere. But then it just got a bit crazy - it started to lose something.

"When we were in America we should have been a lot more aggressive. But there were a few in the band who'd never been there for a start, and they were a bit overwhelmed by the country itself. So at the very end there was nothing progressing, and I didnae want to know."

There was a presence from the UK music press at the Paradiso in Amsterdam, a converted church with stained glass windows, which until recently was the city's largest music venue.

The night Frankie played there, there was a steel band playing across the street and the bars were so crowded that people were climbing in and out of the windows. The two female backing singers (Dyan Birch, ex Kokomo, and Karen Lawrence) were a feature of the new line-up. The show featured a number of songs from the *Double Trouble* album including 'Love Waves', 'Good Time Love', 'Have You Seen Me Lately Joan', and 'Stubborn Kind Of Fellow.' There was also a brilliant rendition of 'I Can See Clearly Now' which was the first of three encores.

When asked if Dyan Birch would remain in the band with him when he went to the States, Frankie answered: "I personally could not ask a person like her to be a permanent member. She's too good, she's a solo career of her own to follow.

"I can't afford to keep a full-time band on the road. It's impossible to keep them together, good musicians will always be working. It gives me a chance to work with a brass section, which is a new experience for me as I've never worked with girl singers or a brass section on the road."

When asked if he preferred playing in Europe to Britain, Frankie answered, "Well, you get eggs and bacon in England. I like the people here, even though I can't understand them."

Can they understand you? he was asked.

"Well that's a good point. I was talking to somebody yesterday and they asked me whether I thought the words were getting through or if it was just the sound. My ego immediately goes to the words but apparently, it's only the sound. Shakespeare was good, wasn't he? And so was Dylan, but there's only one Frankie Miller for the words. And I mean that."

Author's Note: And Shakespeare couldny sing!

When asked if he thought that the change of style with each album had given him an inconsistent following:

"Well, if they wanted the next album to be the same as the last they're none of my following. They're my following if they come up to me and say 'I've got all your albums.' And they mention certain songs and you've never really thought about it because you've not been listening to them."

Frankie was also asked if he had thought about recording 'I Can See Clearly Now' and he said that although he could do a better version than Ray Charles could, he wouldn't record it.

In typical Frankie Miller style he said to one reporter: "I'll tell you who I really like - Perry Como, I like that kind of singing, oh he's magic, watch him sing."

From Donna McAllister 'Double Dutch Trouble'

" 'I'm real happy with *Double Trouble*,' Frankie said proudly. 'It's a good fuckin' album.' And his convictions were animated by Amsterdam enthusing over the tracks from his new album.

"After the show he was radiant. Two blazing hell-fires built behind his crazy green eyes as he wildly explained, loudly and clearly, 'I don't drink. It's all image. The thing is if you come from Scotland to England you have an immediate reputation for being an incredible drinker, so people make up stories about you. Somebody once said I drink 18 pints of Guinness. I don't drink Guinness… Ever. I'll have a brandy though!'"

With Dave Mackay daughter Sara

Falling In Love Darlin'

Miller's Tale

As we move into early autumn 1978, Chrysalis announce a new single on September 15th entitled 'Darlin'. It's backed with a new studio version of 'Drunken Nights in the City' complete with a Celtic style fiddle backing.

Miller and his new band, featuring Ed Deane (guitar), Steve Simpson (guitar, accordion, fiddle), Tex Comer (bass) and Fran Byrne (drums) played a warm-up gig at Dingwalls as a forerunner to their planned UK tour later in the year.

David Mackay - Producer
David Mackay's recording career began with EMI in Australia. He later moved into television where he arranged and produced themes such as Coca-Cola's 'I'd Like To Teach The World To Sing' as well as the score for BBC TV show *Auf Wiedersehen Pet*.

That project generated a hit single, 'That's Livin' Alright', by Joe Fagin, which won Mackay an Ivor Novello Award and a BAFTA nomination. He also worked on Bonnie Tyler's first two albums.

Steve Simpson
Joined Frankie Miller in 1978 playing guitar, accordion and fiddle. Steve also spent time in Meal Ticket, The Sutherland Brothers, Ronnie Lanes Slim Chance, and had a longstanding working relationship with Roger Chapman of Family.

Terry (Tex) Comer
The song 'How Long' was written about Comer leaving the band briefly to play with The Sutherland Brothers and Quiver and his subsequent return to the band.

Fran Byrne was with Bees Make Honey before he left to join Paul Carrack and Ace.

October 1978 Edinburgh University
With 'Darlin' racing up the charts, Frankie was again appearing on *Top of the Pops* and guesting on shows like *The Leo Sayer Show* and becoming something of a celebrity! We were lucky to get up close and personal with the low stage at Edinburgh University.

This was my first Frankie Miller gig for a year (which seemed like a lifetime) and I took along a number of friends, always including seasoned campaigner 'Tiny' Burns.

It was our first Frankie Miller gig since the Full House days and exciting because it was the 'all new band' featuring Ed Deane, Steve Simpson, Tex Comer, Fran Byrne and Nick Judd. I had been so lifted by his *Sight and Sound* show that April, despite the mixed reviews that had flown around during the year.

The venue was fairly packed, but comfortable and noisy as the first year students partied in the upstairs bar.

We were able to sit cross legged in front of the stage for a while as Frankie and his band launched into a series of new numbers. They opened with 'I Can See Clearly Now', 'Have You Seen Me Lately Joan' and 'In No Resistance', after which some student with too many wine gums in him threw a half full plastic beer glass over the stage… If you could see the look on Frankie's face as he quickly and angrily responded: "I'd just like to say something, that somebody threw a plastic pint tumbler here, and if you want to throw tumblers (if you're a punk or somethin'), you come backstage and throw tumblers, but if you throw tumblers here, I'd like the responsible people to tell us who it is if you would, and then we'll get rid of these people because we're here to play music."

He then went on say that they were planning to try some new material and the next song was called 'Hollywood Nightmare', later known as 'Cold And Rainy Night' - I am guessing this was their first attempt as it wasn't part of the Glasgow show that week. Up next came a song introduced as "Probably the new single" - 'When I'm Away From You' was a beautiful rendition with Steve Simpson on accordion.

Then "This is a wee thing from the first album again about a lady from New Orleans. It's called 'Anne Eliza Jane'. I think she came from Edinburgh in the first place!"

The place was now rocking as Steve Simpson belted out his best fiddle work…

Next: "This is a John Lennon number." It was 'Cold Turkey'. What can be said that hasn't been said before about this number? I had seen Frankie perform this in 1969 and he's still pumping it out with as much fire and passion as ever… Great, even with full echo on his voice! The twin guitar sound of Steve Simpson and Ed Deane is also breathtaking as they blast out that famous 'Clapton' riff from the original Plastic Ono Band version. Ed's psychedelic solo is also something to witness.

By this time the "freshers" are pouring down from the upstairs bar and shouting at Frankie through the narrow corridor into the gig as only spoiled little rich kids could and (since the tumbler throwing incident earlier) there was now a change of mood in the audience.

They wanted the ones sitting at the front to stand up, giving them space to push in. Fair enough, but with our relaxed cross-legged positions given up a while back we were now being crushed against the stage just a few feet away from Frankie's mike stand.

Frankie was forced to make a small plea. "Listen, I've been asked to – wait a wee minute – if you could not push a bit forward cos the wires are gettin' a bit - I was gonna swear there but there are ladies in the audience – the wires are getting a bit kinda messed up so if you could keep it back because the PA is gonna be blown out you know then it'll take about 18 hours to get it fixed so if you just maybe keep back a wee bit..."

Then came 'Falling in Love', the beautiful ballad which came at a good time and maybe aimed at calming down the nerdy students in the audience. A lovely guitar solo and general accompaniment from Ed Deane too.

Frankie continues: "I'd just like to explain that the new things we're doing are like eh things that might be on the album when we finish the tour we're gonna be putting them down and just want to get a reaction kinda thing you know. This is called 'Cry to Me'." And it's the best version of the song I've heard him sing. The vocals are spot on and this is good enough to be on a live album Frankie!

Things slow down with "A number from Sam and Dave. The older people in the audience will know it..."

'When Something is Wrong With My Baby'. Well sung and played again, but Frankie is getting distracted by the "freshers" who are pissing everybody off and has to plead with them during the song again - "Keep back, don't be pushing" - amazing at this point that a big fight didn't break out.

We then got 'Be Good to Yourself' and "A song for my bank manager - 'I Ain't Got No Money'" when Frankie announces "We have to take our leave of you."

The nerdy students obviously hadn't heard of Les Harvey, who was electrocuted at Swansea University in 1972, thanks to a student tampering with cables at the front of the stage.

So with the crowd chanting "Frankie - Frankie! We want more!" the promoter wanders on stage and states "Right, listen" - more like a school teacher rapping knuckles than someone issuing a death threat - "If you all move back, and I mean everybody - we don't want broken bones or heads - but the band won't come back on at the risk of life... Now everybody, move back! C'mon. Don't just stand there gaping, move back, otherwise nothing's happening..."

A few minutes later the band re-appears with Frankie telling them again: "Somebody's gonna get electrocuted," and then: "Can you all join in and sing?" So we got 'Darlin' with lovely accordion backing from Steve Simpson.

"Here's another one we would like you to singalong with." It was 'Drunken Nights In The City'. The crowd loved it! Then the show finished with a rousing version of 'Let's Spend the Night Together'.

A riotous audience but, not to be outdone, what a brilliant performance from Frankie and his band.

January 1979
Frankie's Follow Up

Frankie Miller releases a follow-up to his top-ten single 'Darlin' on January 1st.

Entitled 'When I'm Away From You', it was written by Miller, with a new recording of his classic 'Ain't Got No Money' on the B-Side.

This week, Miller goes into the studio to record a new album which will be produced by Dave Mackay. The album is due to be released in March.

Falling in Love (*A Perfect Fit* in the USA) - Sleeve Notes by Michael Heatley and David Arthur

Everybody in music wants a big hit – something to be remembered by. Frankie Miller, the man with the big hat, will, rightly or wrongly, always be identified with his UK hit 'Darlin' which made the chart in October 1978 and soared to number six. Yet there was much more to the man than that one song, however popular, which he didn't actually write. For evidence, investigate the rest of this album which hit the shops in 12-inch vinyl format in early 1979 – not to mention the rest of his finely crafted back catalogue, which Eagle Records have made available in digital form for the first time on a British label.

It had been a long and fascinating journey from Glasgow's Burns Howff pub, a focal point in Glasgow's music scene during the 1960s, to the Top 10. Frankie's first love was soul music, a Caledonian version of which he purveyed in groups like Sock 'Em JB. Next step forward was the Stoics, a quartet purveying progressive pop-rock, which saw Frankie songwriting with, then falling out with, guitarist Jimmy Doris. A German support tour with Ten Years After was to prove the group's swansong, but Chrysalis – TYA's label – had seen enough to sign the talented Scot in his own right.

Many of the musicians on this album, Frankie's sixth (titled *A Perfect Fit* in the US), were active on the UK concert circuit. Three, keyboardist Paul Carrack, bassist Tex Comer and drummer Fran Byrne, had formed the backbone of 'How Long' hitmakers Ace. Carrack had played a major role in co-writing songs for Frankie's last long-player, April 1978's *Double Trouble*, but would henceforth follow a path that, within a year, would take him to Squeeze.

Into the breach as right-hand man came Steve Simpson, lately of Meal Ticket and a capable performer on guitar, accordion, mandolin and violin as well as adding strong harmony vocals. He would go on to become the first lieutenant of another great British vocalist, Roger Chapman, which post he retains today, as well as leading his own band Chuck Farley and working with a plethora of UK and American musicians. As he's commented, tongue only partly in cheek, "I may not be a star... but I know what stars need."

A mutual appreciation society had developed when his band had supported Full House. "I'd heard Frankie singing just before Meal Ticket came along and was absolutely overjoyed to hear this little white Scottish guy who sounded like Otis. I thought I'd love to work with this man. So, during the course of us touring together, I told him 'One of these days I'm gonna work with you,' and he said 'I hope you're serious.' So, when Meal Ticket came to an end and Full House had had its moment, I got the call from (manager) Keith Reid, whom I didn't know at the time, to go and work with the boy."

The album came together in Warlingham, Surrey – a less than exotic location compared with previous Miller recording forays to New Orleans, San Francisco and New York. Producer Dave Mackay had his studio there, where Bonnie Tyler, Cliff Richard, Billy Ocean and others had recorded successfully. "I'm not sure with hindsight whether the Dave Mackay connection was actually good for Frankie and his music," says Steve Simpson, "and I don't think anybody's going to nail me for saying that. But, at the same time, it did produce The Hit."

Falling In Love was recorded on a session basis, Simpson being involved practically every day. "Some days it would just be me playing acoustic, others it would be Tex (Comer) on bass doing the 'road' tunes, stuff we'd worked out live, or Tim Renwick on guitar." Ed Deane, Frankie's road guitarist of the time, also featured, as did Terry Britton, a man with strong Cliff Richard connections.

The ten tracks on the original album release were exactly divided between Frankie's own compositions and outside material. First up was the self-penned 'When I'm Away From You', released as a January 1979 single simultaneously with the album. Almost inevitably it failed to do as good business as its predecessor, stalling two places short of the all-important Top 40, but was undoubtedly a superior song.

Its combination of tough but tender, a Miller trademark, made it a very coverable number, and the Bellamy Brothers, Kim Carnes and Jameson Booker would all make it part of their own recorded repertoire in future months.

'Is This Love' had been a recent (February 1978) hit single for reggae king Bob Marley. Frankie's version owes little to the offbeat rhythm of the original and, maybe for that reason, remains his only flirtation with the genre. "It's a kind of hybrid," says Simpson. "It's not black enough musically, not dark enough to one degree, but it was a nice try. It worked better live that's for sure, being a smaller band. And the road band understood each other more rather than the producer giving it to you and saying 'That's what I envisage, will you play it please?'"

US singer-songwriter John Hiatt's material has proved popular with singers ranging from Bonnie Raitt to Joe Cocker over the years, and Frankie (or, quite possibly, Dave Mackay) spotted a good'un in 'If I Can Love Somebody'. Revived by US chanteuse Marti Jones in the late 1980s, it appears to be a song never recorded by its writer.

'Darlin'' was penned by Stuart (sometimes known as Oscar) Blandamer, at the time a brass player with London club hopefuls the Q-Tips. While singer Paul Young would ride the 1980s charts as a solo act, interpreting the songs of others, Stuart/Oscar has a sizeable pad in the Amersham area, paid for by his royalties.

The success of 'Darlin'' "came right off the wall," admits Steve Simpson, who played accordion and acoustic guitar on the track (the latter with Tim Renwick). And the credit belongs to Mr Mackay. "Dave and Barry Guard, his partner, came up with a whole bag of tunes and said to Frankie 'We think these will fit, let's do it.' As a producer does."

An amusing sidelight on the producer-musician relationship comes from drummer Chris Slade, who'd just quit Manfred Mann's Earthband to become a session man. It was a discipline that didn't at first come easily.

"I can't remember how many tracks I did; all I remember playing on was 'Darlin'', but I'm sure we'd have cut two or three tracks (at the session).

All I remember is Dave saying 'Can you do a simple fill wherever it's needed?' So I did a diddly diddly dum. He said 'Can you do a simpler one?' I said 'Simpler?' questioningly... and never worked for Dave Mackay again!"

Ironically, Tom Jones had a hit with the song in the States, and Chris (who went on to AC/DC) had started his professional life with Tom in the 1960s in the Squires. "I didn't realise it would be successful, not at all, though it was quite a good song."

The lyrical tip of the hat to Otis Redding in 'Pappa Don't Know' confirmed Miller's abiding respect for the late soul legend. Indeed, Otis's brother George and widow Zelma once came to watch Frankie during a US tour, as sometime guitarist Ray Minhinnet recalls. "She did say he had the blackest voice of any white man she'd ever heard – but she also said Otis would've been proud of him, which is the greatest accolade."

'Good To See You' was reminiscent of 'Sailing', the ballad that gave Rod Stewart a transatlantic chart-topper in 1975. The lead break may well have come from Tim Renwick, coincidentally six-stringer with 'Sailing' songwriters the Sutherland Brothers. Renwick was one of five guitarists credited, including Frankie himself.

The song, Steve Simpson recalls, is one that had been in the repertoire for quite a while, as had 'A Woman To Love', which had gone through various different sets of lyrics. "I think 'And It's Your Love' is one Frank was getting that together just before going into the studio because he had a fresh batch of tunes." 'Falling In Love With You' was the nearest thing to a title track, and is, suitably, a self-penned number.

And Simpson is certain Miller should have pushed his songs more. "He probably underrated himself because he certainly had the knowledge. Would Frankie have preferred all his own songs? I think any writer would. But he was open enough to take the chance.

"We had drunken nights on the road, as you'd imagine. We'd spend all evening drinking and end up in maybe my hotel room. He'd be walking me round the room with his arm round my shoulder trying to teach me to breathe like Mavis Staples! His big thing then was 'It's not the notes you sing, it's how you breathe in-between, that's what gives you the character.' And I've never come up against that attitude before. This is big learning steps here. And I'm learning from a master... who happens to be a friend.

"So I know he appreciated all that, the classic roots like the Otis, the Mavis, but I'm not sure he had the confidence in his writing at that point. But then he had stuff up his sleeve like 'The Rock', 'Drunken Nights In the City', 'Be Good To Yourself', which he co-wrote with Andy Fraser. I still think he underrated himself."

It was standard practice for Frankie to include a soul standard or two in his concert repertoire, such as Solomon Burke's classic 'Cry To Me' and Sam & Dave's 'If Something Is Wrong With My Baby'. "That was great," Steve Simpson recalled of the latter, "because I used to do second vocal."

If 'Darlin'' had given Frankie his long-awaited Top 10 hit, he considered it a double-edged sword. And not just because he didn't write it! "That song lost me a lot of following," maintains Miller. "We were doing well anyway, but suddenly grannies and kids were coming to our concerts and they drove away the hard-core fans." Steve Simpson agrees. "Yeah, he thought he was getting the blue tops... 'Good To See You', which was the next single out, was an equally good tune, but it didn't move. That was just a song that came up during the sessions."

Frankie and Steve parted company when the singer decided it was time to diversify and made a move towards acting. "He was going off to do a TV film, so there was a hiatus in his music then." He looks back on his time with Miller as seminal. "Having had Meal Ticket, my first attempt to form a band with another excellent Scottish singer, Willy Finlayson, fold up, the Frankie thing was a relief in one way because I didn't have to drive it. And to have this singer I could relate to."

And from the producer....
"I've been really lucky in terms of always being able to work with really good singers, Frankie being the first – with the biggest hat.

"Only thing I can tell you about my getting to work with Frankie was because Bonnie Tyler had a hit record and she and Frankie have similar raspy vocal style, Chrysalis asked me to record four songs hoping for a hit single. I had heard all his recordings with all those fab virtuoso rock players but opted for a simple open country rock song where his amazing vocal would be front and centre.

"Frankie probably doesn't hold 'Darlin' as a high point in his career but it opened him up to a wider audience. "

Cheers,
David Mackay

Falling in Love extra musicians included:

Backing Vocals – Linda Taylor, Plain Sailing

Bass – Dave Wintour, a British bass guitarist and session musician. He is best known for his active part as a member of The Wurzels from 1995 to 2002.

He played and recorded with artists such as Rick Wakeman, Eric Carmen, Pete Atkin, Kenny Young, the pioneer jazz-rock band If, Clifford T. Ward, Roger Daltrey, Slapp Happy, Steve Swindells, Pretty Things, Stealers Wheel, Russ Ballard and Leo Sayer.

He played bass on the song 'Dammit Janet' on the 1975 *Rocky Horror Picture Show* soundtrack.

Drums – Chris Slade, best known for playing for the Australian rock band AC/DC. He drummed for the band from 1989 to 1994, performing on their 1990 album *The Razors Edge* along with their first live album with singer Brian Johnson, *AC/DC Live*. He returned to the band in February 2015 to replace Phil Rudd for the Rock or Bust World Tour. Slade has also played with Manfred Mann's Earth Band, Tom Jones, Toomorrow, The Firm, and Asia.

Horns – Ron Asperey
Ronald 'Ron' Asperey was a British fusion musician (alto and soprano saxophone, flute, keyboard).

He performed with Chris Rea, Status Quo, Ronnie Scott Keith Richards and Miles Davis. In 1984 John Williams brought him to his crossover band Sky, with whom he also toured Australia. He also led the English Jazz Quartet at the Jazz At The Mill festival in Adelaide in 1988. During his career, there were many guest contributions to recordings by well-known artists, such as Roger Daltrey, Roger Glover, Glenn Hughes, Meat Loaf and Whitesnake.

Keyboards – Chris Hall
Keyboards, Backing Vocals – Paul Carrack
Percussion – Barry Guard

April 1979
Edinburgh Odeon
1979 'Darlin' Tour (Officially called the 'Good To See You' Tour)
Well, what can we say; after the great show at the end of 1978 at Edinburgh Uni we were fired up to see something along the same lines.

I felt really sorry for Frankie that night though. 'Darlin' was the flavour of the month and Tiny and I had stall tickets about eight rows from the stage.

In front of us were the Odeon cleaning staff who screamed for 'Darlin' for over an hour. In front of the stage were young girl 'fans' waving 'Goodbye Rod/Hello Frankie' scarves… I wish I had grabbed one as a souvenir.

As Frankie blew the Odeon away with 'Cold Turkey' and 'When Something is Wrong With My Baby', I don't think half of the audience actually knew what was going on... He was struggling also with a bad throat, which didn't help matters, but again: who actually noticed?

We left during the encore and drowned our sorrows in the pub next door, actually thinking that Frankie's career (as we knew it) was over...

How wrong could we be? Frankie was totally aware that it wasn't his audience and took steps to fix it.

Ray Minhinnett later told *Mojo* magazine that the guy who wrote 'Darlin' was actually a sax player of his, Stewart Blandamer. A few months after it had been in the UK charts, Frankie and Ray were at Dingwalls where they bumped into him. Ray said, "Have you two met? You know Stew is the guy who wrote 'Darlin'..." Frankie went, "You, ya cunt ye!" and took a bottle of tomato ketchup and covered Blandamer in it...

Two weeks later Frankie was interviewed after a gig at the Stardust in Artane - a bit north of Dublin - by Jack Lynch from *Hot Press*, who was perhaps not prepared for the experience.

As Mr Lynch attempted to break the ice and make eye to eye contact, Frankie got in first... "Fire the questions, man, that's your job isn't it?" When the conversation gets around to the subject of music and in particular the Scottish/Irish league of R&B, of course first name up is Van Morrison, whose preference, like Frankie's, is to keep close to the American roots of the style, particularly to the degree of adopting a more-American-than-not accent in singing. Frankie described Van as "One hell of a fuckin' cracker."

The conversation got around to the punks with Frankie saying that he didn't know what was going on with them, saying that is was a "very London thing". But Morrison. Great writer and very intense singer.

Discussing the places in these islands where black music first took hold, he touched on a point that had come up in a *Hot Press* interview with Van Morrison.

He went on to compare Belfast to Glasgow in that it was likely that the "aggressive " music that he and Van had been brought up on had come in through the ports. "Thanks to the GIs from Holy Loch who were coming into Glasgow, I was hearin' records that were unreleased in Britain at the time. I was hearin' these things in the neighbourhood where I lived, which was very musical and aggressive. I'm not talkin' about personal aggression."

The tone of the conversation changed when Frankie was asked about his *Falling In Love* album and the use of strings. He pointed out that he didn't perform songs live that used strings but didn't see a problem (like using horns) on his albums. He pointed out that Steve Simpson played fiddle live on 'Ann Eliza Jane' as it was in context.

When the subject of business cropped up Frankie said that was wasn't interested in that crap and if he was asked about his personal life he would say "Mind your own fuckin' business."

When asked if there was a personal reason for the more mellow feel to the *Falling In Love* album, Frankie said that "people want to hear fuckin love songs." He had wanted to call the album *Love Songs* but Al Green had beaten him to it. He also pointed out that his favourite singers like Ray Charles, Otis Redding and Wilson Pickett all specialised in love songs.

Frankie finished up the conversation by again saying that the New Wave stuff meant nothing to him and that he could have written 'Cool For Cats' with his pinkie. "Woman and man. I've always believed in woman and man. I've done certain political things like, whatever, about prisoners because I feel for prisoners and 'Devil Gun' which was about political governments. So, what the fuck. Governments have always been the same…"

And so the end of the 'Darlin'' era finishes up with a barnstorming gig in London...

Hammersmith Odeon 29/4/1979

"It must be all of ten years since I first saw Frankie Miller perform live and even then looked set for success. On Sunday night he produced a devastating performance which brought the best out of his band. Too often compared to past masters like Otis Redding and Sam Cooke, few would credit him with an individual style.

"As if to prove a point, Frankie performed an astounding version of 'When Something is Wrong with my Baby', a single spotlight picking him out: it was an awesome piece of singing that would have left a lesser artist completely exhausted.

"The question is, where does he go from here? With his rock counterpart Bob Seger shrugging off the depression of the *Beautiful Loser* period to reach platinum status in the U.S. who knows what tomorrow may bring…"

Chris Ryan

By the time Frankie got over to Europe, 'Darlin'' was dropped from the set. He supported Rory Gallagher in Germany, and blew Rory's audience away into the bargain.

So after all, Frankie proved me wrong, and unknown to us in the UK at the time embarked on a Scandinavian and European tour which included a televised gig for WDR Rockpalast at Wiesbaden in Germany… which beamed out to an audience of seven million.

Excerpts from Rory Gallagher fan website:
Rory's present band, drummer Ted McKenna, formerly with the Sensational Alex Harvey Band, and bassist Gerry McAvoy who's been at Rory's side since the split with Taste, played almost three hours of earthy, sweaty, honest to goodness Rock and Roll. You get the feeling that every time Rory straps on his battered old guitar, it's as much a thrill for him as the ecstatic audience.

Earlier, downstairs at the Rockpalast, the fans are giving Frankie Miller a hard time. With his band already on stage and ready to go and an introduction from Rockpalast legend, Peter Ruchels, Frankie appears, bottle in hand, to a chorus of "Rory, Rory" and Steve Simpson tells them "He'll be along later just hold your fucking horses, all right?"

When Frankie's on top form there can't be many singers to touch him.

Tonight he's great. The hoary voiced Scot gradually quells the "Rory, Ror-y" chants and slowly brings the audience around to his way of thinking.

Only after telling them in his inimitable Glasgow style: "He's comin', he's comin', he's probably no' even left the hotel yet…" Frankie then blows them away with 'Cold Turkey' and six minutes later has 5,000 converts, eating out his hand for the rest of the show!

Not one but two encores says it all and a fantastic version of 'Little Queenie' has Rory's fans in party mood after all!

Set over and the camera men start jockeying for positions again for Rory's encore. With the delighted audience refusing to leave, Rory called on Frankie for a "jam session" to end the night.

The set had a soaring culmination with Frankie Miller joining in the fun for a raucous rendition of old standards like 'Walkin' The Dog', 'Roll over Beethoven' and 'Sea Cruise'. The audience I'm sure weren't the only ones who wished the night didn't have to end.

MIG music released the whole show on DVD some years later. Back at the hotel after the reception, after the drink up, after the party, it's knocking on 4 am and no one wants to go to bed.

It becomes all too apparent why the hotel staff regard this bunch with such native wariness and an eye for survival.

Both camps take over a reception room downstairs, Frankie Miller, still almost vertical, starts singing and someone hands Rory a guitar.

They don't stop playing till bewildered cleaning ladies nervously push the doors open at 8 am. They clutch onto their Hoovers like battle shields, rabbit eyes blinking at the swaying, singing crazies.

It's only when the hotel manager arrives to plead with everyone to move ("You vill have breakfast? Please?") that the entourage corporately staggers into the restaurant. The staff there are dosed up on the jitters too and Rory's manager does nothing to allay their fears. "A table for 75, please," he boomed, marching past at the head of the rabble.

After that, they ran. Breakfast became a self service affair.

L to R Ed Deane Ted McKenna Jim Hall Frankie Miller Fran Byrne Gerry McAvoy Rory Gallagher and Roadie

Play For Today

By late 1979 another, and perhaps surprising, side of Frankie Miller was to appear. I still remember where I was when I saw the *Play for Today* on BBC TV that evening.

'Just a Boys' Game' was broadcast on 8th November. We were mesmerised as we were introduced to Jake McQuillan and Dancer Dunnichy.

Written by Peter McDougall and produced by John Mckenzie, Jake McQuillan (Frankie Miller) casually drifts from bar to bar confident in the fact he can handle himself. In fact, it's fair to say he relishes this knowledge and isn't willing to hear anything to the contrary. Flanked by his promiscuous, good time friend Dancer Dunnichy (Ken Hutchinson), Jake is talked into taking a day off from his work atop a crane in a Greenock dockyard.

Meanwhile, Jake's cantankerous grandfather (Hector Nicol) - a former hard-man of the streets - is a sick man and rather resentful of young Jake.

Despite this, Jake seeks respect from his grandfather, but his quest to cement his reputation will end in tragedy.

A quote from dangerousminds.net
"Frankie Miller's performance melts the camera in its intensity"

Martin Scorsese is quoted as saying that the bar room brawl scene and its bleak moody atmosphere made the film the Scottish equivalent of *Mean Streets*.

Author's note: I last saw Peter in Glasgow when I was with Frankie the night before an Eagles gig at Hampden. I also had the pleasure of meeting David Hayman that night. He came up and introduced himself and whispered in my ear "The man's a fuckin' legend."
I also remember organising tickets for Peter for our tribute night in Barrowlands in 2002.
I met him in Baird's Bar and thankfully met him just inside the entrance, which was a far as I dared venture into the place!

From a *Mojo* magazine interview in 2014 (Contract signed re copyright)

Peter McDougall had already cast first-time actor Billy Connolly in his 1976 *Play For Today*, 'The Elephants Graveyard', and now he had his eye on Frankie.
"I knew he was key to the part I'd written," says McDougall of casting the singer in 'Just A Boys' Game', his gritty play about Greenock's razor gangs.
"First day on set, Frankie went up to (director) John Mackenzie," says McDougall. "He says, 'Is that the camera? Well fucking point it at me, then.' It wasn't bravado, it was something more existential."
Miller played McQuillan with convincing steeliness, bringing realism to a film about pointless violence borne out of hard-man bravado and an endemic drinking culture. "When I was younger, I could've taken you anytime," Jake's grandfather, played by Hector Nicol, tells him at one point. He and his grandson detest each other.
Billy Connolly (in the BBC documentary *Stubborn Kinda Fella*) says "I remember Alex Harvey telling me that there was a guy in London owed him money. He phoned Frankie and said, 'Look, I'm going to confront this guy, can you come with me and do that look you did in 'Just A Boys' Game'? You don't need to say anything, just stand behind me.'"
Peter McDougall: "Look, before you go off your fucking rocker here, that look was a theatrical look that I fucking choreographed and wrote.

Secondly, if Frankie was to stand behind Alex Harvey you wouldn't see either of them, because they're both fucking tiny tots. Neither of them could fight Sooty, far less Sweep, so forget all that pish about Frankie being a hard man. He was acting."

Perhaps an appropriate comment with which to end the 70s.

Peter McDougall Frankie Miller Davy Arthur

The 80s A Change Is Gonna Come

Music in the 1980s was all about image, and with the advent and popularity of MTV, the images that accompanied artists became more important than ever. It will also be remembered as the decade of an increase in the use of digital recording associated with the usage of synthesisers and synth-pop music.

The music press as we knew it in the 60s and 70s was rapidly changing and artists like Frankie were slowly being forgotten about as far as the popular music papers like *NME*, *Melody Maker* etc. were concerned.

Pop stars and their music changed in the 1980s with the help of MTV and a greater focus on image. A new breed of mega-stars emerged, becoming iconic mascots for the genre and defining the decade through fashion, talent and persona. Some of the superstars to emerge were Madonna, Michael Jackson, and Prince. They experienced a level of fame and success not seen since Elvis Presley and the Beatles.

The eighties was the decade of one hit wonders, where an artist would achieve massive success with one or two extremely popular songs and then seemingly fade away, never able to re-create their success. Part of this had to do with the expansion of the music industry, facilitated by MTV and technology.

Record companies could now make just as much money by manufacturing one-hit artists in succession while not having to invest the time and money that would transform a musician into a star with more longevity. Trends were also changing more quickly and many artists could not keep up and adapt fast enough.

Referring back to my *Crawdaddy* comments, perhaps Frankie Miller had made the correct decision to take his time, adapt, and be his own man. And adapt he did…

Your love is like… Easy Money

The *Easy Money* album was produced by Hitmen and Frankie. The Hitmen were some of Nashville's finest session musicians at the time (Reggie Young, Bobby Thompson, Larrie Londin and Joe Osborne).

They were session musicians who worked behind the scenes and rarely achieved individual fame in their own right.

Guitarist Reggie Young and drummer Larrie Londin were two who, in my opinion, along with Frankie, should have been hitting the headlines when *Easy Money* was released.

Bobby Bland, King Curtis, Elvis Presley, Dusty Springfield, Johnny Cash, Solomon Burke, Jackie DeShannon, The Box Tops… these are just a few of the many musical heavyweights whose recordings have been embellished by the talents of Reggie Young, Memphis and Nashville's most versatile and in-demand session guitarist.

Reggie Young played with so many luminaries over the course of his career that he said "it was nothing special" for him and his fellow Memphis Boys to be tapped to support Elvis Presley in the studio in the late 60s.

"We played with all the top stars of the time, and Elvis hadn't had any hits for a while and didn't have an album on the charts," he said in a 2013 interview with *Premier Guitar* magazine.

Young could also be self-effacing about his musicianship. In 2016, he also told *Premier Guitar* magazine that regarding 'Son Of A Preacher Man': "I was just sittin' there goofin' off. It's a sort of a Chet Atkins lick because it uses an open string." They call them 'identifying licks'. "That's what you used to do to make records sound different," he said. "It seems like nowadays there's none of that."

Reggie Young opens 'Easy Money' for Frankie with a lovely guitar intro - an identifying lick. Surely this should have been headline news for *Easy Money* and Frankie Miller?

As long as the talent of session guitarists is required, generation after generation will study the work of Reggie Young as a how-to template. But on a larger scale, everyone - musicians and non-musicians alike - who hear 'Son of a Preacher Man', 'In the Ghetto', 'Hooked on a Feeling', and 'Drift Away' will be instantly drawn into those songs through the art of Young's intros, and he will live on in his brilliant music.

Larrie Londin was an American drummer and session musician. He went from being one of Nashville's only drummers to being country music's top studio drummer.

As a session musician, Londin played with a wide range of artists, including Emmylou Harris, Diana Ross, The Supremes, The Temptations, The Four Tops, Smokey Robinson, Wilson Pickett, Lionel Richie, Carpenters, B. B. King, Al Green and Chet Atkins. Londin demonstrated the diversity of his playing ability through playing jazz fusion with ex-King Crimson guitarist Adrian Belew. In the years prior to his death, Londin also recorded and toured with the Everly Brothers. Listen closely to 'So Young So Young' on *Easy Money* for a glimpse of Larrie Londin's amazing drumming talent.

Easy Money Sleeve Notes by Michael Heatley and Davy Arthur

Frankie now found himself in the country-music capital of Nashville, playing with some of the finest sidemen that city could offer. Despite the location, Frankie didn't turn to steel guitar and strings approach but instead came up with a fine album of material with his own distinctive stamp that merged rock, country and R&B. It was cut under the tutelage of four musicians/producers working under the banner of Hitmen Productions.

The major influence of recording in Nashville was the use of local writing talent. Title track 'Easy Money' was the first of five songs Frankie penned in tandem with Troy Seals, a respected country songwriter, vocalist and session guitarist a decade his senior. If the surname's familiar it's because Troy is cousin of Dan Seals (England Dan), Brady Seals (Little Texas) and Jim Seals (Seals and Crofts). He'd left the business after a pop career in the 1960s to work in construction, but the lure of music proved too strong and he came back as a songwriter and Nashville session musician.

Prior to linking with Frankie, Troy's songs had been recorded by Lonnie Mack, Dobie Gray, Percy Sledge, Ronnie Milsap, George Jones, Rod Stewart and many more. Teaming with fellow American Eddie Setser had inspired 'Seven Spanish Angels', a US country chart-topper for Willie Nelson and Ray Charles – one of Frankie's long-time idols – and Setser's name appears three times in the credits here.

Clearly, the experienced pairing would prove useful in schooling Miller in the ways of Music City.

'The Woman In You', also co-written with Seals, was more of an uptempo slide-guitar romp with horn backing.

Like all ten tracks here, it made its point in well under four minutes, suggesting that *Easy Money* was aimed at radio. 'Why Don't You Spend The Night' was the first of two tracks solely penned by country writer Bob McDill, Nashville's Songwriter of the Year in 1976.

The song was also released as a single in the same year as *Easy Money* by blind country superstar Ronnie Milsap, and added Frankie to a list of 'customers' that ranged from Jerry Lee Lewis to Perry Como!

'So Young, So Young' was the best-known song of Australian new wavers Jo Jo Zep and The Falcons. It had already found its way into the stage set of Elvis Costello, and Frankie's version cemented its status as a cult classic.

Coincidentally or not, former Procol Harum member Pete Solley would become Jo Jo Zep's producer and help the group to major success.

'Forget About Me' returned to the Miller/Setser/Seals combination, and proved such a durable song that the Bellamy Brothers would hit the country chart with it four years later.

Taking of covers, 'Heartbreak Radio' would quickly become one of Frankie's most widely interpreted compositions thanks to Kim Carnes, Rita Coolidge, Lee Greenwood, Delbert McClinton, Roy Orbison and the Osmonds. Amazingly it only ever came off the album as a single B-side (remember them?).

'Cheap Thrills', the second Bob McDill contribution to *Easy Money*, would also be recorded by David Allan Coe, Rita Coolidge and Phoebe Snow. But the lyric could well have been written specifically to reflect Frankie's former 'wild' image. "I can't help the things I do/I've always been attracted to cheap thrills/if you ain't supposed to do it, I will."

'No Chance' stems from the pen of US singer-songwriter John 'Moon' Martin, best known for penning Robert Palmer's 1979 hit 'Bad Case Of Loving You (Doctor Doctor)'. It had appeared the previous year on his second solo album *Escape From Domination*, and had also been a minor hit single, which may be where Frankie first heard it.

Nick Lowe, Dave Edmunds, Mink DeVille, Bette Midler, Michelle Phillips and Rachel Sweet have been other customers for Martin's songs. Since this recording, he has moved to Nashville, where he built his own recording complex, Ponyboy Studio.

The swaggering 'Gimme Love' was the album's final Miller/Setser/Seals effort and, with its ebullient delivery and darting horns, certainly had a good time feel.

The opening line "At five o'clock in Kensington" certainly harked back to Frankie's London days a decade earlier. But it was altogether appropriate that 'Tears', the album's only solo Miller composition, should end proceedings, the raw emotion of the vocal pitched against the Hammond organ-laced backing.

'Tears' is also a duet on Bonnie Tyler's *Faster Than the Speed of Night*, which reached No. 1 in the UK Album Chart. Little wonder Rod Stewart once brought him into his dressing room at Wembley and said to those present: "If you've never heard Frankie Miller sing you've never heard a soul singer." This is soul by anybody's definition.

Talking of west London (where Frankie lived in Maida Vale, up the road from Pink Floyd's Dave Gilmour), The Kensington public house – a hotbed of live music in the early to mid 1970s – was where multi-instrumentalist Steve Simpson first encountered Frankie Miller. The pair hit it off and worked together immediately before Frankie's journey to Nashville (it was Steve's acoustic guitar and accordion on 'Darlin'), and he has fond memories of Miller the master singer.

"He really opened my eyes into the ways of singers. In my first band, Meal Ticket, we were a six-piece band with five singers, a rock 'n' roll choir where we all happened to play. But he was just a dedicated singer. His voice was his instrument and I learned so much stuff from him. I don't think he ever did more than three takes on a tune, that's my impression. It was magnificent, this hard voice that he knew how to use.

"He was the first of my big singers. I've worked with Roger Chapman, Dennis Locorriere, Eric Bibb, loads of really good singers, but Frankie was first of the really powerful men. Learning how he did it was an eye-opener to me."

Easy Money's release in July 1980 would effectively end Frankie Miller's link with Chrysalis Records, which had endured through the decade. The connections and impact Frankie made in Nashville would prove both deep and long-lasting, since within the decade he would become one of country music's most sought-after songwriters.

The singer first enjoyed 'outside' success collaborating with Clint Black. "I met him in Nashville," Miller recounted to rock historian Brian Hogg.

"We had a good time – he knows how to have fun – and we cut 'Burn One Down', an old thing I'd had for ages." The song was later lifted as a single and Black's popularity in the US not only won him substantial sales but cemented Miller's reputation there.

Peter McDougall's next project in which Frankie was involved came in 1981. *A Sense of Freedom* is a Scottish crime film which is based on the autobiography of Glasgow gangster Jimmy Boyle (a second cousin to Frankie). It stars David Hayman as Jimmy Boyle and was directed by John McKenzie for Scottish Television.

Jimmy Boyle was a notorious Glasgow gangster and by his mid-twenties had graduated into a ruthless criminal, earning the dubious title of Scotland's most dangerous man. He was jailed for murder in November 1967. Boyle fought hard against prison conditions and was brutally assaulted many times by prison officers. He, in turn, assaulted many staff, including one attack in which an officer lost an eye. He eventually ended up in the Barlinnie Special Unit, which aimed to rehabilitate violent and disruptive prisoners.

The theme music was written by Frankie Miller and Rory Gallagher.

To dream the dream…
back in the USA…
and a deal with Capitol Records…

Aberdeen April 1981 and BBC Scotland in Concert

With the previously discussed *Easy Money* project behind him, I caught up with Frankie in April 1981 at The Venue, situated in the basement of the Douglas Hotel in Aberdeen, and after trading stares, hugs and handshakes, he disappeared upstairs to watch his 30 minute *BBC In Concert* show, which was being broadcast that night. (Thank goodness for video recorders with timers back then!)

With his new band, and a load of new material, it was back to basics, guitar, bass and drums providing the solid backing for Frankie's powerful vocals.

New songs included 'Zap Zap', 'Don't Stop' and brilliant cover versions of Moon Martin's 'Bad Case of Loving You' and 'The Jealous Kind' from Bobby Charles. His performance on said *BBC In Concert* must be one of the finest ever Frankie Miller performances. Frankie even pulled out his harmonica for 'I'm Ready', The Muddy Waters number from *Once in a Blue Moon*. Ed Deane also gave us a slide guitar lesson during a slow-blues version of 'Rock Me Baby'.

The memory of 'Darlin' was quickly becoming a thing of the past.

Frankie brought the band up to Scotland twice again that year and by November (at the much larger Fusion, a Top Rank nightclub) one significant new song was added to the show - 'Angels With Dirty Faces', which Frankie introduced as "the next single."

Frankie's next recording sessions had taken place in Muscle Shoals that summer in a one-record deal with Capitol Records. 'To Dream The Dream' was released on 11th June 1982 and in a just world should have been a smash hit. I heard it once on Steve Wright's BBC morning radio show.

When Eric Clapton first heard Duane Allman's guitar solo in Wilson Pickett's 'Hey Jude' on his car radio, he reportedly pulled over to the side of the road to listen. "I drove home and called Atlantic Records immediately," Clapton said. "I had to know who that was playing guitar and I had to know now."

I had a similar experience when I first heard 'To Dream the Dream'. I had to pull over because there were tears in my eyes.

Again, I was able to provide Michael Heatley with all the background info to *Standing on the Edge* and together we provided Eagle Rock with sleeve notes.

Standing on the Edge Sleeve Notes by Michael Heatley and David Arthur

Released in June 1982, *Standing On The Edge* was the eighth solo album to bear the name of Frankie Miller. It was cut a long way from his Glasgow roots, in the Deep South of the United States at Muscle Shoals Sound Studio in Sheffield, Alabama – but in musical terms it couldn't have been closer to his heart.

"I've always been influenced by American music," he'd revealed in 1978.

"Apart from the bagpipes it's the only thing that's ever said anything to me. The first thing that ever hit me was rock 'n' roll. Little Richard – that was the first guy that ever punched me in the face with the aggression he put out in his voice."

The backbone of the music was supplied by three-quarters of the Muscle Shoals Rhythm Section, the legendary studio team of David Hood (bass), Roger Hawkins (drums) and Barry Beckett (keyboards) that many consider one of the finest in the world. They formed in 1967, setting up their own recording studio two years later. They were the first rhythm section in the US to have the unique concept of owning their own recording studio, as well as publishing and production companies. (Pete Carr plays on this album instead of original Muscle Shoals guitarist Jimmy Johnson.)

The Section participated as musicians and/or producers on such classic recordings as 'Respect' (Aretha Franklin), 'Mustang Sally' (Wilson Pickett), 'Kodachrome' (Paul Simon), 'I'll Take You There' (the Staple Singers) and many others, appearing on over 500 LPs and garnering over 75 gold and platinum discs in the process.

Muscle Shoals Studios left its original location in 1978 for a new state of the art, two-studio complex on the banks of the Tennessee River. Once safely ensconced in the new building, the Section launched their own record label, MSS-Capitol, and Frankie Miller, previously a Chrysalis artist, found himself a Stateside labelmate of such well respected artists as former Amazing Rhythm Ace Russell Smith, Delbert McClinton and the Band's Levon Helm.

There are books dedicated to the history of Muscle Shoals and Frankie Miller is part of that history.

They attracted noted artists from across the United States and Great Britain. Over the years, artists who recorded at Muscle Shoals Sound Studio included The Rolling Stones, Aretha Franklin, George Michael, Wilson Pickett, Willie Nelson, Lynyrd Skynyrd, Joe Cocker, Levon Helm, Paul Simon, Bob Seger, Rod Stewart, Tamiko Jones, Cher and Cat Stevens.

Their initial successes in soul and R&B led to more mainstream rock and pop performers who began coming to record at Muscle Shoals Sound Studios, including Traffic, Elton John, Boz Scaggs, Willie Nelson, Bob Dylan, Dr. Hook, Elkie Brooks, Millie Jackson, Julian Lennon, and Glenn Frey.

Pete Carr

Jesse Willard 'Pete' Carr was an American guitarist. Carr contributed to successful recordings by Joan Baez, Luther Ingram, Bob Seger, Paul Simon, Willie Nelson, Joe Cocker, Boz Scaggs, The Staple Singers, Rod Stewart, Barbra Streisand, Wilson Pickett, Hank Williams, Jr., and many others, from the 1970s onward.

The 1970s were among the most productive of the Muscle Shoals Rhythm Section as the cream of rock, pop, and soul found their way to 3614 Jackson Highway in Sheffield, Alabama. Carr played on almost all sessions recorded at the studio for the next 10 years. A good example of Carr's musical ability and taste is the standout guitar lines he played on the Bob Seger hit 'Mainstreet'. The Rhythm Section (including Carr) co-produced Paul Simon's *There Goes Rhymin' Simon* which earned them a Grammy nomination in 1974. He was also part of Hourglass in 1968 which also featured Gregg and Duane Allman.

Barry Beckett
was an American keyboardist, session musician, record producer, and studio founder. He is best known for his work with David Hood, Jimmy Johnson, Pete Carr and Roger Hawkins, his bandmates in the Muscle Shoals Rhythm Section, which performed with numerous notable artists on their studio albums and helped define the "Muscle Shoals sound".

Among the artists Beckett recorded with were Bob Dylan, Boz Scaggs, Paul Simon, Rod Stewart, Duane Allman, Lynyrd Skynyrd, Southside Johnny and the Asbury Jukes, Dire Straits, The Proclaimers and Phish. He was also briefly a member of Traffic.

David Hood
played bass on albums by Boz Scaggs, Joe Cocker, Albert King, Aretha Franklin, Cat Stevens, Peabo Bryson, Wendy Waldman, Julian Lennon, Paul Simon, Lulu, Shirley Brown, Glenn Frey, Patti Austin, Joan Baez, Tony Joe White, Linda Ronstadt, Paul Anka, Rod Stewart, Solomon Burke, J. J. Cale, Art Garfunkel, Bob Seger, Shelby Lynne, Bugs Bunny, Leon Russell, William Bell, Traffic, the Staple Singers, Frank Black, Odetta, John Hiatt, Etta James, John Altenburgh, Johnny & The MoTones and Percy Sledge. Hood appeared in 2009 on Klaus Voormann's solo album *A Sideman's Journey*. He participated in the Waterboys album, *Modern Blues*, recorded mainly in Nashville, and has been on tour with them.

Roger Hawkins
Hawkins's drumming can be heard on dozens of hit singles, including tracks by Percy Sledge ('When a Man Loves a Woman'), Aretha Franklin ('Respect', 'I Never Loved a Man (The Way I Love You)' etc.), Wilson Pickett ('Mustang Sally', 'Land of 1000 Dances'), The Staple Singers, Johnnie Taylor, Bobby Womack, Clarence Carter, Etta James, Duane Allman, Joe Cocker, Paul Simon, Bob Seger, Bonnie Bramlett, Bobby "Blue" Bland, Boz Scaggs, Albert King, Traffic, Rod Stewart, Dan Penn, Lulu, and Willie Nelson. He also recorded with Eric Clapton in the early 80s.

"Playing with the same guys for so long, well, it's really hard to impress Barry, David, Pete or Jimmy because they've heard me do it before. And it's the same with them. I mean, if Barry plays a hot lick, I don't congratulate him; he's supposed to do that. I don't know what it is, but when the four of us sit down to play, it's almost like a burden has been lifted from our shoulders. It's like, 'Hey, we're home'."

Recording engineer Mary Saums worked on the album under producer Barry Beckett and liked what she saw and heard. "Frankie impressed all of us, mainly because he was as much a workaholic as the rest of the crew. Whether writing a new song or doing a guitar or vocal track, Frankie seemed to enjoy throwing himself into the thick of it – the harder the work, the better he liked it. A real professional."

Saums, who contributed to gold and platinum albums by Bob Dylan, Jimmy Buffett and others, has since made a name for herself as a best-selling fiction author – the central character of her first title, *Midnight Hour*, was a Nashville session singer – so her nomination of the country-flavoured 'Angels With Dirty Faces' as favourite song has some weight.

While the recording location and musicians involved were definitely American, the material recorded was, uniquely for a Miller album, all self-penned. That said, a couple of writing partnerships had come into play, most notably the one with former Free bass player Andy Fraser, which yielded no fewer than five of the ten tracks on offer.

Chris Spedding again features on guitar. "His singing was always very emotional. One of the best rhythm and blues singers that were around in Britain at that time (1970s). He never had the luck of say, Joe Cocker, which is a great shame because, unlike Joe, Frankie was also a pretty good songwriter." Chris's strongest memory of Frankie is his smile and, as a singer, he says that Frankie is "Definitely the equal of Joe Cocker and Rod Stewart. I'm sure Joe and Rod both would agree."

Certainly, the bruising blues-rock of 'Danger Danger' was a promising opening to an album that suggested the then-popular likes of Foreigner had an experienced competitor to reckon with. 'Standing On The Edge', the first Miller-Fraser collaboration, would have been a standout on a Bad Company album if sung by Fraser's former Free colleague Paul Rodgers. As it is, few could surpass Frankie's delivery here, complete with falsetto high notes. This is the album's shortest song, just shy of three minutes, and everything here's designed to be radio-friendly in both length and content.

After another AOR stomper from the same team in 'Zap Zap' comes the anthemic 'To Dream The Dream', quite possibly the album's highlight. It reflects Frankie's acknowledged admiration for Van Morrison and, with its inspirational chorus, deserves someday to be used as the theme for a TV documentary about some worthwhile character – maybe Frankie himself? Then it's back to bass-driven rock with 'Don't Stop', like all the Miller-Fraser songs newly written for the project.

The rootsy 'Firin' Line' was a collaboration with US singer-songwriters John 'Moon' Martin and Pat Robinson – and, indeed, bears a distinct relation to Martin's 'Bad Case Of Loving You (Doctor Doctor)', which had been a 1979 hit for Robert Palmer.

Frankie had cut an 'off the shelf' Martin composition, 'No Chance', on his previous album *Easy Money*. Since this recording, Moon Martin moved to Nashville, where he built his own recording complex, Ponyboy Studio.

'Jealousy' is the fourth and final solo Frankie composition on the album, and harks back to his admiration for Otis Redding with its deep soul feel. You can just imagine the late, great 1960s soul star turning his hand to this one, the longest track on the album but not a second wasted.

As its title suggests, 'It's All Coming Down Tonight' is a rollicking rocker with a killer guitar solo, quite possibly by Chris Spedding.

But even that has to give way to 'On My Way', a superbly optimistic song to close the album, combining a melody reminiscent of 'First Cut Is The Deepest' with a bittersweet lyric of hope and regret that could only be Frankie Miller.

Three singles were released from this album in total: 'To Dream The Dream'/'Don't Stop' appeared in Britain in June 1982, 'Angels With Dirty Faces'/'Jealousy' following two months later. Album closer 'On My Way' was selected for the Stateside market, though it's unclear whether this achieved more than a promotional radio release.

Touring the States to support the album, Frankie ran into a certain amount of comment that he was similar in style to Detroit's own Bob Seger. "I hear that quite a lot," he growled, "especially from this new album. I don't think I sound anything like Bob. I don't really care."

Ironically, Seger was and remains an ardent Frankie Miller fan, having covered 'Ain't Got No Money' (originally recorded on 1975's *The Rock*) for inclusion on his multi-platinum *Stranger In Town*.

Seger had broken big through playing every available venue, then cashing in with a double concert album a la Peter Frampton. And though Frankie never issued a live album he certainly agreed with the work ethic. "If you want to crack it right," he said of America, "the thing is to work on the road, and you're any good at all people will pick up on it. Everything's right about that... and that's why I like this country so much."

Frankie Miller 'Angels With Dirty Faces' (Capitol) Review *Sounds* Magazine
"Frankie's so unhip that you'll probably read more about him in *Melody Maker*. Despite the Bob Seger style production job from Muscle Shoals studios, he does boast a fine voice and this American sounding song is better than most around."

1982 Tour

Ed Deane kindly gave me the 1982 Tour Itinerary for the USA recently and a tour T shirt a few years back and I have to tell you, Ed, I didn't understand why they had bothered doing a Frankie Miller T shirt at that point because we hadn't heard anything in the UK. I am shocked and saddened to this day that there was no coverage in Britain for any of these shows. Thanks to Ed's kindness I was able to research some of the venues the band played. Red Rocks (a year before U2) and the two Franks... Miller and Sinatra were on the same bill in Chicago Pier - in anybody's book,"Oh, my!" Frankie actually appeared on 8th August.

Chicago Fest

Chicago Fest, billed as the nation's largest summer music festival, opened on Wednesday that week and was filmed for national television and picketed by members of the black community.

The boycott apparently did not affect attendance, however. Officials said 7,000 people swarmed through Navy Pier gates during the first hour. One million people were expected to attend the 12-day music and food festival.

That summer, Barry Fey of Denver's Feyline Productions was one of the promoters in America who recognised that an ever-increasing number of tours were being booked in popular outdoor facilities such as Detroit's Pine Knob, Denver's Red Rocks Amphitheatre, Chicago's Poplar Creek Music Theater and Cleveland's Blossom Music Center.

At the 8500-seat Red Rocks Amphitheatre, for example, bookings had increased from forty-one shows in 1981 to sixty-two that summer, according to Fey. And at the 7800-seat Starlight Theatre in Kansas City, Fey says, "I think we might end up having more shows in a three-month period than we usually have there during the entire rest of the year."

These amphitheatres — which range in capacity from 7500 to 20,000 and sell tickets priced, on the average, from $8.50 to $15 — were gaining in popularity primarily because booking agents had finally realised that the teenagers who made stadium-sized shows a safe bet during the 60s and early 70s were now in their late twenties and early thirties and no longer wanted to spend days in a sun-scorched stadium or an evening in the distant rows of an arena, miles from the stage.

Frankie played around 30 of these types of show all the way through July, including Red Rocks and The Navy Pier in Chicago, whose bill included Frank Sinatra... without a word (as far as I know) from the UK music press.

And Red Rocks must be one of the most spectacular venues ever seen!

Author's Note: After Frankie's Dingwalls gig in December 1980, Carol Clark had expressed concern that the new band might not project in larger venues - she had a valid point (I'm impressed!).

But bringing in Mick Weaver again on keyboards after a seven year absence answered her question, as the Frankie Miller Band offered a full sound to large outdoor auditoriums throughout the USA and Europe.

Lorelei

Frankie's third performance for Rockpalast, a live broadcast took place in the summer of 1982 at Lorelei in the heart of the German Rhine Valley, during a long European tour to promote his new album *Standing on the Edge*. Also on the bill that day were David Lindley, Eric Burdon and Rory Gallagher. Joining Frankie on stage that day were Chrissy Stewart on bass guitar, Malcolm Mortimore on drums, Ed Deane on guitar, and Mick Weaver on keyboards.

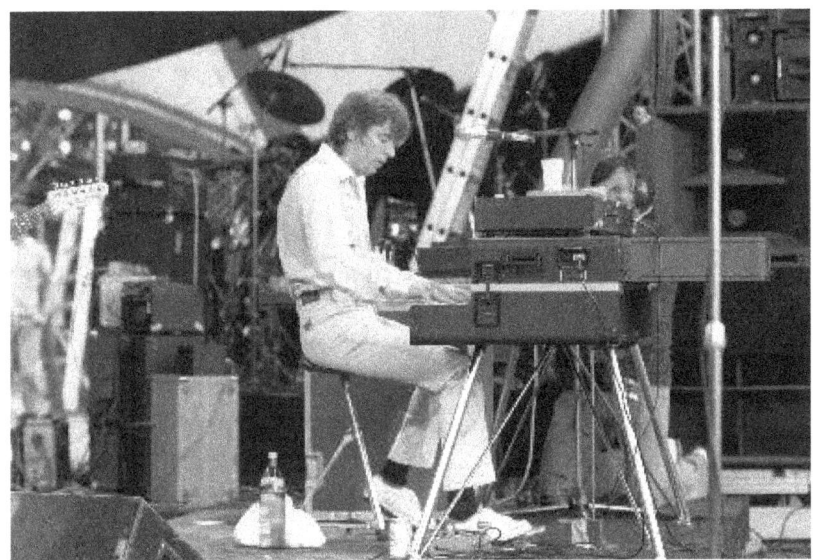

A large, enthusiastic crowd clapped along to the opening 'Ain't Got no Money' and were treated to a few favourites from the back catalogue ('Fool in Love/Be Good to Yourself') before the band launched into 'Danger Danger' from the new album.

Then the show took off as Frankie tore into more new songs from his Capitol release including 'It's All Coming Down Tonight' and a lovely acoustic interlude that included 'Angels with Dirty Faces' and 'To Dream the Dream', a song which should feature in everyone's top ten best records of all time.

The set finished with a rousing version of 'Down the Honky Tonk' before the German audience brought Frankie back for a deserved encore... 'Let's Spend the Night Together'.

The Lorelei is a rock on the eastern bank of the Rhine near St. Goarhausen, which soars some 120 metres above the water line. It marks the narrowest part of the river between Switzerland and the North Sea. Lorelei is also the name of one of the beautiful Rhine Maidens who lured navigators of this river to their dooms with their alluring singing, much as the ancient Greek Sirens did. The name comes from the old German words "lureln" (Rhine dialect for "murmuring") and "ley" (rock). The translation of the name would therefore be: "murmur rock" or "murmuring rock".

The heavy currents, and a small waterfall in the area (still visible in the early 19th century) created a murmuring sound, and this combined with the special echo the rock produces, which acted as a sort of amplifier, then gave name to the rock itself.

The Incredible Frankie Miller Rock Band

So, with it being all quiet on the UK front during 1983, whilst he was in America working on new songs, Frankie returned with yet another new line-up featuring Ex Free/Bad Company drummer, Simon Kirke, Chrissy Stewart on bass, and Neil Hubbard on guitar.

My first gig in Scotland since his show in Fusion Aberdeen at the end of 1981 came when he played the Thornton Hotel in Fife on Sunday August 26th 1984. That weekend, he had also appeared at the East Kilbride Festival, Tam Dhu Stirling and later the Rocking Horse in Carlisle on that trip north.

Frankie had changed his set around and freshened it up with some imaginative covers, including 'Take Me To the River' from Al Green, 'Who's Fooling Who' by Bobby Blue Bland, 'Shaky Ground' from the Temptations and 'He'll Have to Go' by Jim Reeves.

In between, of course, we had a few old favourites, including 'A Fool in Love', 'The Rock' and 'Be Good to Yourself'. He also slipped in a few lines from a new song at the Tam Dhu: perhaps the first public airing of 'Lies Tell The Best Truth Of All'.

When the encore came the sing-a-longs started as Frankie performed 'Drunken Nights in the City'. Then the band returned and we had our first hearing of 'Since I Met You Baby', an old blues classic from Ivory Joe Hunter. Neil Hubbard played with his usual class and style, but nobody would have guessed what was to come before the end of the year!

Billed as 'the incredible Frankie Miller Rock Band', the December 1984 line-up lasted until the end of 1993:
Frankie Miller, Brian Robertson, Chrissy Stewart and Simon Kirke

Brian 'Robbo' Robertson
In June 1974, Thin Lizzy were auditioning for two new guitarists and a session with Robbo was arranged. At 18, he joined the band, along with Scott Gorham. The two lead guitarists provided a critical part of Thin Lizzy's signature sound.

The best known Thin Lizzy songs prove why Phil Lynott, Robbo and co were a remarkably unique outfit, responsible for some of the most long-lasting rock classics in history.

'The Boys Are Back In Town' - Full of swagger and joie de vivre, this seemingly ageless rocker (which referenced Manchester criminals The Quality Street Gang alongside patrons of LA's famous Rainbow Bar And

Grill venue) was Phil Lynott's tribute to macho adventures the world over. It proved a game-changer for Thin Lizzy, hitting the UK Top 10 and paving the way for transatlantic success.

Unquestionably Thin Lizzy's greatest ballad, 'Still In Love With You' was originally demoed early in 1974 by Phil Lynott, Brian Downey, and Gary Moore, and it played a key part in scoring the band a new contract with Polygram Records that same summer. The official studio version (guitar solo by Gary Moore) of the song appeared on November 1974's *Nightlife* album and featured a duet between Lynott and guest vocalist Frankie Miller, but 'Still In Love With You' really came into its own on stage. Embellished by Brian Robertson's sumptuous lead guitar, the eight-minute *Live And Dangerous* version is truly unbeatable. (Robbo had actually refused to re-record the studio version because he didn't think he could better Gary Moore's version.) (Excerpts from udiscovermusic.com)

Brian Robertson suffered a hand injury when trying to protect fellow Glaswegian, singer and friend Frankie Miller in a fracas at the Speakeasy Club in London. Miller had been jamming onstage with the reggae band Gonzalez, and had seemingly offended Gonzalez guitarist Gordon Hunte. Hunte attacked Miller with a bottle in the dressing room, and Robertson intervened, suffering artery and nerve damage to his hand. Allegedly, Robbo subsequently broke Hunte's leg, and broke someone else's collarbone, while another received a "Glasgow Kiss" before being hit on the head with a bottle, rendering him unconscious.

Robertson had formed Wild Horses along with another Scot, Rainbow bassist Jimmy Bain, in 1977, while recovering from his injury.

In May 1982, Robertson replaced 'Fast' Eddie Clarke as the lead guitarist of Motörhead. "That felt totally uncertain," Robertson later told *Classic Rock*. "It only came about because I was helping out some friends and when they asked me to join officially, I said, 'Okay, but I'm not fucking rewriting the 'Ace of Spades'."

Robbo spoke about Frankie during a *Kerrang* interview in January 1994."The best thing that ever happened to me was playing with Frankie Miller. I was on the verge of being that stupid type of Rock guitar player who would actually have a wammy-bar! Fuck that! Miller brought me back down to earth. He brought out of me what he brings out in his singing and I owe everything to him. You can print that and I wish to God you would…"

Simon Kirke
found fame as a drummer with Free (along with Paul Rodgers, Paul Kossoff and Andy Fraser) and Bad Company (along with Paul Rodgers, Mick Ralphs ex-Mott the Hoople and Boz Burrell ex-King Crimson).

In 1970 Free had a number one hit in more than 20 countries with 'All Right Now', which by the year 2000 had received more than two million radio plays in the UK alone.

1974 saw Bad Company's biggest hit single, 'Can't Get Enough', which also became an enduring rock radio hit. All told, Bad Company sold more than 40 million records worldwide. In April 2025 it was announced that Bad Company would be inducted into the Rock 'n' Roll Hall of Fame.

Brian Robertson and Simon Kirke

From Simon Kirke:
I first met Frankie back in the early 80s. I got a phone call from him when I was reading in Chiswick.

I got a message from my manager to call him. I left my number and he called me the next day. He was doing a show at a club in Putney and wondered if I'd like to play drums. There was also a chance of playing on an album that he planned to make later in the year.

As Bad Company was on a break I jumped at the chance. Frankie possessed a voice that always impressed me. Along with Paul Rodgers and Stevie Marriott he was a favourite of mine. So I went down to see him at the club where he was rehearsing. He was there, with his trademark hat. He was quite smaller than I had imagined. With that amazing voice of his I somehow figured that he was quite a big guy. This was not the case.

Playing bass was Chrissy Stewart, and I believe Neil Hubbard was on guitar. I climbed up behind the kit and we ran through a couple of songs. Instantly I felt at home. We were all smiles and I really wanted to take this further down the line. So we did about 10 or 12 songs, did the gig, and it went down really well and Frankie was very happy.

Then we went down to Glynn John's house in the country.
Glynn was slated to be the producer on Frankie's new album. And I'll never forget, it was a very hot day and we got to Glynn's house and he had a pool so I asked if I could have a dip and in I plunged.

I believe Chrissy came in as well. Frankie didn't. After about ten minutes and to my astonishment, Glynn came out of the house completely stark naked and stood by the pool as we swam around. Very strange! When we climbed out and dried ourselves off, we came into the house.

Frankie gave Glynn the cassette of the demos that he had made and we sat around while they were playing. Not much was said until after the final song.

And Glynn kind of shook his head and said, "Quite honestly Frankie there's not much here." I was crestfallen because I thought most of the songs are pretty damn good and I expected Frankie to erupt in anger. Instead Frankie just said, "Och, Glynn, you're very harsh…"

And that really, not surprisingly, was the end of the afternoon for us.

We made some small talk - maybe some adjustments could be made to the songs etc., etc. - but we drove back to London fairly dispirited.

And then Frankie asked me if I'd like to do some shows up in Scotland, eight shows. I said I had to talk to my wife about it just to make sure that we weren't in conflict with any Bad Company dates.

I found out that everything was fine and I had a couple of months off so I called Frankie and I agreed to do it. And then I said, "Well, Frankie, how much you gonna pay me?"

And there was a silence at the end of the line, and then Frankie said, "Well, Simon, I can give you £400."

And I thought, £400 a show. I got a lot more than that with Bad Company.

So I said, "Ok, Frankie, £400 a show. I'll do it for that because I love playing with you."

And then Frankie said, "No, it's £400 for the eight shows. £50 a show."

I kind of swallowed and sat down and had to laugh inwardly at Frankie's cajones.

I could see there was no sense in haggling because it would've demeaned me to try and get £30 or £40 a night more. And impossible, too… So I said, "Ok Frankie, I'll do it for that."

And he said, "Thank you, Simon." There was a short silence and he seemed to lean into the phone and whispered conspiratorially: "Oh and by the way, don't tell the others…"

Which made me think they were getting substantially less than £50 a night!

I then started a memorable couple of weeks touring around Scotland in a van with the three other guys and the worst roadie you could imagine. The very first trip that we did after leaving the hotel, he forgotten to close the back doors and we took off with a lurch and most of the equipment fell out onto the road.

Musically the shows were wonderful. Attendance wasn't too good except when we got in and around Glasgow where clubs were packed. Frankie was a hometown boy. We recorded an album together, *Dancing In The Rain*, which remains one of my favourite albums I've ever played on. Frankie was in superb voice… And Brian Robertson and Chrissy Stewart were five-star players.

We went to Germany and Holland playing clubs. It was a reminder to me of how Free and Bad Company started out.

I wasn't particularly worried about the money. I was comfortable from my earnings with Bad Company and all that mattered to me was that we were making great music together.

One time we were in Amsterdam and the plan was for the band to go on before Frankie and start 'I'd Lie to You for Your Love', which is just a basic A to D, A to D sequence, while Frankie would come on after about 20 or 30 seconds. So we kicked it off and we kept playing it and playing it - no Frankie!

I kept looking at Chrissie and Robbo, as if to say "Where the fuck is he?" After what seemed to be an eternity, I saw the familiar hat bobbing through the crowd accompanied by the head of a Fender Telecaster. The dressing rooms were at the other end of the club, by the way. Well, Frankie climbed up on the stage and plugged in without acknowledging the rest of the band by saying "Sorry guys I'm late" or whatever.

At the end of the gig when we were towelling down in the dressing room I said to Frankie, "Hey, what happened at the beginning of the show?"

And he looked at me with this little smile and said, "Sorry guys, I ran into a girl who made me an offer I couldnae refuse…"

He came to my house in Chiswick on many occasions.

We jammed, wrote some songs… I have a cassette with Frankie, Ronnie Wood, Keith Richards, Boz Burrell from Bad Company… My daughters loved him; he was so polite and genuine.

I was so sad to hear of his stroke. The fact that that wonderful voice of his was stilled and he would never sing again was such a tragedy. Before I

moved to New York I did see him at his apartment in Maida Vale. He made noises in his throat and gripped my arm and we both shed a few tears.
A few words on his songwriting:

Frankie by his own admission was not a great guitarist. He only knew a few chords and seem to take a leaf out of Otis Redding's book. It's what he did with those chords that mattered.

He was very simplistic. He had a little radio cassette recorder that he brought on the road with him and I believed he used that most of the time in his songwriting. He was not a technical person; he just wanted to press the red button and start recording. That was his style. Plain and simple - and from that humble approach he wrote dozens of amazing songs.

The times that I toured with him and played with him were some of the best I can ever remember. He was one of the finest singers ever to come out of Scotland and a wonderful songwriter as well.
Simon Kirke

Chrissy Stewart
was once described as one of rock's most durable bass players. Chrissy played bass with numerous bands including Spooky Tooth, Ronnie Wood, Joe Cocker, Eric Burdon, Terry Reid, Jim Capaldi, Graham Bonnet, Eire Apparent and The People. Born in Belfast, Chrissy spent much of his playing career based in London.

For over 20 years, Chrissy was the driving force in Frankie's bands and remained a loyal friend. He passed away at 73 years old on 16th May 2020.

Phil Taylor joined Motörhead in 1974 and left in 1984, then joined Brian Robertson to form the band Operator. He joined Frankie's touring band in 1986, including the Bob Seger tour to America, later that year, when Simon was unavailable due to Bad Company commitments.

"Philthy" Phil died on 12 November 2015 in London at the age of 61. Lemmy was quoted in *Classic Rock* as saying "I think this rock 'n' roll business might be bad for the human life."

An advert in the Scottish *Sunday Mail*...

'The incredible Frankie Miller Rock Band' playing The Mayfair, Sauchiehall Street, Glasgow in December

I was on the phone to my mate Tiny and off down the road from Aberdeen to Edinburgh to pick him up! Everything was dropped again to get to a Frankie Miller gig.

By early evening we are outside the venue and totally unprepared for what comes next: the poster not only advertising the gig but the line-up...

Frankie Miller on vocals, Chrissy Stewart on bass, Simon Kirke on drums. Brian Robertson on guitar... No way! It can't be Robbo from Thin Lizzy? Anyhow, we retire to the pub across the road... a tad excited at the prospect!

I had told Tiny so much about the previous show in August and hadn't shut up about it all the way along the M8.

It was, after all, our first Frankie gig together since the 1979 'Darlin' tour when we sat and cried in our beer after the show, thinking Frankie Miller's career was over!

We soon got our answers as when the band were announced, Simon, Chrissy and Robbo appeared on stage, and the packed audience went crazy as Robbo opened up with the intro to 'Take Me to the River'. Very Loud and Very Heavy - and Frankie still wasn't on the stage yet...

He appeared to a loud roar in his customary black pipe-hat and full length black waistcoat and you just knew this was going to be something special.

I had never heard such a heavy rock sound from a Frankie Miller band since the Stoics days (although since 'Darlin' he had certainly been heading that way with his stripped-down four piece lineups and occasional keyboards). 'The Devil Gun' was followed by 'A Fool in Love' with Robbo on backing/harmony vocals - and cracking the funnies - and it seemed strange but exciting to hear screaming guitar solos in Frankie's songs, especially after witnessing Neil Hubbard's laid back/classy versions only a few months before.

'Be Good to Yourself' and 'Woman to Love' followed (being regulars in the set for years), and by now the band was cooking and Frankie's smile - and patter - began to appear.

A new song, 'I Don't Need the Aggravation', was introduced and to this day remains one of my favourite FM songs. I was disappointed that it didn't appear on *Dancing in the Rain* but the demo that Frankie gave me some years later (although great) lacked the fire of the live version.

I think Brian Robertson's heavy chords are incredible and married with Frankie's powerful and emotional vocals totally justified the 'incredible rock band' billing…

This was followed by another old favourite, 'The Rock', which actually shows off Robbo's versatility as a guitar player because he plays it with a lot of feeling, and it's not a song you would associate with a Thin Lizzy/Motörhead guitarist.

Then came another two songs that Frankie hadn't done live before. 'Game of Love' was introduced as "a number we've just recorded" and came across on first hearing as very Free/Bad Company... Then the hilarity started. Frankie was trying to tune-up his guitar over the din - I remember saying to Tiny, "I think this is 'Jealousy'" - Frankie is meanwhile suffering the usual 'McQuillan' comments - "Your teas oot Frankie!" - when he suddenly shouted at the top of his voice "Shadupppp!! I'm trying to concentrate!" while from the other side of the stage, Robbo butts in with "Let him concentrate cos I can't remember the chords!!"

The crowd by this time were in raptures with the "pure Glasgow" humour now filling the room and Frankie shouted out again "Shaduppp!" and then broke out into his famous smile and said "It's the first time we've ever done this number... live!" (the band and audience are now in total raptures) and then continued "There's hope for everybody!"

It was hilarious and Frankie loved this rapport with the audience - when the mood took him!

He then belted out 'Jealousy' and it was magic. Four new songs already, and 'Jealousy' was followed by 'Shaky Ground' from The Temptations. Again it was the perfect platform for the new 'incredible rock band'. Another old classic followed: "This is a Jim Reeves song" and Frankie loved it when the crowd sang along. "He'll Have To Go!"

Back to the up tempo stuff with Buddy Holly's 'Rave On' and 'Bad Case of Loving You' from Moon Martin, a number introduced in 1981 which would remain a firm favourite in Frankie's shows for the next nine years. Frankie had also discovered Moon Martin as Capitol stable mates.

By this time I was standing on a table which was holding up the PA and having my head blown off! It was worth it because I got some great photos of the band in action. Then it was all over too soon and Frankie returned to give us 'Drunken Nights in the City' and a super 'incredible rock band' version of 'Since I Met You Baby' which also stayed with Frankie for the rest of his live career. Another super vehicle to showcase Brian Robertson's talents.

It also became a favourite sing-a-long song in Frankie's shows for years to come and brought to an end another classic 'night on the town' with Frankie Miller.

The band continued to tour Europe continuously. From the mid-eighties onwards, the live performances had gone back to a rockier side with former Free/Bad Company drummer Simon Kirke (for a few months Phil Taylor) and Brian Robertson from Thin Lizzy joining Chrissy Stewart to form a powerful backing band to complement Frankie's voice.

Dancing in the Rain

Released in April 1986, Frankie wrote or co-wrote all ten songs on the album. His collaborators included Brill Building legend Jeff Barry and Funkadelic guitarist Eddie Hazel.

Dancing in The Rain tracklisting:
I'd Lie To You For Your Love
Do It Till We Drop
That's How Long My Love Is

How Many Tears Can You Hide
Dancing In The Rain
Shaky Ground
The Boys & The Girls Are Doing It
Game Of Love
Gladly Go Blind
You're A Puzzle I Can't Put Down

A number of impressive names took part in this recording, which took place in New York, as well as Frankie's band, which was:

Guitar – Brian Robertson
Bass – Chrissy Stewart
Drums – Simon Kirke
Guitar – Chris Spedding, Hiram Bullock, Mitch Perry, Mitch Watkins, Ricky Byrd, Tim Renwick
Trumpet – Wayne Jackson
Backing Vocals – Bonnie Bramlett, Chrissy Faith, Elaine Caswell, Eric Troyer

Mitch Perry
Featured in the 'I'd Lie to You for Your Love' MTV promo video which was filmed in London at the Mean Fiddler.

When I asked Frankie why Brian Robertson wasn't in the promo, he explained that Mitch Perry actually played lead guitar on the recording and was flown over to London to take part... an education for the author for sure!

Author's Note: Robbo told me recently that the sessions were "fucked" after he finished.

Mitch began his career around the age of 18 when he flew to Los Angeles and collaborated with the virtuoso bassist of Weather Report and Santana, Alphonso Johnson, in January 1980. He also played with ex-Deep Purple singer Glenn Hughes and recorded with Graham Nash.

Tim Renwick
is best known for his association with Al Stewart in his early career and for his long-standing role as lead guitarist for the Sutherland Brothers and Quiver. He did session work for Elton John, Procol Harum, David Bowie, Mike Oldfield, Gary Brooker, Roger Waters, Eric Clapton, China Crisis, and Pink Floyd plus many others. Other career highlights include touring with Roger Waters during his The Pros and Cons of Hitchhiking tour.

Among the other musicians in Waters' band was Eric Clapton, with whom Tim toured the following year, on Clapton's Behind The Sun Tour. He appeared as a member of Clapton's band at the Live Aid Concert July

13, 1985 in Philadelphia, PA. In 1987, David Gilmour invited Renwick to tour with Pink Floyd as a session musician, and recordings from the August 1988 shows were released in the double live album *Delicate Sound of Thunder*.

Wayne Jackson (Memphis Horns)

was an American soul and R&B musician, playing the trumpet in the Mar-Keys, in the house band at Stax Records and later as one of the Memphis Horns, described as "arguably the greatest soul horn section ever". His musical partner was Andrew Love, with whom he created the signature horn sound at Stax on hit records by Otis Redding, Sam & Dave, and others.

After the years recording at Stax, they incorporated themselves into the Memphis Horns and began freelancing, recording on sessions for such artists as Neil Diamond, Elvis Presley, Al Green, and Dusty Springfield.

In 2012, the Memphis Horns received a Grammy Lifetime Achievement Award for outstanding artistic significance in music.

Bonnie Bramlett

is an American singer known for performing with her husband, Delaney Bramlett, as Delaney and Bonnie. They were signed to Stax records and toured Europe with Eric Clapton. With frequent drop-in performances by other noted musicians like Duane Allman, George Harrison, and Dave Mason, the group became known as Delaney & Bonnie & Friends.

Bonnie was inspired by Tina Turner to pursue a singing career. In her teens, she saw Ike & Tina Turner perform at a club in nearby East St. Louis. Bonnie became the first white Ikette in the Ike & Tina Turner Revue.

Later, as a solo artist, Bramlett continued to contribute vocals to recordings by other artists, including Little Feat and the Allman Brothers Band. She continues to sing as a solo artist.

Chrissy Faith

earned two Grammy nominations for her recordings, one as the voice of Demi Moore in Columbia Pictures' *No Small Affair*. She spent most of her time as a busy session singer in New York and touring with various artists such as Robert Plant, Cyndi Lauper, Lou Reed, Madonna, Celine Dion, Neil Diamond, Whitney Houston, Paul Simon and many others.

Eric Troyer

Singer, songwriter and occasional guitarist who is best known as a member of ELO Part II.

Troyer has performed on various albums as a session musician and backing vocalist, including albums by John Lennon, Bonnie Tyler, and Celine Dion.

Elaine Caswell
is a singer, heard on many recordings, and live appearances. Although her name is not instantly recognised she has performed as a backing singer with many major stars. The list includes albums by Cher, Celine Dion, Meat Loaf, Bonnie Tyler, Phyllis Hyman, John Waite and Jennifer Rush, and Whitney Houston.

Together, they cut *Dancing in the Rain* in New York and the album was released in the spring of 1986.

The album contained several collaborative compositions with Jeff Barry, whom Frankie had met when a plan to re-record a slowed-down version of the Crystals' 'Da Doo Ron Ron' was mooted. When the record didn't happen, they instead came up with a batch of new songs which feature on the album.

Again, regarding the UK music press, it was difficult to track the band's activities but there were some notable shows during the promotion of *Dancing in the Rain*.

The 1986 Park Pop Festival in Den Haag was broadcast on Dutch Radio (Simon Kirke on drums), as was the Commonwealth Games party in Edinburgh for Radio 1. The show at Ingliston was notable because 'Philthy' Phil Taylor had stood in on drums for the tour as Simon Kirke was touring again with Bad Company in the USA.

One German TV appearance featured 'That's How Long My Love Is'.

Germany June/July 1986

With Phil Taylor (ex-Motörhead) and Brian Robertson (ex-Thin Lizzy and Motörhead) in the line-up plus the wonderful Chrissy Stewart on bass, what else would you expect but a high octane blues/rock show?

Stuttgart 3rd July
The audience here were obviously in party mood and of course that transferred to the stage - and Frankie and the band responded with a fun-packed gig with a surprise new number thrown in.

Set List
Take me to the River
A Fool in Love
Be Good to Yourself
I'd Lie To You For Your Love
Do It Till We Drop
Jealousy
Shaky Ground
Game of Love
That's How long My Love Is
(I Don't Need This) Aggravation

"Here's a song about…you know…when, eh…you've got somebody round about your door and when you turn your head away, they're sniffing round your woman; you know what I mean. You guys will know what I'm talking about…listen to all the ladies having a good laugh; that's what this song's about… "

I saw Frankie performing this back in 1984 but the band have it nailed now and Robbo's incidental guitar chords in particular are so powerful, I still get shivers all these years later. And Frankie's voice, as ever, raw with emotion! What a song - and again, shame it didn't appear on *Dancing in the Rain*… Oh, the 80s!!

A Woman To Love
Ain't Got No Money
Bad Case of Loving You
Since I Met You Baby
Let's Spend The Night Together
Where Do You Go….

An unreleased song of Frankie's and performed in a very Buddy Holly/Dion DiMucci early sixties, up-tempo style.

"I want to know…where do you go?" (Frankie throws in a couple of Dylan-style, almost spoken/spontaneous lines.)

"My heart's on fire, my body's burnin now, we got to get to the bottom of this shit somehow…" - finishing the sentence on a high note… Anyhow, in the moment it's hilarious, and re-emphasises how special Frankie's shows could be: full of humour, passion, power and aggression all mixed in.

White doo-wop style, I think someone called it!! And Robbo finished off the number with some great playing again.

Park Pop 1986 (The Hague, Netherlands)
Acts on the bill that day included Madness, Bangles, Frankie Miller Band, INXS, Ten Ten, Gill Scott-Heron and Doctor & the Medics

This show was broadcast live on Dutch Radio and continued to promote *Dancing in the Rain*. Of course the announcer messed up - and Frankie, using his best sarcasm, announced it as the album they released about six years ago, in line with the announcer's introduction!

It was a great gig, on a hot, sunny afternoon.
The Commonwealth Games show celebrated the end of the 1986 games in Edinburgh with 10,000 people attending.

Putting Runrig on the same bill as 'The Incredible Frankie Miller Rock Band' may not have been the greatest idea and, as Frankie later commented, "It was a horrible night. Ten thousand athletes who didn't have a clue. We're not the kind of band to party to unless you're into blues music and a bit of drink. There was a mile between us and the audience."

However, as the radio broadcast shows, the band turned in a fantastic performance, opening with an unbeatable version of 'Take Me To The River' and continuing with a similar set to those of the European Tour, again with a focus on numbers from *Dancing in the Rain*.

The band also appeared (worse for wear) at short notice in the Albert Hall Stirling the following evening, after a late cancellation by Jack Bruce. The gig was also notable for a wonderful performance by Edinburgh band and great friends of the author, Blues 'n' Trouble.

The band continued to tour Europe until the late 80s with a number of television appearances thrown in, notably in Denmark, Germany and Holland.

A few one-off gigs also took place in London, at The Astoria (guest guitar player Dave Edmunds), Mean Fiddler and The Half Moon, Putney.

An American tour supporting Bob Seger came along in October/November. Brian Robertson told me some great stories about the flight and trip over to the US.

The band were in high spirits after several large Bloody Marys during the flight and eventually landed at Miami Airport. On arrival and into the security area the Americans were confronted by two-thirds of Motörhead with Frankie and Chrissy closely behind. 'Philthy and Robbo' - the permanent rock stars - were leather clad and covered in metal jewellery and other similar adornments.

They were backed up by Frankie, who warned them "Don't touch the Rolex." Panic spread amongst the guards, who stood back and let them through, un-challenged!

Bob Seger had also asked the band to dress-up in stage gear, which they refused to do. Robbo suggested that "We blew Seger off the stage anyway."

One evening in Detroit (Bob Seger's home town), on a night off between gigs, Robbo, Chrissy and Frankie had arranged to meet Phil Taylor in a downtown bar. On arrival, Robbo opened the door and there was 'Philthy 'propped up at the bar and surrounded by, and loudly entertaining, a gang of tough locals with his Motörhead stories.

So much were the others afraid of the surroundings that they refused to go in and join him!!

LOOK FOR
FRANKIE MILLER
ON TOUR WITH
BOB SEGER

10/28-29	Philadelphia, PA
11/7	Tulsa, OK
11/9-11	Dallas, TX
11/13-15	Houston, TX
11/17	San Antonio, TX
11/18	Austin, TX
11/20	Baton Rouge, LA
11/23-24	Tampa, FL
11/26	Daytona, FL
11/28-29	Miami, FL
12/1	Jacksonville, MS
12/3	Birmingham, AL
12/4	Nashville, TN
12/6-7	Kansas City, KS
12/9	Des Moines, IA
12/11-12	St. Louis, MO
12/15-16	Chicago, IL
12/21-22	Atlanta, GA

FRANKIE MILLER "SHAKEY GROUND'
from the Mercury LP
"Dancing In The Rain" (422 876 647-1 M-1)
PRO 461-1

It wasn't until late '89 that Frankie announced that he was returning north for some shows. It was met with great excitement by both the Scottish mainstream press and fans alike.

This announcement marked the end of the 80s and the beginning of the 90s, with the Frankie Miller Band booked to appear in Frankie's home town, Glasgow.

John Martor would again step in temporarily to replace Simon Kirke on drums.

1990 Scottish Homecoming

Frankie had announced to the Scottish *Daily Record* that he was planning to work with ZZ Top producer Bill Ham. The band performed a private show at The Shelter in Glasgow in December 1989, then three gigs there in January 1990.

Tickets were like gold dust and as the first night sold out the same day, two extra nights were added to meet the demand. These were Frankie's first public appearances in Scotland since August 1986. It was another homecoming after a three year absence from Scotland.

Each gig was performed in a party atmosphere and that atmosphere continued all the way through 1990 as the band returned several times to Scotland during the year.

April 12th/13th Hattonrigg
April 15th O' Henrys Aberdeen
May 30th Victoria's Glasgow

June 1st Hattonrigg
This was the night that fans were camping in the hotel grounds and some without tickets were offering 50 quid to get in! It was another raucous party event at the band's Scottish HQ and was the night that I had given the boss (and Frankie's friend), Joe Campbell, copies of the flyer I had photocopied to try and get some sort of fan magazine set up for Frankie. I had no idea what we were going to do and if it would ever work, but we thought that if we could at least start a fan group we could inform each other of up and coming gigs in future for a start, instead of relying on the *Sunday Mail* entertainments page and word of mouth.

Set List
Ain't got no money / A Woman to Love / Down the Honky Tonk / A Fool in Love / Beautiful Lie / Jealousy/ When I'm Away from You / The Rock / Dreams to Remember /Darlin/ Dead Flowers/It Must be Love / Be Good to Yourself/ Bad Case of Loving You /Rave On / I'd Lie/Drunken Nights / I'm Down

June 2nd Cochrane Hall Alva
June 3rd O' Henrys Aberdeen
June 4th Edinburgh Preservation Hall

The venue was packed to capacity on a warm June evening in Edinburgh, and I was standing in my favourite spot with right arm against the pillar and foot on the stage. Frankie spotted me as he came on stage from the far side, and walked off again, shouting out "No you again" in a joke. Lots of people in the crowd to see Robbo, which was great, and notable for me because I asked Frankie to sing 'To Dream The Dream' and he did, last number in the encores.

The dressing room was a bit busy and I remember when I stuck my head in the door, Robbo shouted out "It's the cheeky wee c**t from Aberdeen!"to which I replied "I'm not from Aberdeen, I'm from Edinburgh." Can you imagine the look Frankie and Robbo gave each other as I watched the two of them burst into tears of laughter at my failed attempt to redeem myself… After seeing the 'McQuillan' hecklers off the premises with phrases like "Are ye away then?" (you need a broad Glasgow accent to make this one take full effect), we got back to talking about our favourite subject - music - and I remember asking Frankie where he had got 'Jealous Kind' from and he told me about meeting up with Delbert McLinton in the States; another chapter in my musical education.

September 11th Aberdeen Caesar's Palace
September 12th and 13th Edinburgh Venue
September 14th Bowmore Hotel Islay

Big George and the Business were support for the two nights in Edinburgh and Robbo was hilarious as he ran around the downstairs bar area shouting "He's got a fucking wah wah pedal!"

Mr Ross-Watt was, of course, laying waste to the audience upstairs. Well, the party was again in full flight on the 13th and we had a huge surprise because in the downstairs dressing room bar that night were ZZ Top's engineers, over to hear Frankie's live sound prior to their projected recording sessions in 1991. Due to an over indulgence in Otard brandy matters, I'm damned if I can remember the guys' names but they were really nice and a bit shocked when I started to pull their legs by telling them I had actually never heard of *Afterburner*.

The other guy was an Atlantic Music executive and I was brought down to earth when I asked him where he was based. "London, Los Angeles and New York" came the answer. After having asked them all if they had heard of the Stoics, the attempted piss taking stopped right there in that moment.

And for once I realised that much respect would be required in his company.

After the show and with lots of back slapping, hand shaking and leg pulling (Robbo doing his best to compare me with Alex McDonald looks wise!!), Frankie said, outside, "Why don't you jump in the van? We're playing in Bowmore tomorrow…" Being full of Otard and Crabbies Green Ginger I was sooo close to jumping in, but I would definitely have lost my job…

1991 I'll Call You On The Phone Some

By the late 80s, I had been going to Frankie Miller gigs for over 20 years. Apart from a few chance meetings, stares from the stage, banter and hand shakes around venues - and a few backstage visits - I had kept a relatively low profile.

Meanwhile I had been collecting photographs, press cuttings, concert posters etc, until early January 1991 when my phone rang around tea time one Friday evening.

The voice said, "Can I speak to Davy Arthur please?"- to which I replied, "It's me - who's calling?"

"Frankie Miller."

So I said, "Fuck off Billy and Happy New Year" - thinking it was my younger brother winding me up.

"It's Frankie Miller!!"

"C'mon Billy, fuck off... Happy New Year."

"IT IS Frankie Miller!!!" Then the penny dropped. It was indeed Frankie Miller.

During 1990, Frankie's band had used the Hattonrig Hotel at Bellshill as an HQ for accommodation and rehearsals during their brief tours of Scotland, and Joe Campbell, the boss there, had passed some flyers and photos I had taken on to Frankie. Hence the phone call!

"What are your plans regarding T shirts and magazines and what are you up to?"

When I got over the shock of actually realising it was indeed Frankie's voice on the phone, I blurted out that I was fed up of reading about gigs in places like the Scottish *Sunday Mail* - on the day of the show - dropping everything and sometimes driving hundreds of miles to make it!

So I had decided to try and start a fan magazine. I expected a negative response, but I could not have been more wrong: Frankie smiled and agreed. Then he announced that he had a gig at the end of the month in London.

He asked if I would like to come down and meet up that weekend. "Here's my number and address and be at the Hackney Empire Theatre at 1pm on the 2nd of February. Just give your name at the box office. They will be expecting you.

"See ye..."

That Friday night phone call became the first of a series of weekly chats (as long as Frankie was around) and if I was lucky he would play me new songs he had just finished and ask my opinion on them...

We had great conversations (mostly about music) and I remember hearing new songs he had finished almost 20 years before they were released.

A lovely, trusting friendship grew out of that and remains strong to this day.

Three weeks later I was on my way down on the train with my mate Dave Stuart and six bottles of Cairn O Mohr. I think we had planned to take some of the Scottish fruit wine as gifts but we partied all the way down the road (including with other passengers) and the lot was gone!

Saturday afternoon…

Arriving at the empty theatre bang on time was an amazing experience, as who was actually on stage (with Big Charlie from Glasgow, the legendary Thin Lizzy roadie) but Brian Robertson, blasting his guitar out to his audience of two in a soundcheck!

I had no idea what was ahead of us that day as we made our way up to the dressing rooms to meet Frankie: a two hour rehearsal (including four numbers with Kirsty McColl) then at 4pm, the arrival of Ronnie Wood to perform with a 14 piece show band called the Wilfs. We had arrived on the third day of a charity weekend called Rock-A-Baby, a charity organised to raise money for East London hospitals. Committee members included Lorraine Kirke and Patti Clapton.

I moved around between side-stage and the front row as Frankie's band ran through their set, 'Dreams to Remember' and 'Jealousy' (twice). It was just like having your own personal and close-up Frankie Miller show.

When Kirsty McColl appeared with two or three of her musicians, she pulled out a Walkman and held it to the mike. I had never seen the trick before as the songs blasted out through the PA for the assembled musicians' and technicians' benefit.

So now with Frankie on backing/harmony vocals and Robbo taking over the musical director role (yes he did!) we were treated to some Buddy Holly classics including 'That'll Be The Day' and 'Brown Eyed Handsome Man' plus 'There's a Guy Works Down The Chip Shop Swears He's Elvis'.

Great fun and banter on stage, especially when Frankie shouted for a re-run of 'The Fish Shop song!'

Mid-afternoon Ronnie Wood arrived… Frankie hadn't told me this was all planned so I didn't know what was going on that day until it all actually happened. Dave Stuart and I were sitting on flight cases at the side of the stage when Ronnie Wood came running up the stage-door steps at the back of the theatre.

Ronnie was lovely, and when he came up the back stairs, I nervously blurted out "Here's Honest Ron!" (If you don't get it, read the sleeve notes on *Every Picture Tells a Story*). Then, with a big grin, he asked "Wot you doin' 'ere?"

When I told him I had been invited down by Frankie he gave me a huge smile and hug and said "Where's Frankie?" The funny thing was I didn't think about a Rolling Stone in our company because I still saw him as one of The Faces. But what a lovely, friendly guy! So, armed with a couple of cans of Guinness in his pockets, he asked where Frankie was. There had been a break in the music, so I explained that Frankie was behind the black curtains on-stage. After a few minutes of mayhem, the rehearsals got underway again as Ronnie Wood and the Wilfs assembled into a 14 piece band with acoustic guitars, mandolin, fiddles, and saxophone.

We then retired to a pub for a tea time beer behind the theatre in readiness for the evening's events. When I caught up with Frankie in the dressing room, he was sitting quietly on his own and said to me "I wish Simon (Kirke) was here."

"Why's that, Frankie?"

"Because he usually writes out the set list!" Anyhow, we got that sorted out and had the most amazing evening you could imagine. The beautiful Hackney Empire Theatre was packed and I was walking on air.

During Frankie's set Kirsty MacColl and Frankie duetted on 'Brown Eyed Handsome Man', 'That'll Be The Day', and 'There's a Guy Works Down The Chip Ship'.

I don't think I sat down the whole day or evening!

We were stopped from taking photos during the Wilfs' actual performance but Ronnie kindly let me take one or two during the afternoon. What a day!!!

Highlight for me during his show was a twenty minute version of 'Little Red Rooster' with fiddle solo, sax solo and of course an incredible slide guitar solo from Mr. Wood!

Davy Arthur   Frankie Miller   Dave Stuart

During Frankie's 1991 USA recording sessions, I kept in touch with Jeremy Salmon on Frankie's progress and got another shock when he calmly announced that Bill Ham's wife had been abducted and murdered.

Bill Ham was the maverick businessman who managed ZZ Top for more than 30 years. He also owned the Hamstein publishing company, with whom Frankie recorded a number of demos. Then tragedy struck.

Spencer Corey Goodman had been on parole less than 24 hours when he abducted and murdered 48-year-old Cecile. Goodman was apprehended about five weeks later and executed by the State of Texas by lethal injection in 2000. Ham witnessed the execution.

That event helped put an end to the music project but one successful collaboration from the trip was with Clint Black, with whom Frankie had written 'Burn One Down'. Clint Black's version reached number four in the US Country Chart.

Caledonia's Been Everything I Ever Had

During the run-up to the UK General Election, the 'Caledonia' advert started to appear on ITV. There was never any initial announcement as to who was singing but it was rather obvious who the vocalist was.

The story revolved around a homesick Scot in London, who quits his job and returns home to his roots...

The first publicity in the press for 'Caledonia' came when it was announced that Tennents had offered Frankie to record a full-length version of the song, after the amount of interest shown in the popular TV commercial which featured his voice.

Frankie said that they hadn't been prepared to pay him for doing the job right and so he told them to forget it.

Tennents said that every time the ad was shown, their switchboard was jammed with inquiries from people who wanted to buy it. They had never experienced such a response before.

Months later, Frankie was in the headlines again after actually agreeing to record the song.

His emotional rendering of Dougie MacLean's 'Caledonia', which accompanied the advert, led to a huge demand for the song to be released as a single. A new generation of Scots were introduced to the gruff Glaswegian voice of Frankie Miller.

'Caledonia's success led to his band hitting the road on a ten-night tour, but when 'Caledonia' was released it faced problems. First, Tennents took the advert off the air on the grounds that it could drum up nationalist support before the general election. Then Radio 1 refused to include the song in its playlist for DJs. If you don't make the playlist, you can forget about the UK Top 40.

Yet 'Caledonia' made it to number one in the Scottish charts for a four week stay.

The singer claimed the decision not to play the song was a political move. Said Miller: "I'm very into the Scottish National Party and I would like it to have helped them. But the People-That-Be all over the country don't want to take votes from Labour or Conservative.

"Any SNP vote is going to take away from Labour."

Some SNP activists adopted Miller's version of 'Caledonia' as an election theme, playing it outside polling stations and from campaign cars.

Frankie said at the time: "I don't mind that at all. In fact I quite like that. Anything that's actually Scottish, I'm up for."

The BBC's decision not to put 'Caledonia' on the playlist was supposedly taken on the grounds of musical value. Miller was less than convinced.

"That was just words, an excuse," he claimed. Criticism of the decision in the Scottish press was understandable, but Miller felt it backfired.

"There are certain things you don't do with the BBC. I think the attitude was to get the press to phone up the BBC and say: 'What's happening, why isn't this playing?' The BBC don't go for that sort of blackmail. That was the biggest damage done to it.

"I never felt bad about it, I just felt a wee bit bad about how it was handled."

Regarding the upcoming tour, Frankie smiled, "They're in for a shock, they really are, and I ain't just blowing the trumpet. We've got some incredible stuff. I don't think there's anybody can touch us. The band's excellent."

Apart from the years spent in the United States, London had been his home since 1970. Work dictated that he lived in a city he did not like and visits to Scotland were arranged as frequently as possible.

He always maintained that he missed the people back home and it hurt - sounding a bit like the bloke in the advert.

"If I had his job I would never have gone in the first place. Or maybe I would have had to," he added with regret.

The 'Caledonia' advert was not the first he'd done the backing for. His was the voice heard on the 'I've Got Mine' adverts. The ads weren't shown in England, much to his relief. Frankie said at the time, "I don't like listening to my voice. I know I can sing a hell of a lot better than a hell of a lot of people but it's not a thing I indulge in."

Jeremy Salmon faxed me the provisional dates for the Scottish tour and it was thrilling for me as it was to kick-off in the 1300 seat capacity Music Hall, Aberdeen. Being made a guest on the tour was also pretty special.

The tour manager was a guy called Andy Roberts and two days before the band were due in Scotland Frankie asked me to design a tour T shirt and co-ordinate with Andy. We tried and failed as no company around at that time was able to arrange artwork and production in such a short lead time as two days.

Cliff Richard had promoted a tour called 'Access All Areas' and our plan was to create a design using a Scottish Saltire with the words 'Caledonia Tour 1992 - Excess All Areas'.

It may have sold more units than the single!

My friend Rab Howat played guitar on 'Caledonia'. He said:
"I can remember being disappointed that Frankie never turned up for the guitar sessions... but the thing I remember most is the awe of playing behind THAT VOICE! However, his girlfriend at the time, Patricia (ex Pans People), gave him my phone number and he rang to thank me. Frankie did make an offer to tour with him (I think it was Germany). I was making so much money at the time that I turned him down! Idiot!

"I can still remember playing dominos with Frankie when I was a teenager in the Burns Howff in Glasgow - we all ended up really pissed!

"I also remember the first time I ever heard Frankie. I was around 15 and trying to sneak into The Electric Gardens in Sauchiehall St. Luckily that night they let me in. The Stoics were playing and hearing Frankie sing was just a magical experience which will stay with me till the day I die...

"And I end up playing on one of his records. Isn't life strange?"
With Simon Kirke back on drums for the 'Caledonia' tour, Frankie and his band performed to sold-out venues all over Scotland.

The Moat House Hotel, Glasgow

4th November 1993

Frankie was about to perform for two evenings at Glasgow's Renfrew Ferry, after appearing at The Lemon Tree in Aberdeen on the 2nd November (his birthday). Legendary drummer Ian Wallace (ex Bob Dylan/King Crimson etc) had been drafted into the band.

Ian told me over a dram after the Aberdeen show that he had waited ten years to play with Frankie!

I was having morning coffee at The Moat with Frankie's manager Jeremy Salmon when he calmly asked me... did I think that if Joe Walsh joined the band it would help to sell out the Renfrew Ferry? I nearly fell off my seat!! Even allowing for Jeremy's understated style, I still wasn't sure if he was pulling my leg or what!

I was sworn to secrecy that Frankie and Joe Walsh were planning to work together and off I went to enjoy two incredible sell out Frankie Miller shows in Glasgow!

When I eventually managed to have a quiet moment with Frankie some days later, he blew me away even more. "Aye, and Nicky Hopkins is joining to play piano!!"

Nicky Hopkins had been around the top bands as a session player for years, including The Who, The Jeff Beck Group and The Rolling Stones, and had appeared on over 500 albums. My only thought was... God, I'm really going to meet those guys!

Depending on The Eagles' future plans to tour, Frankie was planning to take his new band on the road in America and the project had a provisional name of Fires Brimstone. He even invited me to go with him!

Christmas 1993
Extract from Procol Harum Newsletter *Shine On*

"Few who have witnessed the Miller magic on stage would deny that he is one of the Great British Voices and he has also been described as on of the finest interpretative singers in the U.K..."

"For Gary Brooker, 1993 concluded with Gary Brooker's Christmas Bash at Chiddingfold, Surrey. Two gigs were organised by Gary's wife Franky in aid of charity and must have been witnessed by in excess of 800 folk.

"Following a lively support set from the Big Town Playboys - Bill Wyman's favourite band right now - the gig began in earnest with No Stiletto Shoes (Gary's kick-ass rock band) covering some great rock 'n' roll and rhythm and blues numbers. These were followed by guest vocalist

Maggie Ryder's sweltering version of 'Steamy Windows', delivered with more panache than Tina Turner, and that's saying something!! Shoes guitarist Andy Fairweather-Low followed this with his Amen Corner hit 'Bend Me Shape Me'. Gary proceeded to sing his single, 'Two Fools In Love', a hit single in Holland some years back for Gary and Lori Spee as a duet.

"Next up was a special guest, Frankie Miller, who simply stole the show with four timeless soul standards, namely Wilson Pickett's 'In The Midnight Hour', Allen Toussaint's 'Brickyard Blues' (written for Frankie Miller's *High Life* album), Jim Reeves' 'He'll Have To Go', and Otis Redding's 'Dreams to Remember'. Frankie's vocals were particularly spine-chilling on 'Midnight Hour' and 'Dreams To Remember', the emotional intensity matched by some of the most sensitive horn/sax playing I've heard this side of Stax/Volt from Frank Mead. Needless to say Frankie and the Shoes brought the house down with cries of 'More!'

"The Shoes also included Geoff Whitehorn on guitar, Henry Spinetti on drums and Peter Stroud on bass."

1994

Frankie flew out to the States in the spring of 1994 to record with his new band in Chatanooga.

I'll never forget speaking to him on his return and how excited he was about being in the studio with Joe Walsh. Apart from Joe's obvious talents on guitar, Frankie was blown away by the fact that Mr Walsh had turned up in true style with four guitars and four technicians - one for each instrument! 'Guilty of the Crime' and 'He'll Have to Go' were recorded during these sessions.

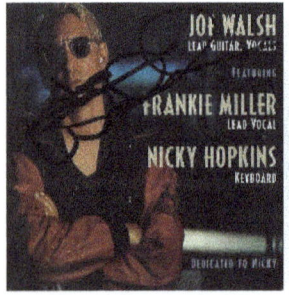  

Before he departed for the USA, Windsong had released the *BBC In Concert* CD.

Fred Dellar from the *NME* had given Windsong my details and promo copies dropped through my mailbox… When I phoned Frankie to tell him, he asked "What does the album start with?"

'Free and Safe (On The Road)' came my reply, then after a few seconds' silence, Frankie said "I forgot all about that song! It was actually one of the tracks recorded at His Masters Wheels in 1975 but never made *The Rock* album."

Excellent sleeve notes came with the package, from Allan Gardner. Here is a sample…

"There are few white rhythm and blues vocalists who can stand comparison with the best (or even second best) black exponents of the music, and fewer still who are British: Van Morrison, Chris Farlowe, Rod Stewart, Joe Cocker, Paul Rodgers. Frankie Miller, whose voice can suggest the mellowness of Sam Cooke or the rasping urgency of Ray Charles, is another member of this select group. It's a talent that has also been appreciated by more discerning record buyers and that is heard to the full on these *In Concert* recordings."

The last two gigs…ever.

One on Monday 15th August 1994 at the Marktrock Festival in Leuven, Belgium, and another in Wervick on Friday 19th.

Andy Newmark on drums, Chrissy Stewart on bass and Neil Hubbard on guitar.

I don't have much information on these shows other than that I had tried to get flights but Aberdeen-Brussels in those days was no easy task for someone still in a nine to five job. I phoned Frankie on the morning of departure and he was already away and rehearsing with his band.

I couldn't make it - and how I was to regret not trying harder! Frankie then returned to the States to team up again with Joe Walsh and plan their recording and performing future together. He went to see the Eagles live in the Giants Stadium, New York, and afterwards the hand of fate dealt out a shocking blow.

In A New York Minute

It was the morning of Saturday August 27th 1994. A normal Saturday morning, until I returned home after my morning walk with the dogs. Approaching my back door, I was met by two ashen faced friends who calmly asked if I had heard the news about Frankie Miller.

They handed me a copy of the morning paper with a front page headline "Rocker Frankie Fights for Life". It stated that "Scots rock legend Frankie Miller was last night fighting for his life following a massive heart attack in New York."

He was said to be "critical" in the city's St Vincent Hospital. In a state of shock and panic I immediately phoned the hospital, and after several attempts to contact the correct department and speak to someone who could give some answers, I was coldly told that Mr Miller had been discharged. I also tried Frankie's home number in London in the vain hope that somehow there might be someone on the end of the line with some news. No such luck. The following morning, Sunday 28th August, the headlines rang out: "Family prays for Frankie".

"Prayers were being said for Frankie Miller, the Scots rock legend."

I quickly realised that phoning the hospital was always going to be a waste of time and that in any case, others, including Frankie's family, had more right than me to any confidential news. I knew that Jeremy Salmon would give me any updates, but unfortunately at the time and until he could get to New York himself Jeremy knew as much as we did… What a terrible and hopeless situation!

"His family said he'd had a brain haemorrhage in New York on Thursday, contrary to earlier reports that the 44-year-old singer had suffered a heart attack."

"Doctors at St Vincent's Hospital, New York, were said to have diagnosed two blood clots."

As the news dried up, Monday's papers by this time were down to four liners stating that Frankie was still fighting for his life in a New York Hospital. Meanwhile, on 9th September, I had a phone call from ex Rory Gallagher keyboard player Lou Martin (I had met and kept in touch with Lou through his Blues 'n' Trouble years) to tell me that Frankie's new piano player, Nicky Hopkins, had died of complications from abdominal and heart ailments.

More tears - and I immediately played 'Girl from Mill Valley' in tribute. Another sad day.

As the weeks passed and with Frankie in a coma, and still no news of Frankie's wife Annette's whereabouts, it was announced in the press that Frankie had undergone major surgery to remove a blood clot and that it had been a success.

He had indeed suffered a brain haemorrhage that was to leave him in a coma with even the most optimistic prognosis offering little hope. A two per cent chance of survival was the best projection Annette heard during the 20 agonising weeks at his bedside while Frankie lay unconscious, contracting infection after infection.

October 16th 1994

The press announced that Frankie had been flown home in secret from the United States. He had in fact been flown home (still in a coma) to the National Hospital for Neurology and Neurosurgery in London's West End.

Unbelievably, Frankie's showbiz friends had rallied round to help pay his crippling £800 a day medical bills in the US - he had had no medical insurance!

I kept trying Frankie's home number and suddenly the answering machine had changed from Frankie's voice to Annette's so I knew then that they were indeed back in London.

Visits to the hospital were restricted, so news of Frankie's progress was slow in getting back to us in Scotland, with Annette quite rightly not taking calls.

Frankie was to spend six months in a coma, until March 1995, during which time he also suffered pneumonia, liver infection and meningitis and had five operations. When Annette was eventually able to take phone calls again it was just a massive relief to know that Frankie had survived, but was obviously still seriously ill, with an untreated second aneurism, unable to speak properly and paralysed down his right side.

London 1996

During 1996, with Frankie now safely back home, I said to Annette that I would just love to shake Frankie's hand, and she said calmly one morning: "Why don't you?" I didn't hang around and booked my flight to London without a second thought!

Frankie and Annette had recently allowed their first visitor from the press (Billy Sloan) to visit and publish the first photographs since August 1994, so it was exciting and a privilege to be added to the "guest list".

All sorts of things were buzzing through my head... How did Frankie look? What if he couldn't remember me? I turned up at his house armed with gifts and a huge card to be greeted with a huge smile and hug! I needn't have worried!

One of the first things Frankie did was to put on a recently received CD from Billy Connolly with a song called 'I Wish I Was in Glasgow'. Although he couldn't speak properly he could say "Aye!!" loudly and proudly and could attempt words if prompted to do so.

His communication skills were there in abundance and Frankie's wicked sense of humour certainly hadn't deserted him!

As the stories unfolded of all the happenings of the last 2-3 years Annette and Frankie proudly announced that they had been approached by a record company to release a new album but couldn't agree on the last few tracks.

I bravely suggested that it may require a "fresh ear" and amazingly I was to hear a number of unreleased Frankie Miller songs!! After a listen to a good number of songs, Frankie agreed to my five suggestions, and to my astonishment I was becoming involved in a new Frankie Miller album.

We went for lunch to a local bar and Frankie went speeding off in his electric wheelchair without a care in the world, leaving Annette and myself to walk some metres behind.

When we got back to Frankie's he decided to go for an afternoon nap and I thought it was my cue to leave, as I didn't want to outstay my welcome… I couldn't have been more wrong because Annette's reply was "What? And leave me here on my own?"

It hit me like a ton of bricks that she needed to talk, and it was then that the whole story of the trip to New York and the terrible consequences started to unravel.

Annette had saved Frankie's life by giving him mouth to mouth resuscitation and calling an ambulance. He died again and she revived him again! He was rushed to the hospital in Manhattan and put on a life support machine.

He had indeed travelled without insurance and Annette had been forced to leave their hotel and lodge with nuns. Frankie had been placed in a huge tub of ice to keep his temperature down.

After Frankie's eventual discharge from hospital Annette wrote to her local MP, "screaming and shouting" because the UK health service were not prepared to provide proper occupational therapy. Doctors had written Frankie off as a vegetable.

They had even told Annette to walk away from the situation. Annette couldn't accept that and fought every step of the way to get physiotherapy and speech therapy for Frankie.

The letter worked and Frankie was given a place in a rehabilitation unit.

The music charity Nordorff Robbins also arranged music therapy via The Drake Music Trust.

The trouble was, nobody was sure whether Frankie could understand what was being said! Then one of his friends, Graham Lyle of Gallagher and Lyle, shoved a guitar in his strong left hand and while he strummed asked Frankie to "play a C" and Frankie did it! This was a major turning point and Annette immediately knew that Frankie was back and ready to set out on the long road to recovery. The comeback had begun.

Annette immediately told the doctors that vegetables definitely couldn't play guitars!!

He was now able to walk a bit by himself and was even climbing stairs in his apartment block. Frankie had confounded the experts and Annette reckoned they should be writing a medical paper on him. In a moment of self-doubt she had asked Frankie if he was glad she had saved him, to which he answered "Aye!" That answer and the look in his eye were all she needed to make the decision to devote the rest of her life to his care.

She said, "I am with him all day every day and there is nothing that I wouldn't try if I thought there was even a slight chance that it would help in some way."

In the late evening, when it was time to say my goodbyes, I did my best to put on a brave face for Frankie, but as I walked down to the tube station that night, I cried my way down Edgware Road.

1997

I had my own down time with bowel cancer, which exhausted me from late 1996 – I had an operation in April/May 1997 - and strangely enough, my rocks were Annette and Frankie Miller!! I had regular phone calls and cards, CDs and tapes (Frankie and Annette made me my own personal collection of songs!!!), and orders to consume huge amounts of vitamins sent, which I will cherish as long as I live.

This is not something that has been in the public domain but shows the spirit and unbelievable love and caring that Frankie and Annette are capable of showing, even during their own times of hardship.

During 1997 one of Frankie's unreleased songs, 'Sending Me Angels', was released by Kathy Mattea, and her version of the song brings a tear to my eye to this day.

I played it every day that summer and it was an inspiration to me. Annette was even able to find a beautiful card to send me with gold angels which reads "Me and Frankie are sending you angels." Needless to say I made a full recovery…

This song stood out as one that helped ease the pain of that summer and indeed a version of it by Delbert McClinton dropped through my letter box from Annette and Frankie later that year.

I will also never forget Ed Deane's kindness in sending me these tour T shirts and beautiful note.

1998

Into 1998 and I had a call out of the blue from Elaine Donnelly at the BBC asking to speak to Davy Arthur. "We are making a documentary on Frankie Miller and Annette and Frankie have asked me to contact YOU…" When I phoned Frankie's to tell them the beeb had been on, Annette calmly said, "Well, you know more about Frankie than Frankie does!"

It was another huge sign that Frankie was willing to allow the outside world into his life, and it was a brave step allowing BBC camera crews to film both in and around his home and hospital ward to witness first hand his remarkable rehabilitation.

So we arranged interviews, tried to cover his younger days and some career highlights, tell the New York story as Frankie and Annette try to re-build their lives… all in 30 minutes!

The resulting *Ex–S* documentary, *Stubborn Kinda Fella*, was shown on BBC 2 at the end of year and repeated on Hogmanay 1999. It was an impossible job to tell Frankie's story in 30 minutes but Rod Stewart and Billy Connolly, among others, contributed. It was a huge honour to have been asked to be involved in that project, which took around six months to complete. Annette's comment regarding the press misprint is a classic! One newspaper in its TV guide section listed the programme being about Frankie Miller who had recently passed away. That resulted in Annette telling Frankie "I can't talk to you any more, you're dead!"

Some memorable quotes from and about the documentary:
Shirley Whiteside (*Glasgow Herald*) revealed "The remarkable courage of Frankie Miller…"

"He has a raw, rasping singing voice that hints at the pain and hardship of growing up poor on a dirt farm in Alabama or maybe a one-room shack in Tennessee. To the uninitiated it is always a surprise to learn that the gritty, soulful growl belongs not to a black American bluesman but to Frankie Miller, a gallus Glaswegian who showed the world that a white boy from Bridgeton could sing the blues. "

In another headline:
"Tomorrow's BBC Scotland *EX-S* documentary charts the 48-year-old singer's progress from being written off by doctors as a 'vegetable' to his triumphant return to songwriting."

"Frustrated by the reluctance of medics to offer any hope of recovery, Annette administered her own occupational therapy to coax Frankie back into action."

Annette said: "With every week that goes by you can see another improvement.

"I never gave up hope. I felt sure he would make it. He wouldn't give up.

"Frankie is just so stubborn...
"I SUPPOSE IT'S BECAUSE HE'S SCOTTISH!"
"He died... and I revived him again."

Billy Connolly said about Frankie that he "used to be a wee bit grumpy" at the height of his stardom but now exuded "sheer goodness."

Author's Note: A reader in the Scottish *Daily Record* begged to differ, reciting a story from Frankie's days with the Stoics… He remembered, as a wee boy, standing in the pouring rain outside a scout hut in Drumchapel, when the band were rehearsing inside. Frankie appeared at the door and shouted: "You boys…" As the lads started to run away, Frankie continued: "Come inside out of the rain!"

From Tom Shields in the *Daily Record* 10/9/2002

"You either have the life force or you don't, and Frankie has it by the bucket-load." – Billy Connolly

"He's the only white guy that ever brought a tear to my eye." – Rod Stewart

"He's got a swagger - he's got a swagger you could dry a washin' aff!" – Peter McDougall

From Shirley Whiteside in the *Glasgow Herald*

"The contrast between the slim-hipped seventies rocker wearing his trademark black hat and the middle-aged man of today, able to frame chords on a guitar with his left hand but not yet able to strum with his right, is sobering. Pity is not something Frankie Miller would thank you for nor does his attitude inspire it.

"Every day his speech and mobility improve and he is obviously happy - serene even - and enjoying every moment of his life. He has a wicked sense of humour and brief glimpses of the bad boy rocker from the old days still survive as, with a mischievous glint in his eye, he flirts outrageously with the female physiotherapists during one of his regular therapy sessions."

Fans, and those who cared about Frankie, were now becoming aware of Drake Music Project, a charity which promoted integration between disabled and able-bodied musicians. He had been working with project tutor Cormack O'Kane, and a celebrity band featuring Bonnie Tyler, Paul Carrack and Jools Holland played one of his new songs, 'Sun Comes Up, Sun Goes Down', at a fund-raising concert for the charity.

Will Jennings, co-writer of Celine Dion's monster hit 'My Heart Goes On', had written the words to music by Frankie.

Annette never considered deserting Frankie, even when she became so exhausted from the constant care that she began hallucinating.

"In a half-hour programme there is not time to include material from every public figure with something to say about the former electrician who began writing songs when he was ten years old. "

Billy Connolly gave a rare interview, Rod Stewart took time off from touring and figures as diverse as musician Jools Holland and Celtic great Jimmy Johnstone gladly agreed to be filmed.

Billy Connolly says of Annette: "She has done the most staggering job. When Frankie was successful he was a grumpy little character. Now he glows."

But any omission from the story was always going to hurt the woman who has done so much to bring quality to a life torn apart.

Annette says: "I feel guilty. I saved his life but people have told me they wouldn't want to live if something like that had happened to them.

"But at the start I asked Frankie if he was glad to be alive and he said 'Aye'.

"Our roles have been reversed. When we met he was very protective of me. Now I'm doing the looking after."

"I want him to achieve all he can. If he could sing again, that would really be something – but just to have a conversation would be nice."

The truth is, if Frankie had had a brain haemorrhage in Britain they'd have switched the machine off, after three months in a coma. In America they are too aware of lawsuits.

She said: "That's why I think football star Davie Cooper could have been saved.

"They only gave him 18 hours on life support."

When Annette was asked who supported her, she calmly replied, smiling: "Nobody, really."

"The doctors told me to get on a bus and get on with my life. But that's not me."

There have been other joys along the way. After a gig last year, Rod Stewart pushed Frankie's wheelchair along his dressing room and declared to the throng, "This is the Frankie Miller, the best singer on the planet."

Later, Rod, Frankie and Annette went along to a Bob Dylan gig in London and afterwards Dylan walked off stage and spoke to no one – he simply hugged Frankie. From that moment Frankie uttered the words "Bob Dylan."

The milestones in the singer's rehabilitations have been hard won. It was fifteen months before he could leave hospital. Three-and-half years learning to walk again. He still can't read or write, and can't talk or sing much, either, but he and his partner have adapted accordingly.

"Frankie's got a memory like an elephant and he can communicate pretty well by drawing pictures," says Annette. "Don't play us at Pictionary – you'll lose!"

Frankie's record shelf bulges with the work of his beloved Ray Charles and Annette explained that Frankie once had a chance to meet the jazz legend.

During his recovery at Northwick Park Hospital in London, Frankie pleaded with Annette to sneak him out to a Ray Charles concert at Wembley. At the aftershow Frankie was within two feet of his idol but was too mesmerised to say hello.

"In hindsight I thought this was a great move by Frankie," says Annette. "Can you imagine? Frankie can't really talk and Ray Charles couldn't see – it would have been your worst nightmare."

Rod Stewart also, again, spoke about Frankie and laughed as he told the story about how Frankie again brought tears to his eyes – after a night of heavy drinking.

"He came round to my house in Beverly Hills one night in 1977 and we hit the brandy. As it happens, I drank him under the table. Frankie then had one drink too many, and threw up all over the sofa. I couldn't believe it. But he's a great character. I love him. "

Rod also revealed a dream wish for the coming year. "I'd love to sing a duet with him. And I'll be looking to record a Frankie Miller song on my next album. After me, Frankie is the best white soul singer ever." Rod laughed again: "No, seriously, he is the best."

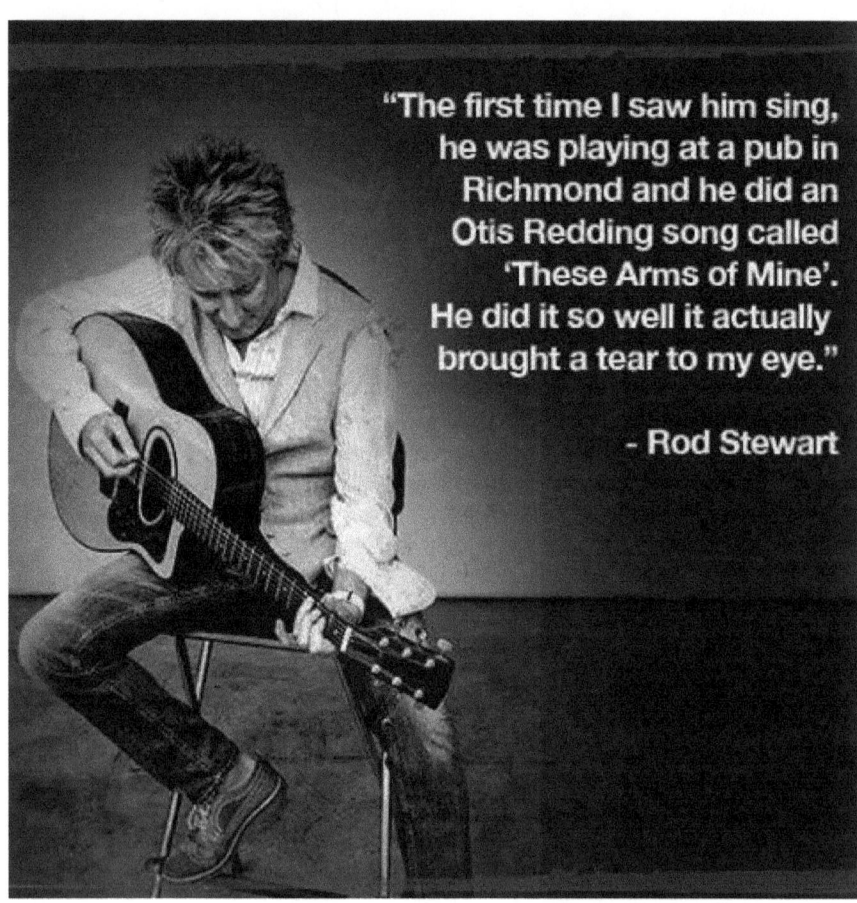

"The first time I saw him sing, he was playing at a pub in Richmond and he did an Otis Redding song called 'These Arms of Mine'. He did it so well it actually brought a tear to my eye."

- Rod Stewart

May 2002

Leading up to the September 2002 Barrowlands concert and the accompanying album, *Something Old, Something New, Something Borrowed, Something Blue*

From Fish (Marillion)
"I got back from London on the 26th May, hungover from a night out... On the 27th, I recorded a session for the Frankie Miller tribute album at CaVa Studios in Glasgow. Rather than fill you in here on Frankie's history, why don't you visit www.frankiemiller.net to find out about one of Scotland's most famous voices.

"Since his aneurysm Frankie has lost much of the control of his right side and has been fighting to regain the power of speech. He is still fully aware of everything around him and his memory is sparkling (much to some people's dismay:-)

"Thanks to Music Therapy he has recovered some of his voice and the mischievous look in his eyes still smiles as strong.

"The last time we were out together was in Berlin in 1985, when after his gig there, we went along with Brian Robertson to Annabelle's Nightclub, which at the time was owned by Tammi's boyfriend. Mainly due to Tammi's presence as a waitress I hung out there quite a lot, much to the annoyance of the guy.

"On the night in question we settled into a session and the bill started to run. Frankie headed off early as I think he knew what was coming and left Brian and I to take point on the Dawn Patrol. At about 4am the club was closing, and the bill duly arrived and I presented my credit card to take care of the 400 mark bill.

"They didn't accept credit cards and Brian and I considered a drunken sprint for the door. The boyfriend came over to the table which had been served most of the night by Tammi and ripped up the bill! A big score for him in his eyes and a big score for Drunk Musos Utd:-

"Brian had come up for the session at CaVa and the first thing I said to him was that he still owed me the money from '85. The tribute album looks like being a very happening project with Rod Stewart, Lulu, Maggie Bell and a host of other artists from past and present contributing a rendition of one of Frankie's songs.

"I had originally wanted to sing a song that Stuart Adamson wanted to record and had thought that after Stuart's death (16 December 2001) I would be asked to fill in. I was very surprised when I was asked to sing 'Caledonia'. It was No 1 in the short-lived Scottish Charts mainly due to Scottish sales inspired by the use of the track on a Tennents beer advert.

"I immediately agreed and when I found out the backing band that was on offer I couldn't have refused in any case. The band consisted of Brian Robertson on lead guitar, Ted McKenna (drums), Zal Cleminson (guitars), Chris Glen (bass) and Hugh McKenna (keys), the entire Sensational Alex Harvey Band! Add to that an 25 piece BBC Orchestra, a 25 piece Gospel Choir and the Shotts and Dykes Pipe Band and you have an amazing collection of sounds and musicians.

"It was also the first time I worked with my new keyboard player, Irving Duguid, who had arranged the track and the strings for the orchestra. He is definitely a find and no-one will be disappointed with his addition to my new line-up. As a writer, I firmly believe he will make a major contribution to the new album.

"The track has turned out well beyond expectations and is being considered as a single release in September by Eagle Records, the record company dealing with the project. Tennents have also expressed interest in a repeat of the advert with the new version.

"Magic moment of the session was Frankie's arrival from London. It was great to see him again and as I mentioned before, he has lost none of his spirit. Funniest moment was definitely 7 musos trying to work out what Frankie wanted from the pub as part of the 'carry-out'. As Frankie got more frustrated, 7 musos went through their own game of alcohol charades - vodka, Frankie ? Naw! Brandy? Naw! Whisky, Frankie? Naw! Sweet! Malibu, Frankie? Creme De Menthe, Frankie? NAW! etc. etc. etc. Eventually he drew what he wanted on a bit of paper and it turned out he wanted 3 Snickers Bars. The entire room, including Frankie, was on the floor laughing!

"I was so proud when he came up and gave me a big hug and said 'Thank You, Thank You' and made a sign for singing.

"To be given a compliment from a man with one of the greatest blues/soul voices from our wee country is something I will cherish for a very long time.

"After the session I was in the hotel by the Clyde Auditorium and spent too long in the bar with the band. When I eventually decided to go to catch the last train and get a taxi to the station the entire Auditorium exited and the concourse swarmed with punters who had been at a David Cassidy concert! Tres Fellini as I sat with the SAHB's, a Thin Lizzy guitarist and Frankie Miller! The 70s strike back.

"Needless to say I missed the train and got home thanks to Frankie's fan club organiser, Davy Arthur, at 4am. Worth every lost brain cell...

Author's Note: My own memory of that day was arriving late at CaVa and seeing Frankie being driven away and back to the hotel for a break. I had missed the pipe band part, the orchestra and the choir but Robbo, Fish and SAHB were still in the studio. It was still only early afternoon and the 'Caledonia' track would eventually take 10 hours in total to record.

So, not having seen Robbo for a few years, there was lots of banter to be had, as well as the serious side of recording. I had some vinyl that Robbo still hadn't signed for me so armed with the silver pen, I laid one or two 12"singles on the large mixing desk for him to sign... We carefully peeled back the cellophane cover that had been signed by Frankie, Chrissy and Simon a few years back - so this was Robbo's turn. After signing with his usual "Yodel" postscript he said to me: "Blow on it to dry the ink before you put the cover back on," and without thinking I said "Na, you do it, it will dry quicker!!!" True story - and Robbo loved that kind of banter. Few would get away with that with "yer man".

I'm sure that was also the day that SAHB recorded 'Dancing in the Rain' with Dean Ford. I also watched that session but sadly lost the hard drive that housed the digital photos!

Around 10pm I drove Robbo and Soren back down to the City Inn where we hooked up with Frankie, Annette and Chrissy Stewart with his wife Pat. For my part I remember Robbo getting out an acoustic guitar and singing 'Jealousy' and having a singalong with Fish and assorted SAHB members too. And witnessing the 40 quid a round Jack Daniels orders in which I was NOT involved.

At which point we should pick up on Fish's story again. When he shouted out that he had missed his train, Frankie's wife Annette suggested that "Davy Arthur lives near you." The rest is history... we travelled through to Edinburgh together, excited about the new 'Caledonia' recording as we listened to Fish's new favourite CD (the soundtrack to *Blackhawk Down*.) When we got back to his lovely farm, we listened to the 'Caledonia' mixes and sat until dawn, before I wearily set out for home.

When news of the Barrowlands project broke it was Joe Walsh who made the headlines.

In a phone interview with Billy Sloan:
"I pray I'll be able to hear that amazing Frankie Miller voice one more time," said Joe, 54, in a voice cracking with emotion. "I've always been in total awe of Frankie. I think he's the best rock 'n' roll singer ever... period. And I've heard some good singers. Frankie is also a fighter. With him, anything is possible. Wouldn't it be great if he could sing again? I wouldn't put it past him."

Joe has never forgotten the first time – 30 years ago – when he heard that amazing Frankie Miller voice. "A mutual friend called Bob Pridden, The Who's sound engineer, let me hear Frankie's song, 'Be Good To Yourself'," he recalled. "I thought he was a black guy from the Deep South of America. I couldn't believe it when I found out he was a white guy from Glasgow.

"Frankie could do rock and country. He could sing the blues, too. It was a voice which could do anything. From that moment on, I wanted to meet him because I thought so much of his talent. I never dreamed I'd actually get to work with him."

The first time Joe and Frankie actually met was in 1989. They spent a weekend at Bob's house in the English countryside and cemented their friendship. But Joe was struck dumb when he heard Frankie sing in person. "We went to the local pub for a few drinks, then back to Bob's and sang around a piano," revealed Joe. "But I didn't want to open my mouth. I just wanted to listen to him. I was sick of my own voice – I wanted to hear Frankie Miller."

September 2002 Barrowlands

My recollections…

It must have been the year 2000. During the year when Frankie was receiving music therapy thanks to the Drake Music Trust, I was asked by Annette to contact a guy at the BBC in Glasgow by the name of Alec Downie.

Along with Tom McCafferty, we arranged to spend an evening with Alec and get to know him better. We hit it off with Alec immediately and he seemed to have the same passion for Frankie that we had.

He had met one of the Drake employees, Cormac O'Kane (Cormac had been giving Frankie some music therapy which included sessions with an acoustic guitar and singing together), on a trip to Ireland and Frankie's name came up. After that chance meeting, Alec had it in his mind to research and produce some kind of "tribute album and possible concert" to Frankie and other Glasgow stars of the 60s/70s (SAHB, Maggie Bell etc). Hence our meeting at Frankie and Annette's request.

Naturally at the time I was also keen to keep Frankie's name out there and help if I could to raise money for a worthwhile cause. My idea, if a gig was to happen, was to try to model it on The Band's The Last Waltz where we could form a "house band" and have guests appearing to perform Frankie's songs.

It took two years out of my (and others') lives, but likely candidates for a contribution to an album would be acts like Rod Stewart, Maggie Bell,

Nazareth, SAHB, John Martyn, Ray Wilson and a host of other Scottish artists.

So we proceeded to make up a list of would be/suitable recording artistes for the album and those willing and able to appear for a tribute gig, with Barrowlands being the favourite venue - a 2000 standing capacity, east end location in Frankie's home city fitting the bill perfectly. Obvious candidates for a house band would be Frankie's ex band members and other Scottish musicians who may be available.

Simon Kirke - Free, Bad Company, Frankie Miller 1984–1993; Ted McKenna - Teargas, SAHB, Rory Gallagher. Simon was otherwise engaged with Bad Company but Ted accepted immediately and was another powerhouse and comrade throughout. Having known the Teargas guys also since the late 60s, it was another fitting FM connection.

Also, living locally, Ted was able to give of his time both in rehearsing, recording and assisting in the lead-up to the show. I was lucky enough to spend a day in the studio with SAHB and guest vocalist Dean Ford and watch them perform 'Dancing in the Rain'. It was one of my favourite tracks on the album.

Our friendship and contact remained right up until late 2018, when we were arranging to meet up in Holland with Gerry McAvoy and Marcel in the new band they had created, Band of Friends. What happened to Ted was a tragedy. RIP my friend Ted McKenna.

Chrissy Stewart on bass - NO others considered.

Brian Robertson on lead guitar - it seemed an obvious choice, and I will take credit for pushing for Robbo as we had retained our friendship and contact and he had, after all, pre-Joe Walsh recorded and toured with Frankie for 10 years! I knew Robbo could ably support an array of different artistes performing Frankie's songs (not only heavy rock which made him famous in Thin Lizzy and Motörhead). Robbo is also an accomplished keyboard player and drummer.

I had watched him one afternoon in London, rehearsing with Frankie's and Kirsty McColl's bands, and he spontaneously took over the "musical director" role, directing Kirsty's band. I saw a new side to Robbo that day and it did nothing but endear him to me even more.

He did something similar for the Barrowland project and spent eight hours on stage on the night… we then spent hours together (he and I) in the hotel bar and were escorted to our rooms at 7.30 the following morning. Good bless you Brian!

Paul Guerin on second guitar and slide guitar. Paul became a leading light in the Quireboys and the Down 'N' Outz with Joe Elliot. It was a master stroke from Robbo, bringing in his old pal and ex Clan band mate Paul, whom I had met a few years earlier on their tour. Paul also spent most of his evening on stage and especially loved the experience, not only of performing Frankie's music but standing strong alongside all the great people who performed that night.

It must have been early 1995 that Robbo came to the Cathouse in Brown Street, Glasgow, with a band called Ain't Lizzy (including the aforementioned Paul Guerin and a vocalist Wayne Ellis, bass player who had won a TV talent show as "Phil Lynott"). My mate Dave Stuart and I gatecrashed the party early that afternoon and ambushed Robbo. We shared a few hugs and tears as we discussed Frankie's current predicament and then he took me to the bar to meet two people I would be interested in meeting: his lovely parents.

Hugh McKenna (SAHB) on keyboards. A perfect fit also and a great connection to Frankie since the 60s.

From memory I am sure that Nazareth were first to agree to participate and go into the studio to record. Their lighting guy, roadie and all round amazing guy, Ronnie Dalrymple, got involved at that point and did - along with his partner Bev Harrison - an amazing job of organising the production office/T shirts/lighting on the night, and hosting Sunday afternoon tactical meetings in their home over what seemed to be an endless summer in the run up to the gig.

For a non-smoker I managed to float home on numerous occasions thanks to their hospitality. Pete and Dan were around a lot during that spell and of course the subject almost all of the time was Frankie Miller. I will never forget Pete telling me a story about the Shadettes days in the 60s when he also owned and ran a music club bar in Dunfermline. He arrived in the place after one of his own gigs to a packed venue full of locals, including screaming girls, being blown away by Sock 'Em JB. Frankie was immediately banned from ever playing in Pete's club again.

The weekend of the actual gig was mayhem and there are a few gaps... Artistes HQ was The City Inn. Friday night we were in a small group which accompanied Frankie and Davy Bryson round all the old haunts in south east Glasgow. (Davy was a character and a lovely guy who mixed monitors for Rod Stewart for over 20 years. He also worked for Tom Petty, The Beach Boys, and Diana Ross. There was a rumour that his ashes ended up in Tom Petty's Rickenbacker.)

Saturday was full-on with sound checks starting early afternoon. It was already raining talent. Joe Walsh had his hideaway down in the depths of the backstage corridors then blew the place away during rehearsals. I guess there must have been less than twenty of us watching at the time. Cold shivers ran down my spine...

Smokey Wendell had ordered that his artist would not be filmed or recorded during his performance. I hid behind the PA during his performance later on and stood about 2 or 3 metres behind Chrissy Stewart and sometimes crouched down and peered through the keyboard player's legs. During 'Rocky Mountain Way', Joe came marching towards me just as he tore into his last solo... and I stood up strong, clicking my camera with full zoom and thinking (jokingly) "This is my gig, ya baaastard!!" As I peered through the lens, Joe looked like he was right on top of me!! Sorry Smokey, but excited beyond belief didn't even come into it. (And I have lost the footage too!)

After the Barrowland show and probably around 3am, I bumped into Dan McCafferty and helped him find our way upstairs and out of the place, and into the swirling Glasgow rain (Dancing in the Rain). I was so mentally and physically exhausted after that evening that I can't actually remember the journey back to the City Inn apart from the all-night red wine session in the restaurant with Robbo! We were ushered to bed by the breakfast staff around 7.30am.

The gig run over had finished so late that there was no time for any formal aftershow party. It was a case of last man standing back at the hotel bar - me and Mr Robertson!

Looking back, it really was an amazing gesture from Joe Walsh to come over to Scotland and play his music in tribute to Frankie that night.

Also, for me, meeting the amazing Smokey Wendell, Joe's manager, was an experience I won't forget either!

"This one's for you Frankie"

Afterwards, in a press review, James Halbert wrote "Much of Glasgow's musical history is bound up in the story of Frankie Miller, one of rock's lost talents, stricken by a brain haemorrhage. Miller's friends offer hope - and one last great night."

Joe Walsh announced "This is for you, Frankie" then aired an emotionally raw version of 'Amazing Grace'.

He picked out some highlights, including (the truly heartbreaking) 'Still in Love With You', which was sung with great power and emotion by Ray Wilson, and not forgetting Brian Robertson's beautiful guitar solo. It was also a timely reminder that Frankie had duetted on the original track with Phil Lynott on Thin Lizzy's 1974 album *Nightlife*.

I thought that Mr Halbert was a bit hard on Clare Grogan, who he described as "easy on the eye - and hard on the ear - as ever" WTF! It was a charity night and the artists all entered into it with a spirit of great camaraderie. She performed 'Angels With Dirty Faces' and I had the best view in the house. I was crouched a few metres away on stage and hiding behind the amps. She looked stunning and in my opinion should be given credit for being brave enough to add a feminine flavour into what was essentially a male-dominated rock concert. (Not to mention the backstage mayhem that was going on in the bar!)

Joe Walsh returned for 'Life's Been Good' and 'Rocky Mountain Way'.

"The latter was simply awesome. A fatter, more toothsome intro riff you will not find, and being close enough to Walsh's eccentric, accentuating grimaces was a rare treat."

Brian Robertson   Joe Walsh

As the show (it ran from 7.30pm-2am) began to reach its climax I will let James Halbert describe it.

"It's hard for a Glaswegian living in London to convey what it meant to see Nazareth and SAHB at Barrowlands, but I'll try. Suffice to say your scribe was hearing the music filtered through decades of shared history. This you see was the same ballroom that I frequented as a Teddy boy, while notorious Glasgow hoodlum (and second cousin of Frankie Miller) Jimmy Boyle terrorised the neighbourhood."

So, Dan McCafferty was described as "grey-haired and avuncular", and Chris Glen as "portly through good living". But when Zal Cleminson played the granite-solid riff of 'Faith Healer' however, we were instantly zapped back to a time when Vambo rooled (sic). "Even without the legendary Alex, SAHB were stunning."

By the time the whole cast reassembled to celebrate Frankie, most punters looked as trashed as the Barrowland's plastic-strewn floor. Only Robbo, comping chords with a lecherous grin, looked ready for another Jack Daniels.

Meanwhile, at this point, I sat at the back of the auditorium in a secure area with Frankie and watched the quiet delight on his face. His old Glesca Pals had made him incredibly proud. See you back at the ranch Robbo!!

Headbangers and Heroes

We were contacted by a young Glasgow artist, Catherine Heffernan, who had a plan to organise an art exhibition celebrating the city's rock culture, using Alex Harvey, Jamie Barnes and Frankie Miller images. She asked if I had any suitable photos that she could use as inspiration for her sketches.

Catherine's plan was a light-hearted tribute to Glasgow and its music featuring three of its finest performers.

Here are some examples of her brilliant work…

Well, Long Way Home

During my first visit to see Frankie at his home in 1996 I found that he and Annette had chosen a dozen or so tracks for a proposed new album but needed around five more for the record company. Of course I had responded by blurting out, "What you need is a fresh ear"... and my life changed in yet another direction, when the studio door opened and I was presented with an unbelievable list of Frankie's songs!

I was in seventh heaven as song after song blasted out of the speakers. Rockers, ballads, you name it, but one hit me so hard it made my cry: 'Long Way Home'. It just seemed to sum everything up about the situation; a tearjerker, make no mistake.

Anyhow, the plan with that particular company fell through, and I probably asked a million times over the next wee while: "What about the new album?"

During my regular phone conversations with Annette and Frankie, the topic of conversation invariably got back round to the album we had discussed a while back...

But first of all, in early 2004, Eagle Records decided to re-master eight of Frankie's albums, up to and including *Standing on the Edge*. I was asked to help source and select bonus tracks for all of them and help with sleeve notes. (Not as easy as it sounds, by the way). I flew down and accompanied Annette to meet Mike Howell at Eagle, where, on the first day, we ran through some old 4 track tapes which were the out-takes from *Once In a Blue Moon*.

It was exciting for me to see the list of songs that didn't make the album, but when we put them into the tape machine, they were so old and brittle they didn't play back properly... so Frankie's versions of 'Heard it Through the Grapevine' and 'Ain't Too Proud to Beg' are lost forever. The challenge now was finding songs in the archive that were recorded around the same time (early 70s so that his voice matched that of the album(s)).

It was a huge learning experience for me but we did it. We got around the problem with some of the later albums by putting live versions on, which I think worked a treat. The albums sold out and these versions are almost impossible to find copies of nowadays. Ironically, we found out-takes from some of the albums later on (after the releases) but if you've never seen Frankie's filing system...

Well, regarding any new album, the final choice of tracks still had to be decided, so next thing I know I'm on a plane down to London again, to spend five days (and nights) with Frankie, going through his catalogue of unreleased songs!

To cut a long story short, I was asked to get the headphones on and sit in his home studio and first of all break the songs down into different categories, ballads/love songs/country feel/rockers/soul/you name it - not an easy task - whilst noting stand out songs for the album.

Frankie and I had some fun going through his music, I can tell you! I had heard a demo of 'Long Way Home' during my visit in 1996 and it made me cry. Many more had a similar effect and another title contender stood out, and I suggested to Frankie we consider it. Frankie replied with a one word answer, "No," so that idea was shelved.

But we were making great progress and day one was a great success. Back to it next day and another huge lesson for Davy Arthur: don't mess with Frankie Miller! While going through more tracks, I re-played the rejected one from the day before and tried it on with Frankie. It was 'True Cry of the Heart'.

I got the famous stare and an emphatic NO exclamation mark!! It was just a wee test but a lesson I would never forget. Frankie retains an ear for music that to me is out of this world, and as if to emphasise that he rejected my choice of the 'Long Way Home' version that I had recalled and shocked me by producing, from nowhere, a master recording with a completely different vocal which rattled the walls of his home - full blast! If I had any doubts about Frankie's ability to show that he was still a master of his craft, they were eradicated that morning!

Five days came and went and it was time to head back to Scotland. By then, 'Long Way Home' had established itself as favourite for an appropriate album title, and the next step for us was to decide on a design concept while Annette and Frankie decided on the final selection of songs.

I also fell in love with Frankie's version of 'You're the Star', which Rod Stewart had released as a single a few years back, and the version of 'He'll Have To Go' which had been recorded in Chatanooga with Fires Brimstone. We had the foundations of a potentially great album!

By luck one day as I was walking through Buchanan Galleries in Glasgow, I came across a painting which featured Frankie's home area of Bridgeton Cross. The painting is called Bridgeton Reflections by John M Boyd and to my mind would be a perfect backdrop to the *Long Way Home* theme.

Annette and Frankie loved it and we went about getting permission to reproduce the imagery for the cover. Result!!

In the meantime, we had struck up a friendship with the Quireboys and became regular guests at their gigs both in Glasgow and London. Their record company at the time, Jerkin' Crocus, said they would be interested in releasing Frankie's new album, so that really set the wheels in motion.

Billy Sloan in the *Sunday Mail*
It's Miller Time

SCOTS rock legend Frankie Miller is to release the album fans thought he would never live to hear. The singer has completed the CD *Long Way Home*.

"These are a collection of great songs recorded when Frankie was fit and well," said David Arthur, who handles incoming enquiries on the singer's website. "Frankie still has a lot of songs in the vaults he wants to work on. We hope to bring out more albums over the next few years."

The cover of *Long Way Home* will feature an archive painting of Bridgeton Cross in Glasgow, where the singer grew up.

The CD is being released on record label Jerkin' Crocus thanks to Mick Brown and will be mastered by US rock star Dan Baird of The Georgia Satellites.

David said: "Dan is a huge fan of Frankie's music. In 2005, when he visited the UK, he invited Frankie to one of his gigs and offered to help. 'Guilty of the Crime' had appeared on the *Robocop* TV series soundtrack album and a promo single CD was kicking around in the States."

Allan Laing

FRANKLY, it's the kind of news which makes you feel the opposite of what you should feel. You hear that Frankie Miller is releasing a new album and your heart sinks.

For a start, it can't be true. The boy from Bridgeton suffered a near-fatal stroke in 1994 which, sadly, has left him severely and, it seems, permanently disabled. A rare talent cut down in his prime. So for "new album" read "old stuff". B-movie material which has languished in the vaults for more than a decade. Why? Because it probably wasn't worth releasing in the first place. Which is the point where your heart sinks.

How wrong can you be. All you have to do is listen to the first few chords of the opening track, a blistering rock solid R&B song, 'Guilty of the Crime', and you swiftly realise that this ain't second-rate Frankie. This is vintage Miller and just about as good as he ever gave.

Dear Frankie Brings a Tear to the Eye Once Again
"The Glasgow pop legend has lost his extraordinary voice, but it lives on in a new collection of songs."

Fiona Shepherd's *Scotsman* review is included here because it came from the heart. Here is an excerpt:

It has been 20 years since his last album, *Dancing In The Rain*, but in the period prior to his stroke, Miller had established himself as a songwriter in Nashville and started work on a solo album, co-writing with Will 'Up Where We Belong' Jennings, and a band project, Fire and Brimstone, with Joe Walsh of the Eagles, Nicky Hopkins of the Jeff Beck Group, Ian Wallace, who has played with Bob Dylan and King Crimson, and bassist Chrissy Stewart, a long-term associate from the Frankie Miller Band.

Long Way Home has been compiled from this wealth of recorded material, and is an undeniable treasure trove for patient Miller fans, who will find this album impossible to approach without sentiment. Record companies are notorious for milking respected musicians' back pages dry after they have died. Let us, for once, enjoy the still-fresh fruits of an outstanding singer while he is alive and can take pride in this fertile cache.

From a review by Doug Collette at *All About Jazz*
Frankie Miller's fame, such as it is, derives from his 1978 hit 'Darlin', combined with songwriting credits for artists as diverse as Bob Seger and Bonnie Tyler.

The fancy digipak enclosing *Long Way Home* illustrates the duality of the music inside, as well as Miller's relative distinction: his hoarse voice is his most profound means of communication.

The front cover graphic outline of the Scotsman in a familiar bowler hat is in stark ghostly contrast to the inset 1977 stage photo of a vibrant young soul man at the top of his game.

Frankie Miller was stricken by a brain haemorrhage over fifteen years ago, shortly after most of these tracks were recorded. There is an undeniably sad irony in hearing him sing of personal reinvention in 'Guilty of the Crime', especially if you are a long-time fan of the artist.

Joe Walsh plays a perfectly drunken slide guitar on that tune, plus all the guitars on 'He'll Have to Go', where engineer Bill Szymczyk also lends the production talents the Eagles utilised so extensively.

Will Jennings, Miller's regular songwriting partner, plays and produces on *Long Way Home* too. And, as on 'Over the Line', the vocalist demonstrates how he meets the greatest challenge of the interpretive artist: to unify a variety of songs and styles through the strength of his own personality and performance.

Miller's gifts as a singer are such that he can bring a ring of truth to otherwise stock imagery, as with the gambling motif of 'Win Lose or Draw'.

He always sounds like he's singing as hard as he can, whether on mid tempo tunes like this or the markedly more subdued acoustic country waltz 'Lovin's Too Easy'.

Long Way Home is a testament to the living, breathing quality of music at its most inspirational. While on the one hand it's a tragedy that we may never see Miller perform the wrenching confessional that is 'The Rose', we must consider ourselves blessed to have this collection of songs to savour. It might be selfish to want more of the same, but that hope for something more is simply a reflection of the very foundation of Frankie Miller's personal and artistic ethos.

Long Way Home
Frankie Miller
by Doug D'Arcy

Long Way Home is Frankie Miller's first new album for twenty years. I've been listening to it and reflecting on his life whilst I recover from a back injury suffered when a wave rolled over me in India. I've known Frankie since he was in the Stoics, a Glasgow band that moved to London around 1970, changed their name, played the Isle of Wight festival and split up quite soon afterwards.

The Stoic philosophers who expressed the idea of enduring suffering without complaint may not have had in mind the dangers of getting up to sing in a Glasgow pub but there at least they were in the right area. In fact Frankie ended up singing in a London pub in Kentish Town called the Tally-Ho where a lively mix of Scottish roadies and Irish builders had chosen to congregate and drink.

They were part of an old story. When Scottish and Irish immigrants had travelled first to England, and later America, they brought with them their songs and melodies, and when they met the music of early Afro-American blues it created a mix, which is the basis of pretty much everything we think of as popular music today.

A typical example was 'The Unfortunate Rake', a funeral song that first appears in Cork in the 1790s, first written in the 'Irish Musical Repository' of 1808. It reappears in England in the mid-19th century as 'The Buck's Elegy' or 'The Unfortunate Lad', a cautionary story about the lethal dangers of sexually transmitted diseases, and the same song later appears in many different variations, 'a Trooper cut down in his Prime' or 'a Sailor cut down in his Prime' or even 'a Young Girl cut down in her Prime'.

They share the common theme of young people deprived early in life by such dangers as drink, gambling or simply ill health, and what goes with those risks and losses. The song becomes in America both a cowboy classic titled 'The Streets of Laredo' and the jazz classic 'St James Infirmary'.

Nick Tosches has followed many of these connections in his book *Country* if you want to know more. As he tells the story, words and melodies flip flop backwards and forwards between country and blues. This history shaped every part of the music, indeed one of Frankie Miller's greatest influences Ray Charles had himself yodelled in a hillbilly band the Florida Playboys, long before his greatest R&B innovations and success, and long long before he recorded one of Frankie's most enigmatic songs, 'I Can't Change It'.

In the 1970s I saw Scottish soul meeting the deep south yet again when Frankie joined Allen Toussaint to complete the writing of his *High Life* album in New Orleans, later to be recorded in Atlanta. Frankie's passionate and whole-hearted singing inspired that unfailingly courteous and charming southern gentleman who had spent his life steeped in the rhythm and blues of New Orleans.

Communication and mutual respect were instant, and whilst Frankie sweated away day after day in an unaccustomed heat and humidity, with the ever-cool Toussaint, they added yet more to the thread of that DNA which links our music consciousness to those early pioneers.

'Shoorah Shoorah', which wasn't a hit for Frankie, was for Betty Wright, which in the mid-80s Pauline Black of ska band the Selecter covered, and indulged me by allowing me to direct the promo in a garage in south London which passed, at least that day, for the French Quarter.

The migration has been constant. Van Morrison, Joe Cocker and the Average White Band all made that same journey, sharing musicians and friendship and a common purpose with each other.

Frankie wrote and recorded many songs and albums over the following years and toured a good deal before being stricken by a brain haemorrhage in New York in 1994. It was a terrible tumble. Our paths had crossed throughout a lot of this and there is plenty to say, never mind all the stories

I could tell, but also a great many musicians have come forward with their own testimony. What are we to make of his story? Well, the music is all there to be listened to.

I think of what Van Morrison called 'the secret heart of music' (or was it 'the sacred heart of music'?) that place where the long threads of the genetic code of notes and words forms itself into the body of our music. It's a place where most music traditions at their core find some common ground if they are performed with proper reverence and belief.

It's within that place that musicians, in my experience, really feel the need to connect, to participate, to belong, and it's to that body of music they must add in order to feel they have really and truly testified. Listening to the title song 'It's A Long Way Home' reminds me more forcefully than ever that whatever else has happened Frankie Miller has done that. Listen to 'It's A Long Way Home'.

Author's Note: Another interesting day in my life happened when I arranged to meet up with Terry Reid in Edinburgh during his 2008 tour. We had met a few years earlier and in the bar after his gig, the topic of conversation turned to Frankie Miller. That evening ended at 3am after a few cognacs and we have kept in touch since. A similar character to Frankie, Terry has a beautiful, distinctive singing style and has to be admired for sticking to his guns in the music industry and following his own career path. On the afternoon of his show at Cabaret Voltaire in my hometown, we sat together before the soundchecks and Terry, with his acoustic guitar in hand, started to sing me a song. "Well the drink's almost finished and the liquor store's closed. And the girl with the cheque book's gone to powder her nose."

I was in awe as Terry sang through the complete version of Frankie Miller's 'Lies Tell The Best Truth Of All'. An edited version had appeared on *Long Way Home* and here was Mr Reid reeling off the complete song with its extra three or four verses! I am guessing that the song comes from the days when Jude supported Terry Reid in London, or even further back to when Frankie and Terry Reid appeared on the same day at the 1970 Isle of Wight Festival.

I was in such a shock that day that I never got round to asking how the hell Terry knew the song, let alone be able to recite it in its entirety. Frankie and I had also managed (along with Paul Guerin) to get to a Terry Reid gig one time together at Dingwalls in London, but that's another story! We had brilliant fun at the quayside before the gig as Terry recited some Joe Walsh stories from their times together in Hollywood as well as some tales from the 1969 Rolling Stones USA tour on which Terry was a support act along with Ike and Tina Turner. He told us that he was smart enough to bail out before Altamont, thanks to some Ike Turner shenanigans. Terry Reid, another legend if ever there was one, that I had first seen perform in 1969 supporting Jethro Tull.

Terry Reid   Frankie Miller   Paul Gueren

Whilst the better known artists were rightly highlighted in the *Long Way Home* reviews it is worth drawing attention to the other key contributors:

Billy Livsey and Graham Lyle co-wrote 'You're the Star' with Frankie and also contributed keyboards and guitar.

Billy Livsey is an American songwriter, keyboardist and producer who has worked with a number of musicians including Tina Turner and Gallagher and Lyle. He played the keyboard solo on Tina Turner's 'What's Love Got To Do With It', on 'How Come' for Ronnie Lane and on hits for Gallagher and Lyle.

Scottish singer/songwriter Graham Lyle is perhaps best known for being part of musical duo Gallagher and Lyle, who worked together between the mid-sixties and 1980. Hits included 'Breakaway' and 'Heart on My Sleeve' (co-written by Billy Livsey).

Similarly to Frankie, Graham Lyle has had a number of his songs covered by artists including Etta James, Ray Charles and Rod Stewart. His most famous composition is 'What's Love Got To Do With It'.

Mike Brignardello - bass player. A quote from *Bass Player Magazine* describes him as follows: "His smooth vintage tone, his seemingly innate ability to know exactly when to play what, and his willingness to put the song above everything else is why he's credited on over 500 albums and countless demos coming out of Nashville."

Chad Cromwell is an American rock drummer whose music career has spanned more than 30 years. He has toured and recorded with Neil Young, Joe Walsh, Mark Knopfler, Joss Stone, Stevie Nicks, Bonnie Rait and Crosby Stills and Nash.

Other musical contributors include Nick Zala, David Naughton and Scottish drummer Jamie Morrison.

Jamie Morrison is best known as drummer for Welsh band The Stereophonics, whom he joined in 2012.

I also had several tears in my eyes when Mick Brown sent me through samples of the artwork for the *Long Way Home* booklet to check over. Annette and Frankie had dedicated the album to me… and christened me 'The Keeper of the Flame.' That tribute will live with me forever.

March 2006

Not only had we got *Long Way Home* completed, but March the same year saw the funeral of Frankie's great friend Jimmy Johnstone, the wonderful Celtic and Scottish international footballer. It coincided with my birthday that weekend so Frankie and Annette's visit to Glasgow was a sad/happy affair, with the funeral on the 17th and my birthday on the 18th.

We had booked a number of tickets and a table at the Renfrew Ferry to see Maggie Bell with the Hamburg Blues Band, and it was lovely to see Frankie and Maggie meeting up again after so long.

Classic Rock Awards

November 6th 2006 *Classic Rock* Awards, Langham Hotel, London
Hosted by Andy Copping

We had been invited down to the *Free Forever* DVD Launch at The Paper/Cafe Royal, London, on Thursday 7 September 2006.

As we made our way downstairs (myself, my good friend Gordon Grubb, Annette and Frankie), we were greeted and welcomed by Andy Fraser and his lovely LA based manageress.

We were then escorted into a back-room bar, with a full view of the evening's proceedings, and where a number of Frankie's close friends were waiting, including drummer Simon Kirke and Doug D'Arcy.

During the evening, Mick Brown from Jerkin' Crocus asked if we would like an invitation to the *Classic Rock* Awards later in the year, and of course we were thrilled to accept. So another adventure was coming up for 'the naïve brothers', Gordon Grubb and Davy Arthur.

We had flown down to Heathrow on the morning of the 6th with an arrangement to meet Annette and Frankie in the hotel, some time before thereception.

CLASSIC ROCK ROLL OF HONOUR
The Langham Hotel, 6th Nov 2006

TABLE 1	TABLE 2	TABLE 3	TABLE 4	TABLE 5	TABLE 6	TABLE 7
Andy Copping	David Coverdale	Ronnie James Dio	Simon Carver	Chris Ingham	Sefton Woodhouse	David Ridings
Jo Jagger	Cindy Coverdale	Wendy Dio	Rashmi Patani	Al King	Susie Ember	Lou Maloney
Justin Lee Collins	Rod MacSween	Neil Warnock	Bill Edwards	Marcus Ehresmann	Scott Steele	Phil Matchan
Libby Spirits	Tony Zivanaris	Scott Sentinello	Gerry Kelly	Dave Shack	Paul Guimaraes	Darren Haynes
Gerry Slater	Linda Zivanaris	Samantha Henfrey	Mark Palmer	Claire Higgens	William Luff	James Dowdall
Mr Marnworth	Jessica Schroeder	Steve Guest	Michelle Kerr	Sarah Brown	Paul Fletcher	Rose Noone
Mrs Marnworth	Glenn Hughes	Sacha Levy	Kirsten Lane	Lindsay Brown	Debra Geddes	David Bianchi
Johnny Rocher	Mike Moore	Derek Kemp	Derek Oliver	Nicola Munns	Jason Day	Richard England
Ritchie Heavern	Carl Swann	Danny Nozell	Dante Bonutto	Andy McIntyre	Caryn Tomlinson	Jaz Coleman
Sid Glover	Karen Swann	Steve Homer	Lite Kromrey	Michele Clark	Amy Catlin	Ali Walker
Rob Randell	Marco Pierre White	Olly Hahn	Juliette Avery	Annick Barborio	Deby Fairley	Des Murphy
Chris Rivers	Jo Headland	Maria Oullette	David Bower	Ian Rowe	Deborah Armstrong	Jamie Hibbard

TABLE 8	TABLE 9	TABLE 10	TABLE 11	TABLE 12	TABLE 13	TABLE 14
Erik James	Alice Cooper	Ian Hunter	Joe Black	Andy Rust	John Deyland	Lisa Beardsley
Rick Conrad	Toby Morris	Trudi Hunter	Silvia Montello	Simon Parker	Sarah Waddington	Dan Tobin
James Denton	Sir Tim Rice	Tracie Hunter	Lisa McErlain	Simon Maxwell	Chris Hewlett	Giles Green
Joe Anditti	Isabella Duncan	Mick Ralphs	Deb Saunders	Jason Mather	Steve Fenter	Nick Bourne
Philomena Lynott	Sharon Chevin	Campbell Devine	Pete Hill	John Robson	Ian Richards	Jon Richards
Sean Meaney	Justine Ellis	Carl Palmer	Azi Eftakhari	Rob Price	Geoff Downes	Gavin Hilzbrich
Martin Moxon	Sara Bricusse	Katie Palmer	Jon Norman	Adrian Camp	Martin Darvill	Claire Jones
Matt Millbank	Brian May	H. Harbinson	Trevor White	Colvin Hewitt	Steve Houre	Steve Hammond
Holly Fox-Wilcocks	Louisa May	Steve Strange	Nick Hirst	Nicky Hewitt	John Wetton	Jessie Reynolds
Dave Headicar	Emily May	Darren Edwards	Phil Shade	Tim Caple	Nils Moore	Marc Beard
Ian Huffam	Jim Beach	Alan Jones	John Mistrally	Jayne Caple	Kas Mercer	Pippa Moye
Karen Johnson	Viktorija Mamh	David Blizzard	Dan Connealy	Tony Havelhead	Eddie Schilloce	Jean-Claude Mighty

TABLE 15	TABLE 16	TABLE 17	TABLE 18	TABLE 19	TABLE 20	TABLE 21	TABLE 22
Scott Gorham	Bruce Dickinson	Chris Squire	Fifa Riccobono	Frankie Miller	Paul Quinn	Byron Carr	Carl Stroud
Harry Doherty	Paddy Dickinson	Scotland Square	David Albert	Annette Miller	Doug Scarrot	Max Kemp	Serena Davies
Christine Gorham	Adrian Smith	Jeff Beck	Vishti Albert	Mich Browne	Nibbs Carter	Nicola Slade	
Denis O'Regan	Natalie Smith	Ralph Baker	James Cassidy	Zal Cleminson	Nigel Glockler	Jean Garcia	Laura K Jones
Duff Battye	Dave Pottenden	Sandra Beck	Ann Cassidy	Chris Glenn	Harvey Goldsmith	Ian Rosher	Pierre Perrone
Chris O'Donnell	Val James	Siân Llewellyn	Cormac Nieson	Paul Henderson	Biff Byford	Adam Coles	Sean Hamilton
Luke Morley	John Jackson	Martin Talbot	Michael Waters	Martin Jarvis	Roland Hyams	Steve Poarch	Hugo Rifkind
Danny Bowes	Rod Smallwood	Helen Marquis	Will Moya	Kirsten Jarvis	Jessie Hope-Wetton	Giles Ellis	Alex Marnfield
Malcolm McKenzie	David Galvin	Mark Stuart-Wood	Tim Hall	James Brown	Jayne Andrew	Allison Page	Alun Palmer
Peter Shoulder	Mark Eurich	Robin Docksey	Catrina Naylor	Davy Arthur	Geoff Barton	Clara Trng	Simon Rothstein
Scott Rowley	Dorian Dugmore	Ian Camfield	Paul Mahon	Gordon Grubb	Tony Wilson	Peter Christoper	Anita Singh
Jeff Chauncey	Bill Griffiths	Mark Kirtland	James Heatsly	Bruce McKenzie	Ian Portnorn	Aine Marsland	Steven Berkoff
			Dave Bedford				
			Ruth Storrs				

Checking in late afternoon, we were able to peek in on the preparations that were on going in the large ballroom where the awards were taking place. On the two large entrance pillars were the table plans.

We knew in advance that Alice Cooper would be there (to receive a lifetime achievement award) but although that was exciting enough in its own right, we were totally unprepared and hadn't put too much thought into who else might be there.

Brian May, Roger Taylor from Queen, Ian Hunter, Mick Ralphs, Scott Gorham, Jeff Beck! Jeff Beck did it for me... starstruck and now nervous as a kitten!

Gordon commented, as we read through the guest list excitedly, "How did two dafties like us get in here son?"

We made our way down to the cocktail bar and shared a table away in the far corner from the entrance with Chris Glen, Zal Cleminson and co from SAHB. Naturally, we were all in high spirits as we awaited Frankie's arrival.

The room was filling up nicely and as the room got noisier and noisier (lots of Japanese business types too) I glanced over to the bar and in walks Jeff Beck and lady and props himself up a few yards away from us.

Next thing I know is Annette and Frankie have appeared at the entrance and all I hear is "Davy Arthur, where have you been?"

I had been awaiting their call so I could go down and help Frankie in, but in all the excitement and probable loss of signal on the phone, I suddenly felt flushed as I pushed my way past the other drinkers (keeping my head down to as I excused myself to Mr Beck...).

So we said our hellos and exchanged hugs and then I grabbed Frankie's wheelchair. Well of course, as we manoeuvred through the busy bar, where not too many seated customers were aware of our attempts to get to the other side of the room, I wheeled left and drove right over Jeff Beck's toes! I blurted out "Sorry mate!" as we shoved past but I would get my chance to explain who the hell we were later! His polite nod and smile gave me some temporary relief to my utter embarrassment.

As the invited guests started to gather and be very slowly ushered in to their tables it was an amazing sea of familiar faces. One moment we were rubbing shoulders with Tim Rice and his wife, then I spotted Philomena Lynott a few paces away.

I couldn't help myself from approaching and pointing out Frankie to her. She was delighted and immediately asked Sean Meaney (her escort for the evening) to scribble down her phone number for me! She said she would like to come to Henry's gigs with us in Ireland when we came over. We were not even inside yet!

The awards were preceded by a beautiful dinner, and then when the formalities began, so did the fun!

The award winners:
- Best New Band: Roadstar
- Album of The Year: *A Matter of Life and Death* by Iron Maiden
- Band of the Year: Whitesnake
- Best Reissue: *A Night at the Opera* by Queen
- DVD of the Year: *Live... In the Still of the Night* by Whitesnake
- Event of the Year: Return of Monsters of Rock
- Classic Songwriter: Queen
- Comeback of the Year: New York Dolls
- VIP Award: Rod Smallwood
- Tommy Vance Inspiration: Phil Lynott
- Classic Album: *Hysteria* by Def Leppard
- Metal Guru: Ronnie James Dio
- Living Legend: Alice Cooper

For me personally there were several highlights.

The main one, of course, was the privilege of being at a table with Frankie Miller and his other guests, but during the evening there were several wonderful speeches plus opportunities to mingle with the other guests.

Roger Taylor entertained us with some Queen stories, as did Scott Gorham for Thin Lizzy. Bruce Dickinson from Iron Maiden came across as a very witty and intelligent guy as he recalled some of his many flying escapades (he carries a full pilot's licence). Alice Cooper humbly accepted the Living Legend award.

Speech of the night, though, and last one before the interval came, was from Philomena Lynott, at which point I slipped quietly between the tables to get a perfect vantage point for some photographs.

You couldn't hear a pin drop in the room as she spoke fondly of her son "Phillip", during which she pointed down to a table in front of the stage and said to Brian May and Roger Taylor of Queen that she knew that her son had made it in the rock world when Thin Lizzy and Queen toured the USA together in 1977.

Then, in her beautiful, soft Irish accent, she quietly recalled an evening when backstage, during an after-show party, she spotted a quiet young guy, sitting in the corner of the room. She said, "He was wearing a T shirt that quite offended me. It said on the front 'Frankie Who' and on the back, 'Frankie Fucking Miller...That's Who!'"

She then pointed across to Frankie's table and said, "And he's here tonight, and he's one the greatest singers ye'll ever hear!" What a brave and generous woman to turn the spotlight on to Frankie. And what a way to finish her speech, which was greeted with a standing ovation. As she made her way across the floor towards us, I couldn't help but approach and give her a big hug. She whispered in my ear, "I'm just going for a pee, I'll be back in a few minutes."

During the interval, as guests mingled and the artists posed for their official *Classic Rock* photographs, I got my chance to have a chat with Jeff Beck and apologise for running him over in the bar earlier. A huge grin appeared on his face when I explained that it was Frankie Miller who had introduced me to his *Truth* album (from the stage) back in the late 60s. He also responded by saying, "Not a bad album, was it?"

That's an understatement, Jeff! He then went on to recall how he had been sacked from the Yardbirds and Rod Stewart from Long John Baldrey's band, and that's how the two came together!

I then asked if he would oblige by coming to our table as Frankie couldn't mingle so easily and I was blown away when he agreed. So during that interval we had Jeff Beck, Alice Cooper, Philomena, Scott Gorham, Brian May, Ian Hunter and a host of others dropping in to see Frankie.

With Chris Glen and Zal Cleminson already at our table… one can only imagine!

As the evening wound down, yet another unexpected comment came from a guy we shared the lift with as I was seeing Annette and Frankie safely off the premises.

It was the editor from *Classic Rock* magazine, who told me he had got into the business because of Frankie Miller. So God bless you.

Postscript: A day or so after getting back to Scotland, when I phoned Frankie's home number, Annette told me an astonishing story. I didn't know whether to laugh or cry. Allen Toussaint had been in London on the same night as the awards and had phoned…to find nobody home!

On checking, I discovered that he had played in Berlin the night before and stopped off in London before flying back to New Orleans. What an addition he would have been to our table!

Jeff Beck Frankie Miller

Eagles Connection

Sunday Mail May 2009

Billy Sloan interviewed Joe Walsh for the *Sunday Mail* in May 2009 during the run-up to the Eagles show at Hampden Park in Glasgow in front of 50,000 fans.

"Joe would only have one man on his mind... Scots music legend Frankie Miller. Joe jumped at the chance to appear at the national stadium on July 4th as a personal tribute to Frankie.

"Joe said: 'I'm playing this gig for my friend Frankie. I'm totally in awe of him. The first time I heard his amazing voice it made the hairs on the back on my neck stand up. Frankie hit a nerve in my soul. I didn't know if he was black or white. I heard this incredible soulful, almost spiritual voice and couldn't believe it came from a guy from Glasgow. I've never heard anybody sing like that'."

Saturday 4th July 2009 The Eagles Hampden Park Glasgow and Mr Joe Walsh
Another memorable weekend was spent in Frankie's company in Glasgow. To be invited by Annette and Frankie to the Eagles show at Hampden and in the company of some of his best friends; to meet Joe Walsh again and to walk down the players' tunnel with Frankie - can life really get better !!??

We were joined in the secure area by Joe's wife Marjorie, younger sister of Barbara Bach - and she was a bundle of fun during the show.

Barbara Bach, of course, was co-star with Roger Moore in the 1977 Bond movie *The Spy Who Loved Me* and the wife of one Ringo Starr - and Marjorie made us smile afterwards, as she was escorted off by security to meet up with the private jet which would whisk them off south for Ringo's birthday party, due the next day.

The top moment was of course when Joe announced 'Guilty of the Crime'. Joe had persuaded fellow Eagles band members to record the track for their multi-million selling 2007 CD, *Long Road Out Of Eden* – and they performed it at Hampden.

Joe said: "Frankie used up a lot of his financial reserves paying for medical treatment in America so I thought I'd put a word in with the Eagles on his behalf and help him out. I wanted to record the songs as my tribute to a great singer and a great man. And a damn good song it is too. Glenn, Don and Tim fell in love with it and we're playing it every night. "

Joe Walsh

In 2008 Joe married Marjorie Bach, sister of actress Barbara who is wed to ex-Beatle, Ringo Starr. The guitarist has been sober since 1995. He claimed he only ever got drunk once but that it lasted for 25 years. His hit song 'One Day At A Time' deals with his struggles with booze and drugs.

Joe said: "The booze was getting too much. I'd lost my perspective on life. I was drinking all the time and had taken it as far as I could. My quality of life was totally falling apart. I was dependent on booze and knew I was in trouble. When it started messing with my health I figured I had to stop but I wasn't sure I could. I had a great party and great run at it but it had got the better of me.

"Now, life is much better. I feel more healthy and strong." Joe added: "A lot of the guys I ran with – such as Keith Moon – are dead. The Eagles are one of the few bands around where nobody has died yet. I nearly ruined my life with alcohol and drugs. So now I'm a person people will turn to if they're in trouble with that stuff. I've been able to help a whole bunch of people."

Earlier in his amazing career, Joe set out to help the American people when he twice ran for President.

In 1980 – and again 12 years later – he campaigned to enter The White House on a ticket of "Free Gas For Everyone."

He claimed if elected he'd make his hit song 'Life's Been Good' the new US national anthem. But there was a serious message behind his light-hearted campaign.

He said: "I'd love to be President for a day because part of the problem in 1980 was apathy – nobody cared, nobody voted and nobody believed in the government.

"What I was really trying to do was get people up off their backsides. I campaigned actively and it was great fun, I went out into the streets with a bullhorn and placards saying : Vote For Joe Walsh.

"I got a reaction and that's exactly what I was trying to do." Joe did get to The White House years later when the Eagles were invited to the Oval Office by huge fan Bill Clinton. He said: "I thought the Oval Office would be really regal and grand but it was just a little room with a desk and a couple of couches.

"It was great being there because the place has such a mystique about it. I got to know Bill Clinton really well and found out that secretly he was an even bigger fan of my previous band, The James Gang." At the time of his interview, the guitarist was optimistic about President Barack Obama and felt the US was on the verge of a great new beginning.

He said: "George Bush and his administration really did not represent the way this country feels. We were all being judged by Bush's actions and that's a shame. I think Obama has reversed a very dangerous path we were going down. He's a fresh start for us. Everybody is behind him.

"It's scary because he wants to change things and Congress is going: 'We kinda like it as it is'.

"But it's 2009, we've got to change. I never thought I'd see a black African-American as President in my lifetime. That's the most significant change of all. It's a good thing and Obama seems to be a good man. Bush went into The White House and disappeared for eight years. He ran things like a gentleman's club. It had to stop."

Quireboys Connection

Brian Robertson came up to Glasgow, I guess sometime in late 1994 or early 1995, to play at the Cathouse. I had met the owner, Robert Fields, somewhere along the line and contacted him to get into the club in the afternoon in order to ambush Robbo. Ambush him we did, and it was quite emotional because it was the first time I had seen him since Frankie's Renfrew Ferry gigs in 1993.

Anyhow, we hugged and shed a few tears and he said, "Come with me, I've got somebody for you to meet." He took me round the corner into the lounge bar and introduced me to his parents. What a lovely couple; and they welcomed me into their company with open arms. They knew all about my friendship with Frankie and even asked if I would send them a copy of my last fan magazine for their memorabilia collection. It made for a really nice afternoon before Ain't Lizzy took to the stage. Bass player, Wayne Ellis - who had previously won a Phil Lynott lookalike competition - certainly looked and played the part, and it really was an authentic Thin Lizzy tribute.

Brian Robertson Paul Gueren

Robbo also sang 'Jealousy' that night as a nod to Frankie. Before I knew it I was drinking with the guys upstairs and got friendly with Robbo's current manager, Pete Schofield, who told me that there was a new band being formed called The Clan which would feature a mixture of Thin Lizzy and Frankie Miller music.

Next thing I knew, I had a fax of their tour itinerary, which included gigs in Holland. Without Robbo knowing, I planned with Pete's office to make my way to the Zal Struik Club in Heino and ambush Mr Robertson again… I don't remember too much about the four days but the gig was great. A lovely young Geordie lad by the name of Paul Guerin was also in The Clan. To cut a long story short, we retained our friendship, and Paul ended up joining the Quireboys in 2003.

I caught up with the guys one night at The Garage in Glasgow and all I remember is the mayhem in the dressing room afterwards. Ted McKenna was with us that night too.

Naturally Frankie Miller's name came up and the conversation went something like: "Wouldn't it be great to do an album of Frankie's music?"(It was actually Mr Nigel Mogg who first put forward the idea with great enthusiasm.)

These things take time but eventually something did happen!

I had gone down to London to stay at Frankie's for a few days (to help select songs for what would become *Long Way Home*) and during my stay Paul invited me over to his place at New King's Road one day, for lunch.

It turned into a marathon session as we listened to a load of Frankie's songs that I had taken to him that afternoon as possibly suitable for the Quireboys. Paul played live guitar solos over the breaks in these songs and for me it was a fairly mesmerising experience!

He was also working downstairs at the vintage guitar shop during that period in his career, so we popped in to say hello to the guys. As we sat in the back office, chatting to everyone, a guy called Blane "Beej" Chaney joined our company.

Blane had come over from Malibu, California, where, he told me, he owned a recording studio. He said he was over shopping for instruments and that he only used traditional analogue equipment for recording. He shook my hand and looked me in the eye and said something like: "Wow! I can see in your eyes that I can trust you. You have a warm heart." He then handed me something that resembled a peace-pipe and said, "Smoke this as a bond of our friendship." It won't come as a surprise that I lost his business card but I hope he remembers me!

It was only later that Paul told me that Mark Knopfler had recently recorded there and that the studios in question were the Shangri-La studios, which had also been used by Bob Dylan and the Band (they resided there for a long while), Eric Clapton, Ronnie Wood and Van Morrison. Blane had loaded it with the premium vintage audio equipment that is still in use today, including the centrepiece API 32 BUS console.

After missing my teatime back at Frankie's (and rudely not phoning to say I was still in one piece), the remainder of the evening is a blur. I remember being alone and shit scared in an empty tube station somewhere and catching the last train back to Maida Vale!

I must have bought a fish supper somewhere on the way up the road because it was still hot and squashed under my arm when I rang Frankie's doorbell.

Annette went to bed and Frankie and I devoured the fish and chips! Frankie then proceeded to show me how to melt frozen Snickers bars in a microwave and we finished our midnight feast with melted chocolate bars and ice cream. Then it was back to the business of listening to his songs into the late night.

When I woke up on Frankie's couch next morning my T shirt was covered in chocolate stains and I remember Annette asking me if I had had a nice time! I still blush at the thought of that moment!

A Quote From Spike, Lead Singer of The Quireboys

"Frankie just wants his music to be heard. These songs have never been heard before and they've been recorded with Frankie's blessing. They are songs that would have been lost if it wasn't for the desire of a group of his closest friends and biggest fans to do them justice. Frankie Miller was – and still is – a massive influence on so many musicians, myself included. He has a special talent as a songwriter and that talent deserves to be celebrated."

100% Frankie Miller features Ronnie Wood, Andy Fraser, Bonnie Tyler, Simon Kirke, Ian Hunter, Luke Morley, Guy Griffin, Keith Weir, Paul Guerin, Tyla, Chris Corney, Mark Stanway, Mick Roobotham, Matt Goom, Pat McManus, Lorraine Crosby, Stuart Emerson, Cherry Lee Mewis, Simon Hanson and Jimi The Piper. In May 2024, The Quireboys released a single called 'Raining Whisky' featuring Frankie Miller. The song also features on their *Wardour Street* album.

Frankie Miller's Double Take

In March 2014, a *Mojo* magazine article mentioned that a new album was on the way, to be overseen by Ray Minhinnett and David Mackay. The plan was to build new arrangements around vocals carefully lifted from Frankie's home demo archive.

The idea for the album came about when Rod Stewart asked producer David Mackay if he had any unreleased songs by Frankie. David reached out to Annette and Frankie, who provided a bag of demo tapes which were then used to piece together a brilliant album comprised of previously-unreleased material expanded with high-profile guest appearances.

Ray had earlier mentioned to me on the phone that there was a documentary planned to coincide with the album. He asked me whether I would do an interview to give the fans' side of the Frankie Miller story, and also asked me who else could be interviewed in Scotland if the camera crew were to come up. We discussed Ted McKenna, Dan McCafferty and Pete Agnew because of their association going back to the 60s - they would have some amusing stories to tell.

Unfortunately, when I contacted them they were unavailable (at the time) for different reasons.

Annette and Frankie were doing their best to keep me up to date with the project's progress and in early 2016 they asked if I had any suitable photos for the album cover. Not a 70s image, Annette said - I think she wanted to get away from the old pictures and use a more recent, 90s shot. When I asked what the album was going to be called, we realised that there wasn't a title yet, so I offered to go away and have a think about a suitable title and appropriate imagery.

Obviously, if there were to be duets on the album, it had to be something appropriate. I hit on the idea of "Double Take" — all the obvious "duets" titles had been done in the past, and when I looked up the Dictionary.com definition for "Double Take" I was convinced that I had a winner:

"a rapid or surprised second look, either literal or figurative, at a person or situation whose significance had not been completely grasped at first"

It was Frankie to a T, in my opinion.

Annette and Frankie loved it.
I combed through my archive for a cover image, and in spite of what Annette had said, I kept coming back to a shot from 1979, a black and white image which caught Frankie in a quiet moment on stage, when he wasn't screaming into his microphone. I persuaded Annette that it was better than

any more recent pictures, and when I sent it to the designer, Mark Todd, he presented the concept beautifully as follows:

"The double image is an attempt to capture the essence of man and music, not a direct representation of one point in time. A single image would be referential to that one moment the photograph was taken. There is an atmospheric quality among all of the images treated this way that serves as essence and memory.

"Specifically referring to the 'Double Take' concept, the pose suggests Frankie at a moment of self-reflection. A second look that he has taken of himself. But in addition, emphasises this second look at the whole of his talent through this release and obviously (thirdly) the reference to the duets themselves.

"The image portrays Frankie in a classic stance, mic. in hand, a characteristic scarf (as he was always well dressed on stage)…all icons of the man.

"Further, as David Shields has stated, 'It's like looking through a dirty pub window before going in for the best night of your life'…a good description. A simple black and white photo may not embrace that."

Mark is a retired professor of Art and Design at Texas University and a big fan of Frankie; he did all the graphic design for *Double Take* and also wrote some sleeve notes for the booklet:

A4 on the jukebox. And the first time you hear the voice it knocks you over. It resonates as the best voice you've ever heard. Frankie who? Frankie F*****n' Miller, that's who!

It's a voice full of worry, regret, passion and pride. One that's salty and sweet. A voice you can admire in and of itself - that tells the story completely - even without the lyric. It falls apart at just the right moment and then rises, just as you think it's gone.

But then the songs are another matter. There are songs here that you've never heard, but it's as if you've had them in the inner corner of your mind. The craft of songwriting is tricky, that in the hands of less skilled practitioners, shows self-consciousness and effort. But in Frankie's hands, the songs sound effortless and natural.

His storytelling leaves you reading between the lines, where the best of literature and art resides. And it's there, between those lines, that you find the depth in the voice - so much being communicated through inflection and pause. It's the marriage of this stellar songwriting with the voice that is magical and secures a special place in music history for Frankie.

The fact that Frankie's back catalogue of demos is so extensive is a testament to his uncharted talent and his passion for his life's work. We are honoured here to get a glimpse into that catalogue through the efforts of his musician friends - those who wanted to pay tribute to Frankie and are indeed fortunate enough to share "the stage" with him.

It is through their admiration and true affection that this collection and its documentation (in the form of the film *Sending Me Angels*) come to us. In an effort to insure his legacy for history and to serve as a special introduction to those who have not heard him, these recordings have been reclaimed.

Those who were not fortunate enough to see him perform live, this is as close as we get for now. It's like rubbing the grime off a window in a pub in Glasgow to have a look, before you go in for what turns out to be the best evening of your life.

Mark Todd

Mark and I were immediately drafted into the team and spent the next six months or so communicating almost daily, with Universal Music, Dave Mackay, and Annette and Frankie.

Some of my favourite quotes from the *Sending Me Angels* documentary:

Huey Lewis loved Frankie's lyric on 'Way Past Midnight', suggesting that it contained the best first line ever: "I'm back on the street again, where the disappointed take a bow".

Joe Walsh on Frankie in the studio: "He usually would take one take - there are singers who can do that - Frank Sinatra was like that - come in, sing it, I'm done, and Frankie was that good! It was just magic!"

Elton John: "I was bowled over by this man who had written all these great songs."

The following are excerpts from *Double Take* reviews:

"The list of esteemed guests lining up to duet with Frankie Miller on this album speaks volumes of the high regard in which he's held by fellow musicians – Rod Stewart, Elton John, Willie Nelson, and Steve Cropper among them. Pairing him with similarly gritty vocalists (Bonnie Tyler, Kim Carnes, John Parr) is another smart move. A fitting tribute and a welcome opportunity to hear Miller's unreleased songs and performances."

Rich Davenport *Record Collector*

"This album is a triumph.

"Everyone has done their bit to honour the music and the man. The result is a record that hums with excitement and does Miller proud. Of course, his voice is on everything, but you hear him alongside Rod Stewart, Joe Walsh, Elton John and Francis Rossi, among others, as if it's the most natural thing in the world.

"Every aspect of Miller's style is represented, and just to round it off there's 'I Do', which has him on his own. A brilliant addition to the Miller legend."

Edited from Malcolm Dome *Classic Rock* 26 September 2016

"Rod Stewart was obviously influenced by Miller, a contemporary, but 'Mod 'Rod's vocals could never hold a candle to Frankie's incredible soulfulness.

"Nonetheless, Stewart musters a spectacular performance on the duet 'Kiss Her For Me'.

"Kudos to producer David MacKay, who also contributes his not-inconsiderable musical talents to most of these songs.

"Frankie Miller's *Double Take* may be the best album he ever made."
Rev. Keith A. Gordon thatdevilmusic.com

In the accompanying documentary DVD, *Sending Me Angels*, which accompanied *Double Take* in the deluxe package, Joe Walsh (God bless him) did his best to explain how music files were sent back and forward between the participating artists and eventually returned to producer David Mackay at the studio HQ in England.

Each number had its own core contributors (both vocalists and musicians) with David Mackay and his team ready to add any additional parts (backing vocals, additional instrumentation etc.)

Double Take - the Track List
In the same running order as on the album - each track featuring Frankie Miller and a guest artist:

1. 'Blackmail' (featuring Joe Walsh)
Joe Walsh is featured elsewhere in the book but may be best known for his contribution to *Hotel California*.

Frankie Miller once told the author of this book that "Joe Walsh made the Eagles."

Drummer Bob Jenkins is a British session drummer/percussionist who has recorded or performed with an impressive number of artists including Labi Siffre, The Three Degrees, Sandie Shaw, Kiki Dee, Elton John, Chris Norman, Andy Williams, Van Morrison, Roger Chapman, Jimmy Witherspoon, Jack Bruce, Johnny Nash, and Andy Fairweather-Low.

Lorraine Crosby is an English singer/songwriter. She was the female vocalist on Meat Loaf's 1993 hit 'I'd Do Anything For Love' and has recorded and performed with Bonnie Tyler. Husband Stuart Emerson (a background vocalist and session musician) also features.

Bass: Chrissy Stewart
Synths and percussion: David Mackay

2. 'Where Do the Guilty Go?' (featuring Elton John and Steve Cropper)
Elton John, Steve Cropper and Ray Minhinnet need no further introductions but Malcolm Bruce, son of the great Jack Bruce, features here on bass guitar. Jack had also committed to partake in a duet with Frankie on another song, but sadly left us before he could record his vocal.

Choir: Jubilation were recorded in Sydney, Australia, and can be seen on the *Sending Me Angels* DVD

3. 'Way Past Midnight' (featuring Huey Lewis)
This track features Huey Lewis and his Brass "Sports" Section who also feature on the DVD.

Tenor Sax: Johnny Colla; Baritone Sax: Johnny Bamont; Trumpet: Marvin McFadden

Guitar: Geoff Whitehorn and Bob Huff

Geoff Whitehorn is the better known of the featured guitarists and is actually the longest serving member of Procol Harum after Gary Brooker. Geoff also recorded ten albums with Roger Chapman. Whitehorn has also contributed to the recordings and performances of other artists, such as Jethro Tull, The Who, Roger Waters, Manfred Mann's Earth Band, Paul McCartney, Billy Ocean and Paul Rodgers.

4. 'True Love' (featuring Bonnie Tyler)
Bass: Chrissy Stewart
Drums: Bob Jenkins
Guitar: Jerry Stevenson is an English guitar and mandolin player who has worked with Barbara Dickson and Procol Harum. Jerry also features in interview on *Sending Me Angels*.

Piano: Ian Stuart Lynn. Ian also features on the DVD and was responsible for the majority of the film production.

5. 'Kiss Her for Me' (featuring Rod Stewart and Joe Walsh)
The main men need no further introduction and are ably backed by the previously mentioned Chrissy Stewart, Bob Jenkins, David Mackay, Ian Stuart Lynn and Jerry Stevenson.

6. 'Gold Shoes' (featuring Francis Rossi)
Francis Rossi from Status Quo features here, and as well as duetting with Frankie, plays guitar, bass and organ.

His interview on the *Sending Me Angels* documentary is filled with humour and worth checking out.

Mark Prentice is a Grammy-winning record producer, an in-demand studio musician, music director, and hit songwriter for Bruce Springsteen, John Fogarty, Vince Gill, Johnny Cash, Felix Cavaliere and a whole lot more.

7. 'Sending Me Angels' (featuring Kiki Dee and José Antonio Rodríguez)
Kiki Dee is an English pop singer. Known for her blue-eyed soul vocals, she was the first female singer from the UK to sign with Motown's Tamla Records, having previously been a backing singer for Dusty Springfield.

She is best known for her 1973 hit 'Amoureuse', her 1974 hit 'I've Got the Music in Me', and 'Don't Go Breaking My Heart', her 1976 duet with Elton John, which went to number one on both the UK Singles Chart and the US Billboard Hot 100 chart. In 1993, she performed another duet with Elton for his *Duets* album, a cover version of Cole Porter's 'True Love', which reached number two in the UK. During her career, she has released 40 singles, three EPs and twelve albums.

José Antonio Rodríguez Muñoz is a flamenco guitarist, composer and music professor from Córdoba, Spain.

8. 'Jezebel Jones' (featuring Kid Rock)

Kid Rock (from biography.com) is an American singer, musician and record producer who came to fame with his unique blend of rap, heavy metal and country rock.

Kid Rock's musical journey is one that has encompassed underground Detroit rap, heavy metal and country rock, and by finding the perfect blend of all three, he turned an underwhelming career into a huge success. From early controversy over sexualised lyrics to selling 35 million records worldwide and marrying (and divorcing) Pamela Anderson, it's been a wild ride for one of the wild men of rap.

Drums: Andy Golden. Andy gained a wealth of experience by drumming for seminal guitarist Mick Green (Johnny Kidd and the Pirates) for three years and recording with Eric Bell, ex–Thin Lizzy. He also wrote songs, composed music for orchestras and dabbled in music production.

Andy sadly passed away in 2024.

9. 'When It's Rockin' (featuring Steve Dickinson and Full House)

Vocalist with The Reed And Dickinson Band, Steve Dickinson is a prolific Canadian singer-songwriter. His crisp, clear vocals and melodic roots type songs feel reminiscent of his influences, Bob Seger, John Mellencamp and Van Morrison. Alto Reed of Bob Seger's Silver Bullet Band, who was a good friend of Frankie Miller's, recorded a disc on TGIF Records with Steve, 'Tonight We Ride'.

Jimmy "Bones" Trombly

Jimmie Bones (born James Trombly) is the organ/piano/keyboard/harmonica player in Kid Rock's Twisted Brown Trucker Band. The two met while Kid Rock was recording 'Early Mornin' Stoned Pimp' at Detroit's White Room Studio in 1995.

Matt Winch on trumpet

He has performed and arranged for artists such as Bill Wyman's Rhythm Kings, Eric Clapton, Robin Gibb (Bee Gees), Andy Fairweather Low and Paulo Nutini.

Nick Pentelow on baritone sax

Nick is a prolific horn player who has appeared in an impressive number of lineups since the 1970s including Roy Wood's Wizzard, Steve Gibbons Band, Juice on the Loose, Gary Moore's Midnight Blues Band. In the late 90s he performed for Gary Brooker and Roger Chapman.

He also played alongside a number of Frankie Miller's ex-colleagues including Clive Bunker, Fran Byrne, Micky Moody, Paul Carrack and Steve Simpson.

Nick Payn

Saxophonist, flutist and harmonica player, Nick Payn (or Payne) is a famous session musician who's played with almost everyone, live or in studio.

He also appeared in Gary Moore's Midnight Blues Band and features in the 1990 Montreux Jazz Festival DVD.

10. 'Beginner At the Blues' (featuring Delbert McClinton)

Delbert McClinton is an American blues rock and electric blues singer-songwriter, guitarist, harmonica player, and pianist. He and Frankie struck up a friendship in the early 80s during Frankie's spell at Capitol Records. Delbert has recorded a number of Frankie Miller songs including 'Be Good to Yourself', 'Heartbreak Radio' and 'Sending Me Angels', which was released as a single in America.

Richard Cottle on organ and piano

Richard has appeared on an impressive list of recordings for artists such as David Bowie, Tina Turner, Bonnie Tyler, Roy Orbison and Elvis Presley.

11. 'To Be with You Again' (featuring Kim Carnes)

Best known for her massive 1981 hit 'Bette Davis Eyes' from the *Mistaken Identity* album, her voice has been described as "distinctively raspy" and "throaty", leading to comparisons to the voices of Rod Stewart and Bonnie Tyler.

Before becoming involved in the *Double Take* project Kim had previously recorded 'When I'm Away from You' which also appeared on *Mistaken Identity*.

'Bette Davis Eyes' earned both the Record of the Year and Song of the Year awards at the 1982 Grammy Awards. Carnes was nominated for Best Pop Female, and *Mistaken Identity* also earned a nomination for Album of the Year.

12. 'I Want to Spend My Life with You' (featuring Willie Nelson)

During his extensive career Nelson has used a variety of music styles to create his own distinctive blend of country music, a hybrid of jazz, pop, blues, rock and folk. He was one of the main figures of outlaw country, a subgenre of country music that developed in the late 1960s as a reaction to the conservative restrictions of the Nashville sound. The Nashville sound originated during the mid-1950s as a subgenre of American country music, replacing the chart dominance of the rough honky tonk music, which was most popular in the 1940s and 1950s, with "smooth strings and choruses", "sophisticated background vocals" and "smooth tempos" associated with traditional pop. It was an attempt "to revive country sales, which had been devastated by the rise of rock 'n' roll" as a distinct genre from the rockabilly spawned from it.

Willie Nelson has had numerous hit singles including 'Always On My Mind', which was also a huge hit for Elvis Presley.

Mickey Raphael

is an American harmonica player, music producer and actor best known for his work with Willie Nelson, with whom he has toured as part of The Family since 1973. Naming Paul Butterfield as one of his biggest influences, Raphael played throughout the years with a variety of artists, ranging from Elton John, U2, and Motley Crue to Vince Gill, Emmy Lou Harris, The Mavericks, Kenny Wayne Shepherd and Neil Young.

Simon Parrish

Since his first professional gig at the Roundhouse in London when he was just 12 years old, Simon has performed in several major productions including the award-winning *Comedy of Errors* at the National Theatre with Lenny Henry. He also performed in *Buddy* in the West End for five years as well as *Jailhouse Rock*, performing 'One Night With You' on *Top Of The Pops* as the 1,000th number one.

Simon has been involved with The Elvis Years since its concept in 2005 and has worked with Mario and David Mackay on its creation from the outset, playing a major part in building the production to the current levels of success. Simon Parrish is not only the bass player, he is also the associate producer, production manager and company manager for the show.

Mario Kombou

Mario has been performing his tribute to Elvis for over twenty years and has notched up over 6,000 performances to date. He also trained as an actor, starring in film, television and theatre productions around the world.

Mario won the Images of The King competition in 2005 in Memphis, Tennessee and is the only tribute artist in the world to have been officially endorsed by Donna Presley. Mario is also endorsed by Elvis Presley Enterprises.

Richard Alborough is an actor who also featured in *Buddy* and *Jailhouse Rock*.

13. 'The Ghost' (featuring Tomoyasu Hotei)

Tomoyasu Hotei is a Japanese musician, singer-songwriter, composer, record producer and actor. With a career spanning more than 40 years, Hotei claims record sales of over 40 million copies and has collaborated with acclaimed artists from around the world.

Bob Huff

Songwriter, producer and musician Bobby Huff has made a name for himself in the country, rock, pop and film/TV music worlds. He has worked with a great number of artists including Rod Stewart and Alice Cooper.

14. 'It Gets Me Blue' (featuring Paul Carrack)

Paul features early in Frankie's career, and had success with 'How Long' as a member of Ace, but went on to create his own solo career. Paul is an English singer, musician, songwriter and composer who has recorded as both a solo artist and as a member of several popular bands. The BBC dubbed Carrack "The Man with the Golden Voice", while *Record Collector* remarked: "If vocal talent equalled financial success, Paul Carrack would be a bigger name than legends such as Phil Collins or Elton John. "

In 1989, Mike + The Mechanics had a UK number two and US number one hit with 'The Living Years', on which Carrack again sang lead.

Following his second stint with Squeeze, Carrack joined forces with Timothy B. Schmit and Don Felder of the Eagles for an ambitious, but ultimately unrealised, recording project. Schmit and Felder soon reunited with the rest of the Eagles and their *Hell Freezes Over* live album/studio album, bringing with them one of the songs Carrack had co-written, 'Love Will Keep Us Alive.' It was recorded by the Eagles and won an ASCAP award as being the most-played song in the US in 1995.

Richard Cottle

Richard's early session work includes playing keyboards and sax on the 1984 *Keats* album, then The Alan Parsons Project *Vulture Culture* album. This would begin a long association with Alan Parsons, not only on Project albums, but also records produced by Parsons, and sessions with other Project members.

Since the mid-eighties Richard has done session work with everyone from Eric Clapton and Peter Frampton to Maxi Priest and Wham!

Richard has also done many live shows and tour dates, having toured with Alan Parsons and David Bowie (Glass Spider world tour in 1987). In 1992, Richard was part of the band when Mike Oldfield performed his *Tubular Bells II* live at Edinburgh Castle in Scotland.

15. 'Out on the Water' (featuring Stuart Emerson)
Guitars and sequencing by Stuart Emerson

Percussion and synths David Mackay

16. 'It's a Long Way Home' (featuring Brian Cadd)
Brian Cadd is an Australian singer-songwriter, keyboardist, producer and record label founder, a staple of Australian entertainment for over 50 years. As well as working internationally throughout Europe and the United States, he has performed as a member of numerous bands including the Groop, Axiom, the Bootleg Family Band and in America with the Flying Burrito Brothers before carving out a solo career in 1972.
Charlie Morgan
In 1985, Elton John invited Charlie to play with his band at Live Aid. As they left the stage that night, Elton decided to take the band on tour. Charlie would continue recording and touring with Elton for the next thirteen years. Charlie is another who has had an extensive career in the music business.

17. 'I'm Missing You' (featuring John Parr)
John Parr is an English musician, singer, and songwriter, best known for his 1985 single 'St. Elmo's Fire (Man in Motion)', charting at number one in the US and number six in the UK.

18. 'I Never Want to Lose You' (featuring Lenny Zakatek)
Lenny Zakatek is a British singer and musician who has lived in London since the age of thirteen. He is best known for his work with the British bands Gonzalez and The Alan Parsons Project.

19. 'I Do'
Richard Cottle: Keyboards and programming
James Graydon: Acoustic guitar
James Graydon is an American songwriter, recording artist, guitarist, singer, keyboardist, producer, arranger, and recording engineer. He is the winner of two Grammy Awards (in the R&B category) with twelve Grammy nominations, among them the title Producer of the Year and Best Engineered Recording. He has mastered many different music styles and genres, and his recordings have been featured on record, film, television and the stage.
From the late 1960s to late 1970s Graydon was a session musician in Los Angeles, working with such artists as Gino Vannelli, Barbra Streisand, Dolly Parton, Diana Ross, The Jackson Five, Alice Cooper, Cheap Trick, Al Jarreau, Christopher Cross, Ray Charles, Cher, Joe Cocker, Marvin Gaye, Hall & Oates, Wayne Shorter, Olivia Newton-John, and Albert King. One of Graydon's most notable session performances is his guitar solo on

Steely Dan's 1977 hit single 'Peg'.

Photographs and Hand Prints

It must have been around 2010 that I received an email from Neil Everest into Frankie's site with an attachment and a message asking if I knew the person in the picture. It was Frankie Miller with the Stoics (Howl) on stage at the Isle of Wight 1970. The first live pictures I ever saw of the Stoics! Before I knew it I was invited down to an exhibition at Swansea Museum of the work of Charles Everest, Neil's father. Charles was an official photographer at the festival and also has an amazing range of close up shots of Jimi Hendrix, Jim Morrison, The Who, Free and many others.

At the event I saw a face that I recognised then realised it was someone I had seen a couple of years back on *Dragons Den*. I remember being hugely impressed by Guy Portelli, who won over three dragons. Three invested in his business.

Guy is a contemporary British sculptor. His work is found in public and corporate collections in Britain and the USA. Ringo Starr possesses several of his pieces.

Check out Guy's Pop Icons Project where he has produced the most wonderful abstract pieces inspired by artists such as Miles Davis, John Lee Hooker, Frank Sinatra and Jimi Hendrix. Guy has also produced a wonderful bust in the image of Frankie Miller.

The following paragraphs are from Guy as he reflects on the Hand Print project:

Isle of Wight revisited. Frankie Miller Hand Print.

The Isle of Wight Festival started in 1968 and reached such a huge audience in 1970 that it became a victim of its own success. With an audience of 600,000 it was not sustainable as a festival. Hence the title 'The Last Great Event.'

It has been frustrating that the importance of the festival has been lost and should be celebrated in a positive light. Glastonbury, which started in 1971, picked up the mantel mainly due to its annual event that has grown steadily over the years.

At the time of writing, we are now heading towards the 50th Anniversary of the 1970 IOW Festival and it seemed appropriate that some form of remembrance was set in place, by way of a museum or heritage centre. My particular fascination is the hand print as a symbol of humanity, and so the project to collect hand prints of musicians who performed was conceived.

I planned that the creation of the sculpture would start with the 1968 anniversary and finish in time for the 1970 anniversary. I estimated that around 100 hand prints would fit onto the fabricated panel.

The strategy of collecting hand prints is an interesting one. You need to start with a big name. I was fortunate to know a sculptor (John Humphries) who had done an amazing portrait of Mick Fleetwood, and I asked if he might put in a request for a hand print.

The hand print arrived with a nice letter wishing me the best of luck with the project. Those people who are knowledgeable on the subject will say Fleetwood Mac did not play the IOW festival between 1968-70, they played in 2015. My early concept for the sculpture was to cover the whole 50 years, but we collected so many hand prints for the early years we had to change the criteria. Anyway, the Mick Fleetwood hand worked very well.

A list of all the musicians and bands was drawn up and approached in establishing the ambition of the project, which was further reinforced with three hand prints from Jefferson Airplane. The Charles Everest images of Frankie Miller at the 1970 festival were powerful and had a real stage presence.

I had heard through different sources that Frankie Miller was much respected and liked by other musicians and so I tracked him down and built up a good working relationship with Frankie and Annette. In my research for what symbols might reflect Frankie's identity, the hat was unusual and recognisable to any Frankie Miller fan, obviously blue. Both Frankie and Annette are very happy with the inclusion of the hand print.

Frankie Miller by Peter McDougall

The voice to soothe the savage beast and a voice to induce the mild mannered to uninhibited aggressive head-banging…Frankie Miller, a voice of such mellifluous beauty and resonance it can echo in and around the canyon of your heart and simultaneously, has the raw, gallous depth and garrulousness of your darkest of streets; he can put you through the emotional cycle from A to Z and when you get to C, you realise it's for crying.

This singer puffs out more talent in his sleep than most performers manage in the daylight of their careers; a thief of a voice, that'll creep up on you in the night and steal away your soul.

He isn't just gifted, he is a gift… he's crammed more living into an overnight bag than most of us pack into the suitcases of our lives… his songs a testament to it.

Frankie Miller, a man of impish mischievousness with a smile you could warm your hands at, but at the same time, has a swagger about him that could dry a washing; a rummel of contradictions.

It is my privilege, not only to know him as a friend, but to have been present on occasions over the years and watch him magically and spontaneously conjure up music and words, words that wring a tear from a working man's jacket and of course, always prompts the question, and asked with a tight-lipped envy, "How the fuck do you do that?"

Who knows, maybe he doesn't himself, but what is irrefutable, is he can, and does…and that is his achievement.

Peter McDougall
Playwright

It's another friend and bandmate, Joe Walsh, who appears to speak for everyone. "Frankie's one of your national treasures," he says. "Look after him."

It certainly has been "A Long Way Home" for you, Frankie… but as you once said many years ago…

You're Still Waiting… Patiently…

'Reflections on Bridgeton Cross' circa 1938 by John M Boyd
The image we used for 'Long Way Home'

Covers-Selected Highlights

Frankie Miller never wrote for anyone but his songs were covered by an impressive number of legendary artists.

Some have interesting anecdotal stories attached.

With a full listing at the end of this book, here are some selected highlights.

Ain't Got No Money - Bob Seger.
From the album *Strange in Town* in 1978.
Two years before actually recording 'Ain't Got No Money', Bob Seger had written 'The Fire Down Below' on the *Night Moves* 1976 album. In an interview for ultimateclassicrock.com Bob Seger looked across the Atlantic Ocean to find inspiration for the song that became 'The Fire Down Below.'

The traditionally blue-collar songwriter found the feeling he was looking for with the help of Scottish singer Frankie Miller and the blues-powered version of England's Fleetwood Mac as he composed the 1976 song, as he told Uncle Joe Benson on the Ultimate Classic Rock Nights radio show.

"I was a big fan of Frankie Miller," Seger explained. "We're very similar in the way we approach rock 'n' roll... I heard a song called 'Ain't Got No Money' and I liked that swampy middle-rock thing." He continued: "Vocally, I was probably inspired by Frankie."

'Ain't Got No Money' featured in Frankie's live shows from its release in 1975 right through until the early 90s and he would often merge a verse of Seger's song into his, such was the similarity of both.

Ain't Got No Money - Black Rose (Featuring Cher)
In 1980, Cher and her boyfriend Les Dudek wanted to form a band called Black Rose. They were a rock band who played small clubs around Los Angeles but didn't want to trade on Cher's celebrity, so much so that Cher fans were unaware of the project. Dudek also had an impressive track record, having worked with the Steve Miller Band, Stevie Nicks, Cher, Boz Scaggs, and The Allman Brothers Band.

You're The Star, In My Own Crazy Way, When I'm Away From You, Kiss Her For Me - Rod Stewart
British rock and pop singer and songwriter, Rod Stewart was born and raised in London, but is of Scottish and English ancestry. With his distinctive, raspy singing voice he is one of the names mentioned when

journalists have reached out to describe Frankie's voice. Rod is among the best selling music artists of all time, having sold over 250 million records worldwide. He has had ten number one albums and 31 top ten singles in the UK, six of which reached number one. Rod has had sixteen top ten singles in the US, with four reaching number one on the Billboard Hot 100.

He first met Frankie in the 1970s and the two retain a close friendship to this day. 'Kiss Her For Me' also featured on the duets album *Double Take* (Rod duetting with Frankie) and Rod also kindly participated in the accompanying DVD documentary *Sending Me Angels*.

Soul Time – Joe Cocker

Joe Cocker was an English singer known for his gritty, bluesy voice and dynamic stage performances.

One of his most memorable performances came at Woodstock in 1969 with the Grease Band and his rearrangement of 'With a Little Help from My Friends'. Frankie's connections with the Grease Band are detailed elsewhere in this story.

Heartbreak Radio – Roy Orbison

Roy Orbison was one of the rock 'n' roll's most popular and successful artists ever. Thanks to his trademark passionate vocal style, dark ballads and distinctive sunglasses, he was a hugely influential singer and composer. Major hits included 'Crying', 'Blue Bayou', 'Only the Lonely' and 'Pretty Woman'.

In 1988, he co-founded the Traveling Wilburys with George Harrison, Bob Dylan, Tom Petty, and Jeff Lynne, and a new album of songs - such as 1989's 'You Got It' - proved to be very successful, even after his death.

Frankie's song appeared on the 1992 studio album *King of Hearts*, a posthumous album put together from master sessions and demos by Jeff Lynne.

The song featured again on *A Love So Beautiful*, which was released in 2017. The album features archival vocal recordings of Orbison accompanied by new orchestral arrangements by the Royal Philharmonic Orchestra. The album peaked at number two on the UK Albums Chart, becoming Orbison's highest charting album for almost 30 years.

I Can't Change It – Ray Charles

This song was written by Frankie Miller when he was just twelve years old. He recorded it eleven years later for his debut album, *Once in a Blue Moon*. The song was covered by Ray Charles (Frankie's mother's favourite singer) on his 1980 album *Brother Ray Is At It Again*. "Everybody from Etta James to Johnny Cash has done Frankie's songs," Frankie's wife, Annette, once told *Mojo* magazine, "but Ray Charles recording it was a really big deal for Frankie. His mum was still around when that happened and she would never tell Frankie how proud of him she was."

A Fool in Love – Etta James

Etta James was an American singer who performed in various genres, including gospel, blues, jazz, R&B, rock 'n' roll, and soul.

Her deep and earthy voice was described as having bridged the gap between rhythm and blues and rock 'n' roll. Song highlights include 'Something's Got a Hold on Me' and 'I'd Rather Go Blind', which became a blues classic.

Her album 1990 album, *Stickin' to my Guns*, on which Frankie's song appears, was nominated for Best Contemporary Blues Album at the Grammys.

You're the Star, There Will Always Be a New Tomorrow - Dana Gillespie

Dana Gillespie (born Richenda Antoinette de Winterstein Gillespie) is an English actress, singer and songwriter. Originally performing and recording in her teens, over the years Dana has been involved in the recording of over 45 albums, and appeared in stage productions, such as *Jesus Christ Superstar*, and several films. Her musical output has progressed from teen pop and folk in the early part of her career, to rock in the 1970s and, more latterly, the blues.

The song 'Andy Warhol' was originally written by David Bowie for Dana, although her version of the song was not released until 1973. After performing backing vocals on the track 'It Ain't Easy' on Bowie's *Ziggy Stardust and the Spiders from Mars*, she recorded an album of her own produced by Bowie and Mick Ronson, featuring Ronson on guitar, in 1973, *Weren't Born a Man*. Dana remains a close friend to Frankie and Annette. They met when guitarist Ed Deane organised everyone to meet during the 1997 Bob Dylan tour that Dana and her band supported.

Heartbreak Radio, When I'm Away from You, I'd Lie to You for Your Love - Kim Carnes

Kim Carnes' distinctive, raspy vocal style has drawn comparisons to Rod Stewart. In 1980 she released *Mistaken Identity*, which featured the worldwide hit, 'Bette Davis Eyes'. This became the best selling single of the year in the United States, spending nine weeks at number one on the Billboard Hot 100, going gold, and winning the Grammy Award for Record of the Year and Song of the Year. *Mistaken Identity* went to number one on the Billboard 200, was certified platinum, and was nominated for the Grammy Award for Album of the Year.

She was one of the enthusiastic participants on Frankie's 2016 *Double Take* duets album.

Fool in Love, Heartbreak Radio, Sending Me Angels – Delbert McClinton

Delbert McClinton is an American blues rock and electric blues singer-songwriter, guitarist, harmonica player, and pianist. Four of his albums have been number one on the Blues Chart, and he has earned four Grammy Awards: 1992 Rock Performance by a Duo with Bonnie Raitt for 'Good Man, Good Woman'; 2002 Contemporary Blues Album for *Nothing Personal*; 2006 Best Contemporary Blues Album for *Cost of Living*, and 2020 Best Traditional Blues Album for *Tall, Dark, & Handsome*. He has been nominated for eight Grammy Awards as of 2020.

Delbert also features with Frankie on *Double Take*. *Rolling Stone* calls him the "Godfather of Americana Music."

Author's Note: I once asked Frankie what had inspired him to perform 'Jealous Kind' (by Bobby Charles) and his answer was "Delbert McClinton." Praise indeed. (Around 1991-92 I had just returned from a trip to Holland when Frankie invited me down to attend a Delbert McClinton gig with him in London. But sadly for me, a Wednesday night gig was a trip too far and I couldn't go.)

You Always Saw Blue Skies, I'll Never Let You Down, Tears – Bonnie Tyler

Bonnie Tyler is a Welsh singer who is also known for her distinctive husky voice. She came to prominence with the release of her 1977 album *The World Starts Tonight* and its singles 'Lost in France' and 'More Than a Lover'. Her 1978 single 'It's a Heartache' reached number four on the UK Singles Chart, and number three on the US Billboard Hot 100.

In the 1980s, Tyler ventured into rock music with songwriter and producer Jim Steinman. He wrote Tyler's biggest hit, 'Total Eclipse of the Heart'. Frankie Miller is also featured on that album, duetting on 'Tears', but has received little credit for that in the music press.

Steinman also wrote Tyler's other major 1980s hit, 'Holding Out for a Hero' from her 1983 UK chart-topping album *Faster Than the Speed of Night*.

In 2016 she recorded 'True Love' in a duet with Frankie on *Double Take* and the pair still retain a close friendship.

In My Own Crazy Way – Johnny Cash / Waylon Jennings

Johnny Cash probably doesn't need any introductions but it's another huge accolade for Frankie that Cash recorded one of his songs.

Cash was an American country singer-songwriter. Much of his music contained themes of sorrow, moral tribulation, and redemption, especially in the later stages of his career. He was known for his deep, calm bass-baritone voice.

He is one of the best-selling music artists of all time, having sold more than 90 million records worldwide. Notable hits include 'I Walk the Line', 'Ring of Fire', ' Folsom Prison Blues' and 'A Boy Named Sue'. Interestingly Johnny Cash (1969) and Frankie Miller (1975) both performed for the prisoners at San Quentin prison.

Waylon Jennings was an American singer, songwriter, and musician, as well as an actor. He pioneered the Outlaw Movement in country music. He joined the country supergroup The Highwaymen with Willie Nelson, Kris Kristofferson, and Johnny Cash, which released three albums between 1985 and 1995.

Danger Danger – The Everly Brothers

The Everly Brothers were an American rock duo, known for steel-string acoustic guitar playing and close harmony singing. They were Don Everly and Phil Everly and combined elements of rock 'n' roll, country, and pop, becoming pioneers of country rock.

They began writing and recording their own music in 1956. Many of the top acts of the 1960s were heavily influenced by the close-harmony singing and acoustic guitar playing of the Everly Brothers, including the Hollies, the Beatles, the Beach Boys, the Bee Gees, and Simon & Garfunkel. In 2015, *Rolling Stone* ranked the Everly Brothers at number one on its list of the Twenty Greatest Duos of All Time.

Their large number of hits included 'Bye Bye Love', 'All I Have To Do Is Dream', 'Cathy's Clown' (which sold 8 million copies), and 'The Price of Love'.

'Danger Danger' had been the opening track on Frankie's *Standing on the Edge* album.

Guilty of the Crime – The Eagles

The Eagles connection features heavily in the Frankie Miller story, but it is to Frankie Miller's credit once more that a band of this calibre have recorded one of his songs.

Their *Greatest Hits (1971–1975)* is the best-selling album in the United States, with 38 million sold, and primed the public for the late 1976 release of *Hotel California*, which would sell more than 26 million copies in the

US (ranking third all-time for US sales), and more than 32 million copies worldwide. Frankie's connection is covered elsewhere in this book and the close friendship stays strong to this day.

Be Good to Yourself - The Georgia Thunderbolts

The Georgia Thunderbolts are an American rock band from Rome, Georgia. Formed in 2015, the band released their debut album *Can We Get A Witness* through Mascot Records in 2021. They also recorded 'Ain't Got No Money' on their 2024 release *Rise Above It All*, also on Mascot Records.

They began touring by opening up for artists such as Black Stone Cherry, The Kentucky Headhunters, and Blackberry Smoke. They're managed by Richard Young of the Headhunters. After a performance caught the attention of Mascot Label Group's North American President Ron Burman, the group was immediately signed to the label.

Their debut album *Can We Get A Witness* was released on October 15th, 2021, through Mascot Records. *No Depression* wrote favourably about the project, calling it "a good one from some up-and-coming good ol' boys looking for a sweet home of their own." The single 'Be Good To Yourself' was selected by both *Rolling Stone* and *Classic Rock* as one of the best songs of the week.

Singer TJ Lyle and Richard Young have both contributed to this book as follows:

"Hey! Thank you for reaching out! Frankie has become a huge influence to our sound and myself as a songwriter personally! We first found out about Frankie from our manager and partner Mr. Richard Young from the Kentucky Headhunters. We were in the studio working on our first record and we were missing something from our sound and Richard - who grew up with the musical likes of Frankie Miller, Eddie Hinton, Paul Rodgers etc. - the Greats!!! - (also being producer of our record) came up with the idea for us to work up 'Be Good To Yourself', which became one of our best streaming and live performed songs.

"And it changed us musically. From the feel of his melodies to the swing of his shaky, soulful, painful, timbre. He has touched and inspired us! He actually shared our version of his song 'Be Good To Yourself' on his social sites and gave us a thumbs up. A positive input coming from the man himself really gave us the indication that we were doing something right!

"My manager has some amazing things he could share with you about Frankie and his memories and inspiration. If you would like to reach him he would love to hear from you! Thank you so much for reaching out! It's been a pleasure!!"

-T.J. Lyle.

Richard is quoted as describing Frankie as follows: "There's a rare confidence in his voice that only a few possess, and that's what it takes to put a rock, soul and blues song across. It's like a bird crying and it draws you in, like a moth is drawn to a light."

So until the tragic events of 1994, Frankie Miller worked at the highest level, and his association with the Eagles would have taken him to an even higher level; that's the heartbreak.

Davy Arthur with Tj Lyle

A Selection of Collaborators

Jimmy Doris, Robin Trower, Paul Carrack and Andy Fraser all appear throughout this story, but there are a few other high profile names to mention…

Graham Lyle
is a Scottish singer-songwriter, guitarist and producer.
He co-wrote 'How Many Tears Can You Hide' with Frankie on *Dancing in the Rain*.
Between 1970 and 1997, he co-wrote eighteen British Top 40 hits, nine Billboard Hot 100 entries and four US Country number ones. His song writing collaborators have also included Terry Britten, Albert Hammond, Troy Seals, Jim Diamond and his long-time performing partner, Benny Gallagher.
His most famous composition is Tina Turner's 'What's Love Got to Do with It?', which won him the Song of the Year Grammy. He is also well known as a member of Gallagher and Lyle, McGuinness Flint and Ronnie Lane's band Slim Chance.

Troy Seals
is an American singer, songwriter, and guitarist and a member of the prominent Seals family of musicians that includes Jim Seals (of Seals and Crofts), Dan Seals (of England Dan & John Ford Coley) and Brady Seals.
His compositions have been recorded by artists such as Joe Cocker, Eric Clapton, Nancy Sinatra, Randy Travis, Conway Twitty, Hank Williams Jr., Elvis Presley, Roy Orbison, Levon Helm, and Jerry Lee Lewis.
Frankie teamed up with Troy Seals to write 'The Woman In You' and 'Heartbreak Radio' on *Easy Money*.

Eddie Setser
On the same album appeared the name of Eddie Setser. His reputation extended beyond country music. Setser co-wrote Eric Clapton's 1983 pop hit 'I've Got a Rock & Roll Heart.' His songs were also sung by Rod Stewart, Aretha Franklin, Greg Guidry, Etta James, The Four Tops, Rita Coolidge, Isaac Hayes and Delbert McClinton.
The trio of Miller, Seals and Setser co-wrote the title track 'Easy Money', plus 'Forget About Me' and 'Gimme Love'.
'Forget About Me' was also recorded by American country music duo The Bellamy Brothers. It was released in June 1984 as the first single from

the album *Restless*. The song reached number five on the Billboard Hot Country Singles & Tracks chart. 'Seven Spanish Angels' was written by Troy Seals and Eddie Setser. Ray Charles with Willie Nelson recorded the song in 1984 and it has been in turn covered by 30 artists.

Jerry Lynn Williams
was a rock music singer and composer. He wrote such hits as 'Forever Man,' 'See What Love Can Do,' 'Something's Happening,' 'Running on Faith' and 'Pretending' for Eric Clapton. His break as a songwriter came when Delbert McClinton's cover of a song from his second album, *Givin' It Up for Your Love*, reached the Top 40.

Frankie Miller wrote 'Guilty of the Crime' with Jerry Williams.

The Bellamy Brothers
are an American pop and country music duo consisting of brothers David and Howard Bellamy from Dade City, Florida.

Starting in the late 1970s, the Bellamy Brothers found success in country music as well, charting ten number one singles, 25 top ten and more than 50 hits overall on the country charts. To date, they have released more than 50 albums.

Notable songs include 'Let Your Love Flow' which was placed on the BMI list of the top 100 most played songs of the 20th century. They co-wrote 'I'd Lie To You for Your Love' with Frankie and also recorded Guilty of the Crime' and 'Over The Line'.

Jeff Barry
is an American pop music songwriter, singer, and record producer. Among the most successful songs that he has co-written in his career are 'Do Wah Diddy Diddy', 'Da Doo Ron Ron', 'Then He Kissed Me', 'Be My Baby', 'Chapel of Love', and 'River Deep - Mountain High' (all written with his then-wife Ellie Greenwich and Phil Spector) and 'Leader of the Pack' (written with Greenwich and Shadow Morton).

He worked with Frankie on *Dancing in the Rain* and is credited with co-writing a number of songs: 'Do It Till We Drop', 'That's How Long My Love Is', 'The Boys and The Girls Are Doing It', 'Gladly Go Blind', 'You're A Puzzle I Can't Put Down' and 'I'd Lie To You For Your Love' (along with the Bellamy Brothers).

Will Jennings
has written for a variety of artists, including Steve Winwood, Whitney Houston, Eric Clapton, B.B. King, Joe Sample, Mariah Carey, Barry Manilow and Roy Orbison.

With Steve Winwood, he wrote a series of albums including *Arc of a Diver*, *Talking Back to the Night* and *Back in the High Life*, an album that contained the hits 'Higher Love', 'The Finer Things', and 'Back in the High Life Again'. Winwood won the Record Of The Year and Outstanding Male Vocal Performance. Both Jennings and Winwood were nominated for the Song of the Year award for 'Higher Love.'

With Joe Sample, Jennings wrote 'Street Life' (a world-wide hit for the Crusaders with singer Randy Crawford) and several songs for various albums by the Crusaders for guest vocalists, including Joe Cocker ('I'm So Glad I'm Standing Here Today'), and Bill Withers ('Soul Shadows'). Jennings and Sample also wrote 'One Day I'll Fly Away', originally sung by Crawford, which was featured in the film *Moulin Rouge!*

Jennings has collaborated on many songs for films, the most notable songs being 'Up Where We Belong' for *An Officer and a Gentleman*, a song that won the Academy Award in America and the BAFTA (British Academy Award) in the United Kingdom and was a number one hit for Joe Cocker and Jennifer Warnes. In 1997, Jennings wrote the world-wide number one Céline Dion hit 'My Heart Will Go On' for the film *Titanic* with his collaborator James Horner. They won the Golden Globe Award and the Academy Award for Best Song from a Motion Picture.

He co–wrote a number of songs with Frankie, notably 'Long Way Home', and 'Over The Line'.

Scott English
was an American songwriter, arranger and record producer. Famous songs he wrote or co-wrote were 'Mandy' by Barry Manilow (I believe the story is actually about Brandy - Scott's pet dog!) and 'Bend Me Shape Me' which was a hit for the American Breed and Amen Corner. A one-time neighbour of Frankie, he co-wrote 'Baton Rouge' with Frankie and he and his wife were the inspiration for the final version of 'Kiss Her For Me', after the pair had separated…

Frankie Miller, That's Who !!

Frankie Miller Songs Have Been Covered By...

You're The Star – Rod Stewart
SPANNER IN THE WORKS
Released: May 31, 1995

Soul Time – Joe Cocker
HAVE A LITTLE FAITH
Released: Aug 31, 1994

Heartbreak Radio – Roy Orbison
KING OF HEARTS – track 2
Released: Nov 30, 1991

Ain't Got No Money – Bob Seger
STRANGER IN TOWN – track 6
Released: Nov 30, 2000

I Can't Change It – Ray Charles
BROTHER RAY – track 4
Released: Nov 30, 1988

Fool in Love – Etta James
STICKIN TO MY GUNS – track 9
Released: Nov 30, 1998

Sending Me Angels – Kathy Mattea
LOVE TRAVELS – track 2
Released: Nov 30, 1996

Heartbreak Radio – The Traveling Wilburys
THE TRAVELING WILBURYS VOL 4 1/2
Released: Nov 30, 1989

Guilty of the Crime – Joe Walsh
ROBOCOP TV SERIES SOUNDTRACK – track 2
Released: Nov 30, 1995

Heartbreak Radio – The Osmonds
BEST OF THE OSMONDS – track 19
Released: Apr 05, 1999

Gladly Go Blind – Southside Johnny & Asbury Jukes
GOING TO JUKESVILLE – track 4
Released: Nov 30, 2001

A Fool in Love – UFO
NO HEAVY PETTING – track 8
Released: Nov 30, 2002

When I'm Away from You – The Quireboys
TEARS IN HEAVEN – track 3
Released: Dec 19, 2005

When I'm Away from You/I'd Lie to You for Your Love – Bellamy Brothers
BELLAMY BROTHERS GREATEST HITS 2 – tracks 2 & 4
Released: May 22, 2002

You're the Star – Dana Gillespie
STAYING POWER – track 11
Released: Nov 30, 2002

Danger Danger – Voodoo Kings
VOODOO LOVE – track 11
Released: Jul 19, 1999

I'd Lie to You for Your Love – Sister Whiskey
LIQUOR & POKER – track 5
Released: Nov 30, 1998

It's a Long Way Home – Johnny Hallyday
ROUGH TOWN – track 12
Released: Nov 30, 1999

No Beginner at the Blues – Keri Leigh
NO BEGINNER – track 9
Released: Nov 30, 1993

I Know Why the Sun Don't Shine – Paul Kossoff
BLUE SOUL – track 14
Released: Nov 30, 1991

Drunken Nights in the City – Henry McCullough

UNFINISHED BUSINESS – track 12
Released: Nov 30, 2002

There Will Always be a New Tomorrow – Dana Gillespie
EXPERIENCED – track 8
Released: Nov 30, 2001

Nothing to Do With Love – Bonnie Tyler
FREE SPIRIT – track 1
Released: Nov 30, 1995

When I'm Away From You – Kim Carnes
MISTAKEN IDENTITY COLLECTION – track 4
Released: Mar 23, 1999

I Can't Wait Much Longer – Robin Trower
TWICE REMOVED FROM YESTERDAY – track 1
Released: Nov 30, 1995

Feel Love Comin' On – Millie Jackson
HARD TIMES – track 8
Released: Nov 30, 1996

Rollin' Thunder / Lonely Eyes – Bellamy Brothers
ROLLIN THUNDER – tracks 6 & 9
Released: Apr 30, 1991

Lonely Cafe – Hanne Boel
KINDRED SPIRIT – track 4
Released: Nov 30, 1991

The Doodle Song – The Proclaimers
THE PROCLAIMERS THE BEST OF – track 5
Released: Nov 30, 2001

Sending Me Angels – Peter Frampton
MAD DOGS AND OKIES – VARIOUS
Released: August 30, 2005

Baby Come Home – John Martyn
INDEPENDIENTE – track 1
Released: Nov 30, 2003

How Many Tears Can You Hide – Shakin Stevens
THE HITS OF SHAKIN STEVENS VOL 2 – track 9
Released: Nov 30, 1998

Beginner at the Blues/Sending Me Angels – Coco Montoya
JUST LET GO – tracks 9 & 13
Released: Nov 30, 1996

Over the Line/Guilty of the Crime – Bellamy Brothers
OVER THE LINE – tracks 1 & 4
Released: Jul 22, 1997

I'm Old Enough – The Roost
FOUR PENCE AND A PRAYER – track 2
Released: Jul 31, 2005

Sending Me Angels – Delbert McClinton
ONE OF THE FORTUNATE FEW – track 4
Released: Oct 07, 1997

Little Angel – Mighty Diamonds
ICE ON FIRE – track 8
Released: Nov 30, 2000

Heartbreak Radio – Lee Greenwood
GOD BLESS THE USA – track 6
Released: Nov 30, 1999

Sending Me Angels – Chris Farlowe
FARLOWE THAT – track 2
Released: Jul 14, 2003

Eternal Flame – Joel Nava
JOEL NAVA – track 7
Released: Nov 30, 1996

Heartbreak Radio – Kim Carnes
VIEW FROM THE HOUSE – Track 3
Released: Nov 30, 1990

Heartbreak Radio – Lannie Garrett
DOUBLEBACK

Released: Nov 30, 2003

After All I Live My Life – Edwyn Collins
DR SYNTAX – track 13
Released: Apr 01, 2003

Lonely Cafe – Troy Turner
BLUES ON MY BACK – track 4
Released: Nov 30, 2001

Nothing to do with Love/Sending Me Angels – Kelly Richey
SENDING ME ANGELS – tracks 1 & 11
Released: Nov 30, 2000

Lonely Eyes/Ain't Got no Money – Chris Farlowe
BORN AGAIN – tracks 3 & 5
Released: Nov 30, 1999

Nothing To Do With Love – Deborah Coleman
SOFT PLACE TO FALL – track 9
Released: Mar 21, 2000

Burn One Down – Clint Black
D'LECTRIFIED – track 11
Released: Nov 30, 1999

Fool in Love/Heartbreak Radio – Delbert McClinton
PLAIN FROM THE HEART – tracks 12 & 13
Released: Nov 30, 1999

You Always Saw Blue Skies/I'll Never Let You Down – Bonnie Tyler
ALL IN ONE VOICE – tracks 4 & 11
Released: Dec 28, 1999

Beginner at the Blues – Kathryn Cairns
MESSIN WITH THE WRONG GIRL – track 8
Released: Dec 21, 1999

Heartbreak Radio – Delbert McClinton
THE ULTIMATE COLLECTION – track 17
Released: Jun 01, 1999

Nothing To Do With Love – Kenny Wayne Shepherd
TROUBLE IS… – track 10
Released: Nov 30, 1996

I Can't Live Without You – Robin Trower
LOVE MISTY DAYS – track 8
Released: Nov 30, 1996

Sending Me Angels – Bonnie Tyler
ANGEL HEART – track 4
Released: Oct 05, 1992

Burn One Down – Clint Black
THE HARD WAY – track 9
Released: Jul 14, 1992

Season of the Wind – Bellamy Brothers
HOWARD AND DAVID
Released: Nov 30, 1989

My Own Crazy Way – Oak Ridge Boys
AMERICAN DREAMS – track 7
Released: Nov 30, 1988

I'd Lie to You for Your Love – Kim Carnes
LIGHTHOUSE – track 2
Released: Nov 30, 1987

In My Own Crazy Way – Johnny Cash / Waylon Jennings
HEROES – track 9
Released: Nov 30, 1985

In My Own Crazy Way – Rod Stewart
EVERY BEAT OF MY HEART – track 7
Released: Nov 30, 1985

Danger Danger – Everly Brothers
EB 84 – track 2
Released: Nov 30, 1983

Beautiful Woman – Don Williams
CAFE CAROLINA

Released: Nov 30, 1983

Heartbreak Radio – Molly Hatchett
DEED IS DONE – track 8
Released: Nov 30, 1983

Forget About Me – Bellamy Brothers
RESTLESS – track 1
Released: Nov 30, 1983

I'm Ready – Climax Blues Band
SAMPLE AND HOLD
Released: Nov 30, 1982

I'm Old Enough/The Doodle Song – Lou Ann Barton
OLD ENOUGH – tracks 1 & 8
Released: Jan 01, 1982

I'm Old Enough – Johnny Hallyday
HOLLYWOOD – track 4
Released: Nov 30, 1978

Sending Me Angels – Andrew Strong
OUT OF TIME – track 3
Released: Nov 30, 2000

Gladly Go Blind – Jackie Leven
ELEGY TO JOHNNY CASH
Released: 2005

Standing at Your Window – Andy Fraser
NAKED… AND FINALLY FREE
Released: Nov 2005

Guilty of the Crime – The Eagles
LONG ROAD OUT OF EDEN – track 5
Released: October 29, 2007

Cocaine, A Bottle of Whiskey, Kiss Her for Me, So Called Friends – Spike
SO CALLED FRIENDS
Released: May 12, 2008
Jealousy – Bettye Lavette

SCENE OF THE CRIME
Released: September 25, 2007

When I'm Away From You, Kiss Her For Me – Rod Stewart
THE ROD STEWART SESSIONS 1971 – 1998
Released: September 2009

Baby It's You – The Quireboys
HALFPENNY DANCER
Released: 2009

Sending Me Angels – John Oates
1000 MILES OF LIFE
Released: August 23, 2008

Guilty of The Crime, A Woman To Love, I'd Lie To You For Your Love – Reed & Dickinson
TONIGHT WE RIDE
Released: November 6, 2009

Sending Me Angels – Miller Anderson
BLUESHART
Released: September 15, 2003

Guilty Of The Crime – Bellamy Brothers/Bacon Bros
THE ANTHOLOGY VOL 1
Released: September 29, 2009

You Always Saw The Blue Skies – Seth James and Jessica Murray
MILLION MILES OF LOVE
Released: November 16, 2016

Be Good To Yourself - Georgia Thunderbolts
CAN WE GET A WITNESS
Released October 15, 2021

Ain't Got No Money – Georgia Thunderbolts
RISE ABOVE IT ALL
Released August 23, 2024

Discography

Frankie Miller UK Album Releases
Bonus tracks feature on the remastered albums.

Once in a Blue Moon
1973
1. You Don't Need To Laugh (To Be Happy)
2. I Can't Change It
3. Candlelight Sonata In F Major
4. Ann Eliza Jane
5. It's All Over
6. In No Resistance
7. After All (Live My Life)
8. Just Like Tom Thumb's Blues
9. Mail Box
10. I'm Ready
11. I Can See The Train (Bonus Track)
12. Blow My Whistle (Bonus Track)
13. Rules Of The Game (Bonus Track)
14. And It's Raining (Bonus Track)

High Life
1974
1. High Life (Filler)
2. Play Something Sweet (Brickyard Blues)
3. Trouble
4. A Fool
5. Little Angel
6. With You In Mind
7. The Devil Gun
8. I'll Take A Melody
9. Just A Song
10. Shoo-Rah
11. I'm Falling In Love Again
12. With You In Mind (Filler)
13. Brickyard Blues (live)
14. The Devil Gun (live)
15. If You Need Me (live)
16. With You In Mind (live)

The Rock

1975
1. A Fool In Love
2. The Heartbreak
3. The Rock
4. I Know Why The Sun Don't Shine
5. Hard On The Levee
6. Ain't Got No Money
7. All My Love To You
8. I'm Old Enough
9. Bridgeton
10. Drunken Nights In The City
11. A Fool In Love (live)
12. Hard On The Levee (live)
13. Sail Away (live)
14. Drunken Nights In The City (live)
15. Walking The Dog (With Rory Gallagher live)

Full House
1977
1. Be Good To Yourself
2. The Doodle Song
3. Jealous Guy
4. Searching
5. Love Letters
6. Take Good Care Of Yourself
7. Down The Honky Tonk
8. This Love Of Mine
9. Let The Candlelight Shine
10. (I'll Never) Live In Vain
11. Free And Safe On The Road (live)
12. It Takes A Lot To Laugh (live)
13. This Love Of Mine (live)
14. Down The Honky Tonk (live)

Double Trouble
1978
1. Have You Seen Me Lately Joan
2. Double Heart Trouble
3. The Train
4. You'll Be In My Mind
5. Good Time Love
6. Love Waves

7. (I Can't) Breakaway
8. Stubborn Kind Of Fellow
9. Love Is All Around
10. Goodnight Sweetheart
11. (I Can't) Breakaway (Bonus Track)
12. Love Waves (Bonus Track)
13. Good Time Love (Bonus Track)
14. Have You Seen Me Lately Joan (Bonus Track)
15. Double Heart Trouble (Bonus Track)
16. Stubborn Kind Of Fellow (Bonus Track)
17. Goodnight Sweetheart (Bonus Track)

Falling in Love
1979
1. When I'm Away From You
2. Is This Love
3. If I Can Love Somebody
4. Darlin'
5. And It's Your Love
6. A Woman to Love
7. Falling In Love With You
8. Every Time A Teardrop Falls
9. Pappa Don't Know
10. Good To See You
11. Is This Love (Bonus Track)
12. Cry To Me (Bonus Track)
13. Cold Turkey (Bonus Track)
14. When Something Is Wrong With My Baby (Bonus Track)

Easy Money
1980
1. Easy Money
2. The Woman In You
3. Why Don't You Spend The Night
4. So Young, So Young
5. Forget About Me
6. Heartbreak Radio
7. Cheap Thrills
8. No Chance
9. Gimme Love
10. Tears
11. Lock Up Your Secretaries (Bonus Track)

12. The Woman In You (Bonus Track)
13. Beggin' For Trouble (Bonus Track)
14. Lonely Eyes (Bonus Track)

Standing on the Edge
1982
1. Danger Danger
2. Standing On The Edge
3. Zap Zap
4. To Dream The Dream
5. Don't Stop
6. Angels With Dirty Faces
7. Firin' Line
8. Jealousy
9. It's All Coming Down Tonight
10. On My Way
11. Bad Case Of Loving You (Bonus Track)
12. Jealous Kind (Bonus Track)
13. Cold & Rainy Night (Bonus Track)
14. Don't Stop (Bonus Track)

Dancing in the Rain
1986
1. I'd Lie To You For Your Love
2. Do It Till We Drop
3. That's How Long Is My Love Is
4. How Many Tears Can You Hide
5. Dancing In The Rain
6. Shaky Ground
7. The Boys & The Girls Are Doing It
8. Game of Love
9. Gladly Go Blind
10. You're a Puzzle I Can't Put Down

The Very Best of Frankie Miller
1994
1. Darlin'
2. When I'm Away from You
3. Be Good to Yourself
4. I Can't Change It
5. High Life/Brickyard Blues
6. Fool in Love

7. Have You Seen Me Lately Joan
8. Love Letters
9. Caledonia
10. Stubborn Kind of Fellow
11. Devil Gun
12. Hard on the Levee
13. Tears
14. I'm Ready
15. Shoo Rah Shoo Rah
16. Double Heart Trouble
17. So Young, So Young

BBC Live in Concert
1994
1. Free and Safe on the Road
2. Play Something Sweet
3. It Takes a Lot to Laugh, It Takes a Train to Cry
4. With You in Mind
5. The Rock
6. Be Good to Yourself
7. A Fool in Love
8. Jealous Guy
9. I Can't Break Away
10. Double Heart Trouble
11. Stubborn Kind of Fellow
12. Falling in Love With You
13. Goodnight Sweetheart
14. A Woman to Love
15. When I'm Away from You
16. When Something is Wrong with My Baby
17. Darlin'
18. Ain't Got No Money

Long Way Home
2006
1. Guilty Of The Crime
2. Win Lose or Draw
3. You Always Saw The Blue Skies
4. Lovin's Too Easy
5. He'll Have To Go
6. You're The Star
7. Over The Line

8. The Rose
9. Baton Rouge
10. Lies Tell The Best Truth Of All
11. It's A Long Way Home
12. Never Name Drop (Hidden Track)

Frankie Miller's Double Take
2016
1. Blackmail - Frankie Miller featuring Joe Walsh
2. Where Do The Guilty Go - Frankie Miller featuring Elton John and Steve Cropper
3. Way Past Midnight - Frankie Miller featuring Huey Lewis
4. True Love – Frankie Miller featuring Bonnie Tyler
5. Kiss Her For Me - Frankie Miller featuring Rod Stewart
6. Gold Shoes - Frankie Miller featuring Francis Rossi
7. Sending Me Angels - Frankie Miller featuring Kiki Dee and Jose Antonio Rodriguez
8. Jezebel Jones - Frankie Miller featuring Kid Rock and Full House
9. When Its Rockin - Frankie Miller featuring Steve Dickinson and Full House
10. Beginner At The Blues - Frankie Miller featuring Delbert McClinton and Full House
11. To Be With You Again - Frankie Miller featuring Kim Carnes
12. I Wanna Spend My Life With You - Frankie Miller featuring Willie Nelson
13. The Ghost - Frankie Miller featuring Tomoyasu Hotei
14. It Gets Me Blue - Frankie Miller featuring Paul Carrack
15. Out On The Water - Frankie Miller featuring Stuart Emerson
16. It's a Long Way Home - Frankie Miller featuring Brian Cadd
17. I'm Missing You - Frankie Miller featuring John Parr
18. I Never Want To Lose You - Frankie Miller featuring Lenny Zakatek
19. I Do – Frankie Miller
Other Compilations

Frankie Who - Frankie Fucking Miller That's Who (Norway only vinyl) 1979

I'm Only Serious (Germany only vinyl) 1979

Love Letters - a 16-track compilation released in 1996 by Disky (a Dutch company)

Frankie Miller That's Who (Chrysalis box set) 2011

Frankie Miller – Live At Rockpalast (Box Set) 2013 WDR Media Group MIG 90592 (CD ,Vinyl and DVD)

Frankie also appeared as Alveric on *The King OF Elfland's Daughter*, which was a concept album by former Steelye Span members Bob Johnson and Peter Knight.
He features on two tracks: 'Alveric's Journey Through Elfland' and 'Just Another Day of Searching', which also featured on *Full House*.

Ad Fundum - a Belgian feature-length film directed by Erik Van Looy. The soundtrack album contains 13 tracks and Frankie's two songs were both released as singles in Belgium: 'Where Do the Guilty Go' and 'Why Don't You Try Me', which was written by Ry Cooder (who also produced this version) and performed with Sara Beth, and reached number six in the Belgian Flanders Chart. Ironically the film is based on a story about student freshmen in Leuven University, the town in which Frankie played one of his last ever two concerts.

7 Inch Singles

Little Angel
Jan 01, 1974
A Side – Little Angel
B Side – Brickyard Blues

A Fool In Love
Sep 01, 1975
A Side – A Fool In Love
B Side – I Know Why The Sun Don't Shine

The Rock (Single)
Jul 01, 1976
A Side – The Rock
B Side – The Heartbreak

Loving You Is Sweeter Than Ever
Oct 01, 1976
A Side – Loving You Is Sweeter Than Ever
B Side – I'm Old Enough

Be Good To Yourself
May 01, 1977
A Side – Be Good To Yourself
B Side – Down The Honky Tonk

The Doodle Song
Jun 01, 1977
A Side – The Doodle Song
B Side – I'll Never Live In Vain

Love Letters
Aug 01, 1977
A Side – Love Letters
B Side – Let The Candlelight Shine

Frankie Miller…Thats Who! E.P.
4 Track Extended Play (EP) Version
Nov 01, 1977
A Side – Jealous Guy
A Side – Fool In Love
B Side – Brickyard Blues
B Side – Sail Away

Stubborn Kind Of Fellow
Jun 01, 1978
A Side – Stubborn Kind Of Fellow
B Side – Good Time Love

Darlin'
Oct 01, 1978
A Side – Darlin'
B Side – Drunken Nights in The City (Re-Recorded by David Mackay)

When I'm Away From You
Jan 01, 1979
A Side – When I'm Away From You
B side – Ain't Got No Money (Re-Recorded by David Mackay)

Good To See You
Jun 01, 1979
A Side – Good To See You
B Side – Cold And Rainy Night

So Young, So Young
Jun 01, 1980
A Side – So Young, So Young
B Side – Tears

Why Don't You Spend The Night
Jul 01, 1980
A Side – Why Don't You Spend The Night
B Side - Heartbreak Radio

Standing On The Other Side
Jul 01, 1981
A Side – Standing On The Other Side
B Side – Fire In The Furnace

To Dream The Dream
Jun 01, 1982
A Side – To Dream The Dream
B Side – Don't Stop

Angels With Dirty Faces
Aug 01, 1982
A Side – Angels With Dirty Faces
 B Side – Jealousy

Danger Danger
Sep 01, 1982
A Side – Danger Danger
B Side – On My Way

I'd Lie To You For Your Love
Mar 01, 1986
A Side - I'd Lie To You For Your Love
B Side - Dancin' In The Rain

Caledonia
Mar 01, 1992
A Side - Caledonia
B Side - I'll Never Be That Young Again

Where Do the Guilty Go
Nov 30, 1993 (Double T Music Belgium)

Why Don't You Try Me
1993 (Double T Music Belgium)

12 Inch Singles
To Dream The Dream USA
1982
A Side - To Dream The Dream
B Side Danger Danger / Don't Stop / It's All Coming Down Tonight

I'd Lie To You For Your Love UK
Mar 01 1986
A Side - I'd Lie To You For Your Love
B Side – Do It Till We Drop / Dancing In The Rain

I'd Lie To You For Your Love - Holland
Mar 01 1986
A Side - I'd Lie To You For Your Love
B Side – Game Of Love / You're A Puzzle I Can't Put Down

Shaky Ground (Promo Holland)
1986
A Side/B Side Shaky Ground

How Many Tears Can You Hide – Germany
Mar 01 1986
A Side – How Many Tears Can You Hide
B Side – The Boys And The Girls Are Doing It / Dancing In The Rain

Musical Performances By Frankie Miller in TV and Film

All The Right Moves starring Tom Cruise - 'Blue Skies Forever'

Act Of Vengeance starring Charles Bronson - 'Working For The Company' and 'There Will Always Be A New Tomorrow'

The Rum Diary starring Johnny Depp - 'After All (I Live My Life)

Just a Boys Game - 'Rules Of The Game'

Sense of Freedom - 'Sense of Freedom' with Rory Gallagher

Life on Mars - 'I Can't Change It'

Thanks / Acknowledgements

The book has been a long time in the making and the original designs were made by Mark Todd, which Frankie loved. This gave me the confidence to keep going and eventually have something to show the world and make Frankie Miller proud. That is my wish. I will also never forget Mark's brilliance and contributions to the Double Take project. Without Mark the book may never have got to where it is today.

Thanks to Steve Holbrook too for his invaluable help. He is another who pushed me and eventually pointed me in the direction of New Haven.

The photographers who have donated their work to me, Professor Manfred Becker, David Staugas, Marc Marnie and Carlo Chinca also need to be celebrated and reminds one that indeed, "Every picture tells a story, don't it."

Nobby Clark for the professional advice over the years. He once told me that my original photobook was the best biography he had seen. He also pointed out about editing, an area in which I was totally naïve.

Frankie Miller for all the fabulous music, the friendship and great times we have had together.

Annette Miller for showing remarkable courage and compassion in caring for Frankie plus everything you have done for me over the years. Putting others before yourself, as ever.

My family too, who have heard me harping on about Frankie Miller for many years to the point of wanting to commit suicide…or murder. They may prefer the latter.

Steve Holbrook
Eric McLean
Tyrel Gobel
Ian Gomm
Allan Jones
Barbara Charone
Susan Whittall
Angie Errigo
Simon Kirke
Professor Mark Todd
Professor Manfred Becker
Todd Tolces
David Staugas

Marc Marnie
Carlo Chinca
Nobby Clark
Davy Shannon
Peter Hubbard
Glenys and Neil Everest at Cameron Life
Annette and Frankie Miller

"Everybody needs his memories. They keep the wolf of insignificance from the door."

From Mr. Sammler's Planet by Saul Bellow.

www.ingramcontent.com/pod-product-compliance
Lightning Source LLC
Chambersburg PA
CBHW042041240426
43667CB00047B/2942